YOUTH RISING?

Over the last decade, "youth" has become increasingly central to policy, development, media and public debates and conflicts across the world—whether as an ideological symbol, social category or political actor. Set against a backdrop of contemporary political economy, *Youth Rising?* seeks to understand exactly how and why youth has become such a popular and productive social category and concept. The book provocatively argues that the rise and spread of global neoliberalism have not only led youth to become more politically and symbolically salient, but also to expand to encompass a growing range of ages and individuals of different class, race, ethnic, national and religious backgrounds.

Employing both theoretical and historical analysis, authors Mayssoun Sukarieh and Stuart Tannock trace the development of youth within the context of capitalism, where it has long functioned as a category for social control. The book's chapters critically analyze the growing fears of mass youth unemployment and a "lost generation" that spread around the world in the wake of the global financial crisis. They question as well the relentless focus on youth in the reporting and discussion of recent global protests and uprisings. By helping develop a better understanding of such phenomena and critically and reflexively investigating the very category and identity of youth, *Youth Rising?* offers a fresh and sobering challenge to the field of youth studies and to widespread claims about the relationship between youth and social change.

Mayssoun Sukarieh is a Postdoctoral Fellow at the Cogut Center for the Humanities at Brown University.

Stuart Tannock is a Senior Lecturer at the School of Social Sciences at Cardiff University.

Critical Youth Studies

Series Editor: Greg Dimitriadis

Wired Citizenship: Youth Learning and Activism in the Middle East
Edited by Linda Herrera

Youth Rising? The Politics of Youth in the Global Economy
Mayssoun Sukarieh and Stuart Tannock

YOUTH RISING?

The Politics of Youth in the Global Economy

Mayssoun Sukarieh and Stuart Tannock

Routledge
Taylor & Francis Group

NEW YORK AND LONDON

First published 2015
by Routledge
711 Third Avenue, New York, NY 10017

and by Routledge
2 Park Square, Milton Park, Abingdon, Oxon, OX14 4RN

Routledge is an imprint of the Taylor & Francis Group, an informa business

Library of Congress Cataloging in Publication Data
Sukarieh, Mayssoun, author.
Youth rising? : the politics of youth in the global economy / by Mayssoun Sukarieh and Stuart Tannock.
    pages cm.—(Critical youth studies)
    Includes bibliographical references and index.
    1. Youth—Political activity. 2. Young adults—Political activity. 3. Youth movements. 4. Political participation. 5. Capitalism. 6. Social justice. 7. Youth—Employment. 8. Young adults—Employment. 9. Student loans. I. Tannock, Stuart, 1969– author. II. Title.
    HQ799.2P6S85 2014
    305.235—dc23

                                                                    2014007959

ISBN: 978-0-415-71125-8 (hbk)
ISBN: 978-0-415-71126-5 (pbk)
ISBN: 978-1-315-88466-0 (ebk)

Typeset in Bembo
by RefineCatch Limited, Bungay, Suffolk, UK

Printed and bound in Great Britain by
TJ International Ltd, Padstow, Cornwall

CONTENTS

SERIES EDITOR INTRODUCTION

Greg Dimitriadis

Mayssoun Sukarieh and Stuart Tannock's *Youth Rising? The Politics of Youth in the Global Economy* comes at an opportune time for this book series. When I began the series in 2005, I saw it as a venue for critical work on youth that moved across disciplines including education, sociology, and media studies (among other fields). I saw the series as an outlet for creative work that looked to understand a range of social, cultural, and economic phenomena in and through the lives and experiences of youth around the world. Since 2005, the global financial crisis as well as a series of worldwide protests put youth very much into the spotlight. Like many, I have operated under a series of assumptions about the last several years. Youth have been the primary victims of the global economic collapse (as evidenced by ubiquitous unemployment figures) and have responded to these and other injustices through worldwide protest movements (as evidenced by the Arab Spring in the Middle East to the Occupy Movement in the US and elsewhere). This is a narrative that has gripped scholars from across the political spectrum, differences emerging only in their responses to it.

Of course, the focus on youth has been longstanding in critical scholarship, including work associated with cultural studies. For example, Lawrence Grossberg has argued that a "war on youth" has been raging in the US since at least the 1990s. "Kids are being subjected to forms of economic, political, legal, penal, medical, and rhetorical attack" (2005, p. 364). For Grossberg, this war on youth is tantamount to a war on the future itself. "That is, the attack on kids is about the relationship between individuality and time. It is a struggle to change our investment in and the possibility for imagining the future" (p. 366). The struggle over youth is a struggle over modernity—the ability to aspire or to imagine a progressive set of social, cultural, and material relationships.

This work has been critically important for understanding the empirical experiences and conditions of youth today. *Youth Rising? The Politics of Youth in the Global Economy*, however, is a different kind of intervention. Sukarieh and Tannock argue that the discourse of "the future" itself has been hijacked by hijacking the category of youth. More specifically, the volume asks us who is responsible for the ways the category of "youth" has been used by various actors across the political spectrum. As such, it is a necessary and provocative corrective to much of the work done today in the area of critical youth studies—work that would pick up and deploy the term "youth" in seemingly self-evident ways. The heart of this book's provocative argument is that the category of "youth" has been put to use by various social actors for a range of ends often obscured by public discourse. For example, the authors argue that youth unemployment rates have been exaggerated or misrepresented by various neoliberal interests to give cover for free market excesses in the wake of the 2008 meltdown. This is of course counterintuitive. But Sukarieh and Tannock explain in detail how free market interests have not diminished in the wake of the meltdown but have expanded in scope and reach. Creating "panics" around unemployment and youth are one important way these interests have been allowed to advance unchecked. This is just one of the provocative arguments the authors put forward in this important book.

In another provocative example, Sukarieh and Tannock question the relentless focus on youth in the wake of the recent global protests. As they demonstrate, this focus on youth obscures the ways cross-generational strategies have been used by protesters around the world—strategies that have long historical antecedents and did not show up fully formed out of youth. The focus on youth has served to create wedges in what they see as a primary struggle against forces that would perpetrate structural economic inequality for the majority of the world over time. The same focus on youth and possibility has delimited the range of political possibilities available to youth. For example, the authors look closely at the global student protest over tuition fee rises in Chile, Quebec, and other countries. As the authors show, education has been increasingly massified, while opportunities for economic mobility have narrowed for those who have and have not attended school. As they demonstrate, the fight over tuition and debt has foreclosed a thinking through of these fundamental contradictions and critique of higher education itself has not necessarily emerged from these protests. Rather, they have worked to solidify the notion that higher education is the ticket to social mobility.

In these respects and others, the focus on "youth" has served the interests of the elite. The authors demonstrate the truly remarkable worldwide interest in youth and desire to invest in youth, including by a spate of governmental and non-governmental agencies around the world. On one level, this is a positive and remarkable development. On another, Sukarieh and Tannock show how this focus has precluded other kinds of discussions and has worked to keep youth—in their everyday lives—locked into neoliberal logics. This is a sobering critique for the field as a whole. As Foucault reminded us, all knowledge is dangerous and there are no safe spaces. Sukarieh and Tannock make the category of "youth" a dangerous one—including for progressive educators who would want to champion them.

Reference

Grossberg, L. (2005). Cultural studies, the war against kids, and the re-becoming of US modernity. In C. McCarthy et al. (Eds.), *Race, identity, and representation in education* (pp. 349–368). New York: Routledge.

ACKNOWLEDGMENTS

This book builds on a series of case studies investigating the changing circumstances of youth, work and education in the global economy that we have published previously and that are cited throughout the following pages. *Chapter 1: The Neoliberal Embrace of Youth* directly incorporates material that we have written in two articles published in the *Journal of Youth Studies*: "In the best interests of youth or neoliberalism? The World Bank and the new global youth empowerment project" appeared in 2008 in Volume 11, Issue 3 of the *Journal of Youth Studies*; and "The positivity imperative: A critical look at the 'new' youth development movement" appeared in 2011 in Volume 14, Issue 6 of the *Journal of Youth Studies*.

INTRODUCTION

Young people are at the heart of today's great strategic opportunities and challenges, from rebuilding the global economy to combating violent extremism to building sustainable democracies.

(United States Secretary of State Hillary Clinton,
Tunis, Tunisia, February 25, 2012)

In February 2012, United States Secretary of State Hillary Clinton went to Tunisia to speak at a youth conference in Tunis. The conference, which was called "Youth Rising: Aspirations and Expectations," took place just over a year after the overthrow of the Ben Ali regime in Tunisia. According to Clinton, it was the "young people of Tunisia" who were responsible for the Tunisian revolution, and who had struck "the first blows for freedom and opportunity" in the region. More than this, it was the failure of the Arab regimes "to offer young people a better vision for the future" that had led many of them, over the previous year, to "sink into the sand." Clinton told the conference delegates that, across the world, "the needs and interests of young people have been marginalized for too long."

"The world ignores youth at its peril," warned Clinton, because of "what experts call a youth bulge"—the growing proportion of the population of the developing world who are "under the age of 30." "I have fought to put women's empowerment on the international agenda," said Clinton: "I think it's time to put youth empowerment there as well." To do this, Clinton reported that the US State Department had created a new Office of Global Youth Issues in Washington, DC, and was currently creating new youth councils at US embassies and consulates around the world. Clinton also used the conference in Tunis to announce the creation of a new Global Youth Jobs Alliance, which would bring together government, the private sector, universities and non-profits to tackle the growing crisis of global youth unemployment (Clinton, 2012).

Clinton's presence and remarks at the Tunisian "Youth Rising" conference epitomize the growing centrality of youth to contemporary global political discourse. In the context of global development programs, aid and development organizations such as the World Bank, the United Nations, the International Labour Organization and the World Economic Forum have increasingly focused on youth and youth issues as key development priorities. The World Bank's (2006) *World Development Report 2007*, for example, was dedicated entirely to addressing the current state of the world's youth. In the wake of the global economic crisis of 2008–2009, there has been growing concern, in countries around the world, over rising levels of youth unemployment and underemployment, and recurrent talk of the risk of a worldwide "lost generation" (ILO, 2010). In the context of the US-led global war on terror, increased attention has been paid to the destabilizing effects of alleged youth extremism, youth involvement in violent conflicts and militia activities, and the local and global security impacts of the so-called demographic "youth bulge" (Beehner, 2007; USIP, 2010). In the context of the mass uprisings throughout the Arab world in 2011–2012, which toppled governments in Tunisia, Egypt, Libya and Yemen, global media and policy discussions have widely framed and labeled these uprisings as being, above all else, youth-led revolutions (e.g., Feiler, 2011). Over the past decade, national governments, in both the global North and South, have developed and/or expanded national youth policies, youth councils and youth ministries; while in the context of civil society, there has been an explosion of local, national and international youth-oriented NGOs, thinktanks and media channels (Kraftl, Horton & Tucker, 2012; van Dijk, de Bruijn, Cardoso & Butter, 2011).

All of this activity has been echoed by a parallel surge in academic youth studies. The past decade has witnessed a proliferation of research, conferences, articles, books, book series, journals, research and teaching centers, professional societies and academic subfields all dedicated to the academic study of youth and adolescence (Sukarieh & Tannock, 2011; van Dijk et al., 2011). Most recently, for example, the academic discipline of geography has experienced the rapid growth of studies that focus on the "geographies of youth" (Jeffrey, 2010, 2012a, 2012b; Kraftl, Horton & Tucker, 2012). Before that, it was the discipline of anthropology that discovered youth as one of its perennially missing subjects (Bucholtz, 2002; *Cultural Anthropology*, 2011; Durham, 2004). However, as some critical observers of the field of youth studies have noted, despite this growth in academic research and writing on youth, there has been a striking lack of critical reflexivity in asking exactly *why* there has been this dramatic increase in political and academic interest in youth during the contemporary period (Jones, 2009, pp. 26–27; van Dijk et al., 2011). Youth studies today is dominated by empirical research on the lives, experiences and subjectivities of individual young people, and by the normative celebration of reported examples of youth agency, capacity and empowerment.

The theoretical investigation of the political and ideological construction of youth as a social category, and the structural analysis of how youth as a social category is embedded in and shaped by broader changes in global society and political economy—approaches that used to be a central part of youth studies in previous eras—are now much less widely practiced (Furlong, 2009; Mizen, 2002). Paradoxically, for all the talk and writing going on now about young people, there is a sense, therefore, in which the ideological substance and social and political significance of youth itself have often been left largely "invisible" (Jones, 2009, p. 25; see also Griffin, 1997; Mizen, 2002).

In this book, our aim is to analyze and understand the significance of youth in the contemporary global political economy. How is it that youth have come to be seen by so many as being, in the words of US Secretary of State Hillary Clinton (2012), "at the heart of today's great strategic opportunities and challenges, from rebuilding the global economy to combating violent extremism to building sustainable democracies?" How is it that not just youth but "youth empowerment" have come to be taken up as priority concerns of some of the world's most powerful and influential organizations, from the US State Department to the World Bank to the World Economic Forum? How is it, too, that much the same rhetoric of youth and youth empowerment has also been commonly adopted as a "rallying cry" for "radical and revolutionary movements from South Africa to the US inner city" (Venkatesh & Kassimir, 2007, p. 9)—movements that generally tend to view the policies of the US State Department, the World Bank and the World Economic Forum as being precisely what they are rallying against?

Youth, after all, is a concept whose definition and boundaries are notoriously fuzzy. Even the apparently basic question of who is and is not a "youth" is not always easy to answer, as determinations of the ages at which youth is said to begin and end can vary widely, depending upon place, time, individual and institutional context. The social meaning and significance of youth can frequently take on polar opposite forms (Comaroff & Comaroff, 2005). The extraordinary diversity of context and experience of young people of different class, gender, race and ethnicity living in different parts of the world can make it difficult to know what, if anything, such a heterogeneous group might possibly share apart from their common age. Conversely, it is often unclear what the term "youth" marks out that is particularly distinctive or unique in society, that is not also shared by many adults (Mizen, 2002, p. 9). "What do young people want?," asked Hillary Clinton (2012) at the Youth Rising conference in Tunisia. Answering her own question, she declared, "they want the same thing as what all of us want." But such a response, whether true or not, raises the further question of why, then, Clinton and others are now placing so much emphasis on youth as being a critically relevant social category? Such imprecision, diversity and ambiguity have previously led to a long history of social scientific skepticism about the validity and utility of youth as a sociological concept. "La jeunesse n'est qu'un mot," the French sociologist Pierre Bourdieu (1984) once said ("youth is just a word"). Or, as Stuart Hall and his colleagues complained back in the 1970s: "Youth as a concept is unthinkable. Even youth as a social category does not make much empirical sense" (Hall et al., 1976; quoted in Jones, 2009, p. 21).

Our argument is that youth does matter, does make sense, and is much more than just a word. But in order to understand the significance of youth in the current period, it is necessary to do much more than document the lives and experiences of young people, celebrate examples of youth agency and creativity, or call for spaces for youth voices to be heard and youth empowerment to occur. Instead, we need to recognize, first, that the concept of youth, like all social identities, is a social construction, and both its scope and meaning are continually changing. Youth is not biologically given or determined: rather, its duration in the lives of individuals may be said to be shorter or longer, and its social, cultural and political salience as a stage of life and category of identity may be stronger or weaker in different times and places. Second, the shifting scope, meaning and salience of youth are shaped not just by young people themselves, but by a whole host of other social institutions and actors as well, each pursuing different political agendas and ideologies, in the context of the ever-changing social relations and political economy of a global capitalist society. Both youth as a social category and the individual lives of young people are constantly being worked upon, molded, given form and substance—in a word, produced—by the actions of the state, schools, universities, courts, corporations, the media, churches, NGOs and other civil society organizations operating at the local, national and global levels.

To understand the significance of youth in global society, it is thus necessary to look well beyond youth and young people in and of themselves. This is not just because of the wide range of social and political actors involved in shaping the meaning and salience of youth, but also because of the extended scope of referents the concept of youth implicates. Youth functions invariably as a relational concept, one that is defined and given meaning through its contrastive relationships with the concepts of both childhood and adulthood (Wyn & White, 1997). To make claims about youth, then, is to make claims at the same time about adults and children (and vice versa). As Susan Talburt and Nancy Lesko (2012, pp. 2, 4) note, the category of youth "regulates both youth and adults," and "mobilizes actors, both youth and not-youth, to behave in certain ways." Youth is also widely used as a metonym and metaphor—or, in Durham's (2004) terms, a "social shifter"— for making general claims about the state of society and the economy as a whole, and articulating fears about the present and hopes for the future (Clarke, Hall, Jefferson & Roberts, 1975; Griffin, 1993). In this sense, invocations about youth are often made in the context of social struggles and political agendas whose central concerns may only be symbolically or indirectly connected to the lives of individual young people. Finally, ideas about youth (as well as childhood and adulthood), along with the concrete life trajectories and experiences of individual young people, are strongly and inevitably shaped by structures, processes and conflicts based on other identity categories: class, gender, race, ethnicity, nation, religion and so forth. As Sheila Allen (1968, p. 321) once argued, "it is not the relations between ages which explain the changes or stability in society, but changes in societies which explains the relations between ages."

Here we argue that, above all else, it is the rise and spread of global neoliberalism that have led to youth becoming an increasingly popular and productive social category and concept. In neoliberal societies and economies, youth has expanded vertically, to encompass a growing range of ages, as well as horizontally, in terms of the proportion of the population of different class, race, ethnic, national and religious identities that is now widely identified with this life stage. Youth has become increasingly salient politically, socially and culturally; and, in contrast to previous eras, it has been embraced, on all sides of the political spectrum, as a positive identity and social category, more than a pathological, dysfunctional or delinquent one. Three factors, in particular, have driven this expansive embrace of youth. First, youth is widely used to promote the desirability of social change, and package and sell new ideologies, agendas, practices and products. While this use of youth may be found in any political context, it has become especially central in capitalist society, with its emphasis on the transformation of the old, and celebration of the new. Second, youth is often used as a substitute for other, more divisive social categories, such as class, race, religion and nationality, and regularly serves as a universalizing and depoliticizing euphemism that obscures real differences of political interest and ideology. Third, specific characteristics of youth as a social category make it particularly useful for the neoliberal project of renegotiating normative ideas about responsibilities and entitlements from the previous welfare and development state era. These include both its binary and "betwixt-and-between" nature, that combines elements of the child and adult in an ever-unstable mix; as well as its close association as a life stage with the individualizing ideas of personal development, growth and education, aspiration and mobility. In thinking critically about the social politics of youth in the neoliberal era, then, it is essential to pay attention not just to how youth are spoken about, but to the fact that youth is being embraced as a primary social category to begin with. For without understanding the shifting terrain on which youth is understood, invoked and experienced, we are liable to misrecognize the significance of our own uses of youth as a social category and concept as well.

Different Traditions of Youth Studies

There are a number of different traditions for thinking about and studying youth in contemporary society: this book, in many ways, returns to an earlier tradition that has largely fallen out of favor in recent years. For the last couple of decades, two approaches to the study of youth have been particularly dominant. The first focuses on *youth as transition*, and has been characterized by often large-scale, quantitative, empirical studies of the life course trajectories of young people as they move between school and work, from parental homes and families to having homes and families of their own, and from dependent to increasingly independent social statuses. A central claim of this literature is that, in the wealthy societies of the global North in particular, these transitions have tended to become increasingly individualized and complex, and there thus has been a shift away from concern with broad social categories and structures of class, gender and race, etc. (Furlong, Woodman & Wyn, 2011; Jeffrey, 2010a; Jones, 2009). As Andy Furlong (2009, p. 1) notes, in his introduction to the *Handbook of Youth and Young Adulthood*:

> Compared to perspectives developed in the 1970s and 1980s, ... contemporary researchers [in the youth transitions approach] tend to regard individual agency as being more significant, while structural perspectives have become less prominent. There are certainly disagreements over the extent to which individuals are able to exercise choices and shape their biographies, but most new models [in this approach] make some room for reflexivity, even when they are underpinned by an acceptance that individuals are differentially empowered to make choices.

The second dominant approach focuses on *youth as cultural actors* and *youth culture*. This approach tends to employ qualitative, ethnographic and textual research methods to document the subjectivity and agency of individual young people in constructing and consuming objects of mass and popular culture— music, art, dance, fashion, language, sports, media, etc. A key concern here has been to understand what youth means for young people themselves, to view young people not in terms of their future transitions into adulthood but as fully fledged subjects and agents in the present, and to analyze the social and symbolic signifi- cance of youth cultural creativity and practice. Much of youth studies today is centered on the tensions and conflicts between these two approaches. Despite their differences, however, both of these approaches tend to share a preoccupation with emphasizing individual perspectives over structural ones, an embrace of the empirical study of individual young people over the theoretical critique of the construction of youth as a social category in society as a whole, and a general neglect of political economy and close attention to the changing structures and practices of global neoliberal capitalism (Furlong, 2009; Furlong, Woodman & Wyn, 2011; Jones, 2009; Mizen, 2002).

In this book, we return to an earlier tradition of youth studies, prevalent in the 1970s and 1980s, that looked at the construction of *youth as a social category*, and sought to theorize the changing significance and salience of youth in the context of the shifting structures and forces of capitalist society and economy (Cohen & Ainley, 2000; Griffin, 1997; Jones, 2009; Mizen, 2002). This does not mean we do not acknowledge the importance of paying attention to the agency, experience, subjectivity and perspectives of young people themselves; however, we insist that we can only understand such agency, experience, subjectivity and perspective by paying close attention to the broader structural terrain on which these are constructed and negotiated. As Marx (1852) said, in more general terms, "men make their own history, but they do not make it as they please; they do not make it under self-selected circumstances, but under circumstances existing already, given and transmitted from the past." Indeed, the origins of youth cultural studies were located in precisely this area of concern, and only subsequently have tended to lose their focus on broader questions of political economy, and develop an often exaggerated celebration of individual agency and subjectivity (Clarke, 2005; Cohen & Ainley, 2000; Kellner, 1997).

We argue that a renewed attention to global political economy is particularly essential in the current context, where changes in global capitalism have themselves led to an increasing focus on and embrace of youth agency, individuality and subjectity. Thus, a second general frame for the approach we take to youth in this book, that differentiates our work both from the youth as transition and youth as cultural actors approaches, as well as from some of the earlier traditions of studying youth as a social category, is our position with respect to the positive valuation of youth and young people. Youth studies as a whole has tended to frame itself as standing in opposition to negative stereotypes of youth: a key premise is that the core problem of youth in society is that youth are widely seen as a social problem. Youth, it is argued, are predominantly viewed through a negative lens (as a problem, pathology, threat, deficit, etc.) and the task for progressive, critical and radical youth practitioners, researchers and policymakers, therefore, is to promote an ostensibly more accurate and just positive view of youth instead (Finn, 2001; Lesko, 2001; Roche, Tucker, Flynn & Thomson, 2004). The problem with such arguments, however, is that they fail to recognize adequately the broader nature of youth stereotyping in society. Youth as a social category has always been double-sided, encompassing both negative and positive stereotypes. If there is one stereotype in which youth are sometimes said to threaten the very fabric of society, there is a flipside, in which youth are promised to revolutionize society and cure it of its past ills and failures as well. As Jean and John Comaroff (2005, pp. 269, 280) observe:

> Youth are complex signifiers, simultaneously idealizations and monstrosities, pathologies and panaceas. Youth stands for many things at once: for the terrors of the present, the errors of the past, the prospect of a future.... Youth as a sign of contradiction, as the figuration of a mythic bipolarity, is enshrined in the foundations of the modern collective imaginary.... It is crucial ... that we stress its [youth's] intrinsic bipolarity, its doubling.

To adopt terms used by Austin and Willard (1998, p. 2), youth have been widely constructed as "demons of culture"; but they have also long been promoted as "angels of history," viewed alternatively and/or simultaneously both "as a vicious, threatening sign of social decay and 'our best hope for the future.'"

The challenge for critical analysis is not simply to replace negative stereotypes with positive ones. It is, rather, to understand how and why particular kinds of positive and negative stereotypes of youth—or, indeed, invocations of the youth label in the first place—are mobilized by different groups pursuing diverging political projects and visions in changing social and economic contexts over time (Sukarieh & Tannock, 2011).

Finally, a third distinguishing characteristic of our approach that differentiates us in particular from the older, theoretical and structuralist approaches to youth is our interest in paying attention to the social construction of youth in a global context, and looking at the changing salience and significance of youth in the global South, as well as the global North. Older, structural traditions of youth studies overwhelmingly focused on the global North, the United States and the United Kingdom in particular, and tended to adopt nation-state perspectives and frameworks (Griffin, 1993). More recent work in the youth as transition and youth as cultural actors approaches have taken a more global perspective. But these have been limited by the kinds of problems discussed above: a lack of critical reflexivity about the theoretical construction of youth as a social category, an over-emphasis of individual agency and subjectivity, a prevailing focus on culture and consumption, and a continuing neglect of political economy. At a time when so many powerful social actors around the world have become increasingly interested and active in talking about, working on and constructing the object we know as global youth, there is a pressing need to look beyond the immediate perspectives, experiences, practices and life course trajectories of individual young people themselves, in order to understand the significance and salience of youth in the global economy and society today.

Overview of the Book

The remainder of this book is organized into five chapters and a conclusion. We begin in *Chapter 1: The Neoliberal Embrace of Youth* by presenting a broad overview of the promotion and expansion of youth as a social category, used for both celebration and control, in the contemporary period. We argue that the conceptual core of this new model of youth is the rapidly expanding body of theory, research, policy and practice that refers to itself as the "positive youth development movement." We also argue that the embrace of youth has been, in the first instance at least, driven by an elite project that aims to promote and sell neoliberal ideology and agendas, while displacing other categories of identity. The chapter analyses how the promotion of a positive over a pathological model of youth has been exported from the global North to the global South, and examines some of the key actors involved in this process: states, NGOs, international aid and development organizations, corporations, the media, schools and universities, academic researchers, religious and other civil society groups.

The turn to youth in neoliberalism is not entirely new, but is situated within a broader history of close connections between capitalism and youth as a social category. In *Chapter 2: Youth and Capitalism in History*, we trace this link back to the earliest stages of capitalist industrial development, focusing on the construction of youth as workers, youth as consumers, and youth as a category for social control—a framing that has been absolutely pivotal for managing the massive social, cultural and economic dislocations and instabilities that have been caused by global capitalist expansion. The chapter argues that histories of youth are often distorted by a focus on the experience of young middle-class men in the global North, and by a flawed perception that the most salient feature of the emergence of youth in the modern period was the removal of young people from the waged workforce, in the context of the expansion of mass and compulsory secondary education. Rather, we argue that the most notable characteristic of youth in capitalist society is its function in forming a reserve labor force, who are repeatedly pulled into and pushed back out of different forms of waged employment, in the context of social, economic and technological change, as well as recurring business cycles of economic expansion and contraction. The enduring links between youth and employment have long been among the most neglected topics within youth studies; and this neglect has broader ramifications for how we understand other aspects of youth in capitalist society and economy, in particular, the stereotyped construction of youth as the epitome of an unbridled consumerist identity and essence.

In *Chapter 3: The Specter of Youth Unemployment*, we expand on our claims, made earlier in the book, that the current embrace of youth is very often a project driven in large part by elite interests and agendas, by analyzing the growing concern around the world, in the context of the recent global financial and economic crisis, with the scourge of mass youth unemployment and dangers of a "lost generation." The starting point for this chapter are observations that have been made (often by commentators with politics quite different to our own) concerning the statistical mis-reporting and mis-measuring of youth unemployment in the recent economic crisis. However, rather than use these observations to diminish the seriousness of unemployment for young people, we use them instead to raise questions about how and why "youth unemployment" is constructed in distinction to "adult unemployment" or unemployment in general. In particular, we are interested in asking why global business and financial elites have been so willing to frame the labor market fallout from the economic crisis as being, first and foremost, a problem of "youth unemployment." We argue that the youth frame provides elites with an effective vehicle for displacing and reframing critique of their own responsibility for the economic crisis, and for using the crisis of unemployment to continue to roll out changes in policy and practice that support their own ideological and economic interests and agendas. In this chapter, we look at some of the key struggles that have emerged globally around the issue of youth unemployment in the last few years. We also point to the value of going back to some of the earlier literature that was produced in the field of youth studies on the issue of youth unemployment in the United Kingdom and the United States during the 1980s, in order to enhance our critical understanding of the significance of discussions of global youth unemployment in the current period.

In *Chapter 4: Youth as a Revolutionary Subject?*, we take as our starting point another context in which youth has become increasingly prominent around the world in the wake of the global financial crisis: that is the popular uprisings in the Arab region, southern Europe and elsewhere that have widely been framed as youth uprisings and youth-led social movements. The broader question that concerns us here is the relationship between youth and (radical) social change. For youth have long been positioned as revolutionary subjects, framed as agents of change, and supposed to have inherent radical potential. In this chapter, we look back over the long and often contradictory social, historical and theoretical literature that addresses the relationship between youth and social change, radicalism, resistance and revolution, analyzing the formal youth organizations that developed most notably in Europe around the turn of the twentieth century, as well as the global student movements of the 1960s and 1970s. We argue that in order to understand the role played by youth in the global uprisings of the post-financial crisis neoliberal era, we need to recognize both the deep continuities with previous periods in how youth are positioned and represented as revolutionary subjects, but also the ways in which this positioning and representation have been reshaped by dominant (neoliberal) discourses, practices and power relationships of the contemporary period. As with our analysis of youth unemployment, we are particularly interested in the question of who is framing the recent uprisings as youth movements (and why), and how the representations of these events as being youth-led compare to empirical realities on the ground, in terms of the participation and leadership of young people, both during the uprisings themselves and then, a few years later on, in their aftermath.

Finally, we turn to the topic of education, which has long been one of the most important arenas of social policy and practice in the construction of youth—and which is also one of the key sites where the tensions and contradictions of neoliberalism are highlighted most, for society as a whole, but especially for children and young people. In *Chapter 5: Education, Protest, and the Continuing Extension of Youth*, we analyze the significance of the mass student protest movements that recently re-emerged worldwide, for the first time in decades, over tuition fee increases, rising student debt, and concerns over education quality and content, from Chile to Quebec to the United Kingdom to the Philippines. We do this by considering these protests in the context of the decades-long expansion of mass formal education—from the primary to the secondary to the post-secondary level—the continuous promotion of individual social mobility as the ultimate and over-arching ideal for social justice and equality in society (and education as the principal vehicle for achieving social mobility), as well as the concurrent extension of youth as a life stage ever upward in age range, constructed specifically as a time of learning, development, aspiration and mobility. The promise that expanding participation in post-secondary education can lead to better jobs and living standards for all has been argued by a growing number of education scholars to be fundamentally flawed. One of the key questions we are interested in examining in this chapter, therefore, is the extent to which young student protesters are able to develop alternative visions of education that can begin to step outside of and resolve the contradictions and dead-ends of the social mobility model of education—or, in other words, the extent to which student protesters address (or fail to address) the basic problems and contradictions that underlie the extension of the very identity or social category through which they are taking action. In the conclusion to the book, we once again pull together the key themes and concerns for thinking about youth in the contemporary neoliberal period—as well as youth in capitalist society more generally—that run through the book as a whole.

1

THE NEOLIBERAL EMBRACE OF YOUTH

The last two decades of the twentieth century and first decade of the twenty-first century saw a remarkable proliferation of youth policy, programming and research across the globe. In the Arab world, for example, new youth ministries have been formed and national youth strategies produced since the start of the millennium; there has been a surge in NGOs tailored to youth; and youth parliaments have been created to increase political participation among youth. In Egypt, 60 percent of the youth-oriented NGOs that currently exist in the country were created between 2003 and 2006 alone. Many reports about the state of Arab youth have been released: the Arab League dedicated its 2005 and 2006 reports to the subject of Arab youth; and the Arab Network of NGOs dedicated its 2007 annual report to analyzing Arab youth and civil society. Likewise, in Africa, the African Union adopted an African Youth Charter in 2006 and declared 2008 the "Year of African Youth;" and African Union member states—from Ghana to the Gambia to Kenya to Malawi to Lesotho—have adopted new national youth policies (Ansell, Hadju, Robson, van Blerk & Marandet, 2012; Gyimah-Brempong & Kimenyi, 2013). Across the continent, youth have become a new and "major beneficiary" of local, national and international NGO programming, as aid and development organizations have "shifted policy-orientations from the 'rural,' the 'women' or the 'household', to the 'youth' as the new developmental target and hope for the future" (van Dijk, de Bruijn, Cardoso & Butter, 2011, pp. 1–2). Similar developments can be found occurring across Asia, Europe and the Americas: the rise of youth-oriented NGOs, youth-focused development programs, and a wide range of institutions dedicated to increasing overall levels of youth participation and civic engagement, including youth councils, youth parliaments, youth forums, youth consultations, youth mayors and so on (Loncle, Cuconato, Muniglia & Walther, 2012; Luke, 2012; Nenga & Taft, 2013). According to

YouthPolicy.org (2013b), since the year 2000, more than 70 nations from all regions of the world have created or are in the process of creating new national youth policies. While in some cases, these represent revisions of youth policy agendas that have been in existence for decades, in many countries, these constitute the first time there has ever been a national youth policy at all.

In the United States—which, in many ways, has served as the largest and earliest hub of the new global turn to youth—a new "youth philanthropy" movement arose during the mid-1980s, as foundations around the country became increasingly concerned with making youth issues a priority in their charitable giving. By the beginning of the millennium, there were more than 250 youth philanthropy initiatives in the United States, involving some of the country's largest foundations: Ford, Kellogg, Carnegie, Hewlett Packard, Irvine, Rockefeller, Lilly, Kauffman, Mott, Casey, Merck, Surdna and the Open Society. There were also regular summits, conferences and collaborative alliances established with the aim of developing this new philanthropic field (Falk & Nissan, 2007; FCYO, 2013). Largely through foundation support, the United States saw an extensive growth over the ensuing decades of new youth organizations of all stripes and sizes; and new arenas of youth service work that were dedicated to promoting youth organizing, youth activism, youth leadership, youth participation, youth civic engagement, youth empowerment and youth entrepreneurship emerged and expanded (Hosang, 2003; Kim & Sherman, 2006; Kwon, 2013; Mohammed & Wheeler, 2001; Taft, 2011; Watts & Flanagan, 2007). Foundation activity in promoting youth-oriented programming has been closely aligned with state initiatives as well, an alignment perhaps most clearly epitomized by the gathering of five living US presidents for the President's Summit on Youth in Philadelphia in April 1997. The President's Summit was an event that sought to "challenge America to make youth a national priority," and it led to the formation of America's Promise—The Alliance for Youth, a public–private partnership led by former US General Colin Powell and dedicated to improving the lives of youth and children across America (America's Promise Alliance, 2013; Falk & Nissan, 2007; Pittman, Irby & Ferber, 2000).

These local, regional and national shifts to embrace youth as a primary subject of policy and programming have been both mirrored and driven forward by shifts at the international level as well. In 1985, the United Nations General Assembly declared the first International Year of Youth: since then, the United Nations has adopted a World Program of Action for Youth (in 1995), declared an annual International Youth Day (in 2000), launched a biennial *World Youth Report* (in 2003), established an Inter-Agency Network on Youth Development (in 2010), and created a United Nations Envoy for Youth (in 2013). The World Bank has followed suit, forming a worldwide Youth Employment Network with the United Nations and the International Labour Organization (in 2001), establishing a Children and Youth Team (in 2002), creating a network of national Youth Advisory Groups (also in 2002), creating a Y2Y (Youth to Youth

Community) network of young World Bank staff members (in 2004), launching Youthink!, an interactive youth website (in 2006), dedicating an entire *World Development Report* to addressing the state of the world's youth (in 2007), and hosting its first Youth Summit in Washington, DC (in 2013) (YouthPolicy.org, 2013a). In 2011, the World Economic Forum created its Global Shapers Community, which it describes as a "network of Hubs developed and led by young people" who "represent the voice of youth at World Economic Forum events" (WEF, 2011). Similar programs have been launched by a wide range of other aid and development organizations around the world. Not only did the US State Department, for example, create its Office of Global Youth Issues and its global network of Youth Councils in 2012 in order to "empower" youth and "elevate" youth issues as a global policy priority, but in the same year, the United States Agency for International Development (USAID) adopted its first ever *Policy on Youth in Development* (USAID, 2012a). According to USAID (2012b), its new policy aims to reinforce the principle "that young people must be a central focus when developing country strategies and recognizes the need to support, prepare, engage and protect youth today as well as harness the energy and creativity of young people for positive change."

Research and writing on youth and youth issues have also expanded massively over the past few decades. In 1984, a new Society for Research in Adolescence was created in the United States; and over the next two decades, attendance at the Society's biennial conferences quadrupled (Lerner & Steinberg, 2004). A European Association for Research on Adolescence was created in 1988. New journals dedicated to youth and adolescence were launched—the *Journal of Research on Adolescence* in 1991, *Young: The Nordic Journal of Youth Research* in 1993, the *Journal of Youth Studies* in 1998, the *Community Youth Development Journal* in 2000, and *New Directions for Youth Development* in 2002—and the number of people working on and writing about matters of youth have continued to grow exponentially (Dubas, Miller & Petersen, 2003; Lerner & Steinberg, 2004). There has been a boom in book publishing on youth studies, with a growing numbers of handbooks and overviews of the field (e.g., Cieslik & Simpson, 2013; Furlong, 2009, 2012; Jones, 2009; Lesko & Talburt, 2012), and new book series dedicated to the study of youth: Routledge's Critical Youth Studies series, in which this book is published, was launched in 2006; Temple University Press's Global Youth series began publishing in 2011; and the European-based Youth Policy Press was opened in 2013.

What has led to this global turn to youth? Policy makers, practitioners, researchers and others often argue that they have simply been responding to changed social and economic realities that have made youth and youth issues more important and more widely relevant around the world than they have ever been before. Youth as a social category has expanded vertically, in terms of the chronological age range it is popularly understood to cover, and horizontally, in terms of the range of groups of people it encompasses. Children are said to be growing up earlier as a result of the spread of mass media, corporate advertising and consumer society; while adulthood is said to be increasingly delayed for many due to the growing need for post-secondary education and training, the disappearance (or continued absence) of stable career employment, and the corresponding rise in the age of marriage, parenthood, financial independence and moving out of familial homes (Arnett, 2000, 2007a). As secondary and post-secondary educational enrollment levels have expanded, labor market conditions for young workers have transformed, and global mass media and consumer culture have spread across the world, youth has increasingly become a relevant social category and identity not just for middle-class young people in the global North, but for young people across nations, social classes, and racial and ethnic groups in the global North and South alike. The spread of youth as a social category has by no means been uniform or universal: for young people growing up in poor families in some parts of the global South, in particular, who remain outside of formal education, the formal labor market and mass consumer society, the concept and identity of youth, as it is understood elsewhere, continue to have limited relevance. But youth is more widely recognized around the world than it has ever been, and it is a social category and identity that appear to be spreading rapidly.

Other social and economic changes are also said to have contributed to bringing youth to the foreground of global public and political attention. The World Bank's *World Development Report 2007* on the state of the world's youth, for example, highlights five core reasons that it argues are driving the growing concern with youth, particularly in the countries of the global South: a demographic "bulge" that has made the global South's current generation of youth the largest in history; a natural progression from previous successes in addressing the developmental needs of children worldwide, especially in expanding access to primary education and reducing the incidence of childhood disease; an increased demand for higher level skills, which are usually acquired during youth, as countries around the world move from manufacturing and agricultural to knowledge-based economies; a growing threat to world productivity from the spread of HIV/AIDS, which is often transmitted through sexual encounters in adolescence and early adulthood; and a decline in birth rates, population growth and labor-force strength in the global North that has triggered renewed interest in recruiting and exploiting the massive, unemployed and underemployed youthful populations of the global South (World Bank, 2006, pp. 26–44). For the CIA, the US State Department and other core institutions of the US security establishment, it is claimed that it is the (alleged) propensity of youth to engage in violent, militarized activity, combined with the expanding populations of youth in the countries of the global South, that has propelled them to the forefront of national security and foreign policy attention (Hendrixson, 2012).

All of these reasons, however, though they each may contain an element of truth, provide at best only part of the fuller story. For youth as a social category never simply emerges as an automatic effect of social and economic change, but is actively constructed as a tool and technology for managing social and economic change as well. The expansion of youth as a social category, at least in part, is also something that has been driven and shaped by the intellectual, organizational, financial and practical work of policy makers, practitioners and academics themselves: research, policy-making and programming do not just respond to emerging social and economic realities, they help to produce these in the first place (Lesko & Talburt, 2012). If youth as a social category has grown and become increasingly central to contemporary social, political, intellectual and economic activity, this is partly because the social category of youth has become more useful, productive and sensible for a growing number of organizations, agendas and ideologies around the world. One striking example of how this process works over time can be seen in the changing significance of youth in policy and development work in contemporary Africa. Rijk van Dijk and his colleagues at Leiden University's African Studies Centre make the observation that "in a number of countries in Africa, such as Uganda and Kenya, national publics have been discussing whether citizens of age 50 or even 60 should be regarded as 'youth'" (van Dijk et al., 2011, p. 1). The reason for this, they argue, is that:

> the current dispensation of donor funding, relief programmes and international aid [has prioritized] youth-oriented programmes. If the donor-ideology prescribes youthfulness for societal and developmental relevance, it will then dictate practice. . . . Youth has become an ideological project because an arena of interests and scarce resources has been generated around it.
>
> *(van Dijk et al., 2011, pp. 1, 7)*

Similar phenomena can be observed elsewhere. In the Arab world, NGOs that focus on human rights or story-telling or democracy promotion and so on have, over the past decade, often found themselves unable to get funding for their projects unless and until they reframe these projects as being about youth and tailored to youth. In the process, issues and practices that had previously been conceptualized as being relevant to the general population in the Arab world are reconstructed as being particular to youth instead. In order to understand this widening embrace of the social category and identity of youth across the world, we thus have to move beyond simple quantitative assessments of the growing importance of youth, and address more substantive questions: first, of how youth are being talked about within dominant organizations and discourses in the current period; and second, what is at stake in the shift to talking about ever expanding groups of individuals as being "youth" in the first place, as opposed to some other social category (e.g., as adults, or in terms of class, gender, ethnicity, nationality, etc.).

In this chapter, we focus on the nature and significance of the neoliberal embrace of youth by examining precisely these substantive questions. We begin by tracing the emergence of a new set of practices for talking about and working with youth that stands at the heart of the explosion of youth policy, programming and research over the past few decades—a set of practices that are often referred to as "positive youth development." We then address the question of why youth has become such an important social category in global neoliberal society, in particular, by focusing on the core characteristics that youth as a social category and identity has. We examine how the neoliberal model of youth that we describe in this chapter has spread across the world through the direct agency of a dense network of governmental, private sector and non-governmental organizations, and how this model has become hegemonic, even as it is often contested locally by individual young people and others. Finally, we address the question of what has happened to this neoliberal model of youth in the wake of the global financial crisis of 2008–2009, a crisis that many initially argued would lead to the collapse and eventual disappearance of neoliberalism as a dominant ideology, political agenda and set of social, cultural and economic practices around the world.

The Rise of Positive Youth Development

The shifts in youth policy, programming and research in the contemporary period have not just been quantitative, but have also involved a transformation in the principal ways in which youth as a social category and identity is constructed and represented. For, starting in the late 1980s and becoming dominant by the turn of the twenty-first century, a new "positive youth development movement" has arisen that claims to revolutionize the last hundred years of youth development theory, practice and research. This shift in youth work and adolescent study, which has tended to see itself explicitly as a movement and as being self-consciously new and inherently liberating and modern, first began in the United States and subsequently spread across the rest of the world. The positive youth development movement claims to draw on the latest advances in scientific knowledge and theory of what is required for healthy and normal youth development to shape not just youth and educational policy and programming, but a broad spectrum of social and economic policy and programming that impact individuals of all ages and life stages. "The field of youth development," claim the movement's proponents, "has encountered nothing less than a sea change in a remarkably short period of time.... It has been a quiet revolution, with relatively little fanfare or combat" (Damon & Gregory, 2003; see also Benson, Scales, Hamilton & Sesma, 2006; Dubas, Miller & Petersen, 2003; McLaughlin, Scott, Deschenes, Hopkins & Newman, 2009).

In this new positive youth development movement, the most important shift is said to be a turn from a century of pathologizing youth and approaching youth in a negative light, to a path-breaking sense of positivity and a new-found commitment to embracing and empowering the young. When introducing the inaugural issue of the *New Directions for Youth Development* journal in 2002, for example, editor Gil Noam wrote that:

> We have for too long viewed adolescence as a time of crisis and danger, and we need to understand the positive and productive aspects of this important time in life. This journal is dedicated to this shift in thinking. It is unique, created for an amazingly innovative time and an emerging field.
>
> *(quoted in McLaughlin et al., 2009)*

In this more positive view of youth, the agency, contributions and capabilities of the young in society are to be recognized, celebrated and supported. To do this, a whole set of new youth leadership, youth entrepreneurship, youth organizing and youth civic engagement practices, programs and organizations have been developed that are geared, on the one hand, to recognizing and capitalizing upon the inherent abilities of the young, and on the other, to creating, nurturing and guiding these youthful abilities in what are deemed to be socially, politically and economically effective and desirable ways.

More specifically, what positive youth development as a field of research and practice has sought to do is identify the core competencies and characteristics that youth need to have to develop into healthy and "thriving" adults in a "free" and "productive" society and economy; as well as the key factors and conditions that need to be created in order for such healthy development to occur. A key premise is that once these competencies have been identified and conditions created, all youth are capable of healthy or positive development. Thus, Richard Lerner and his colleagues have put forward a widely embraced model of the "Five Cs" that all "prepared" and "productive" youth need to acquire: competence, character, confidence, connection and caring (Lerner, 2004). Peter Benson and his colleagues at the Search Institute, meanwhile, have identified 40 internal and external "developmental assets" that need to be acquired by and provided for all healthy youth (Benson, 1997; Scales & Leffert, 1999). Colin Powell and America's Promise—the Alliance for Youth identified "five promises" that were necessary for positive youth development—caring adults, safe places, a healthy start, marketable skills and community service opportunities—and aimed to use these promises "to mobilize people from every sector of American life to build the character and competence of our nation's youth" (America's Promise Alliance, 2007, p. 5). There are other lists as well: for the National Research Council (2002) in the United States, there are 28 "personal and social assets that facilitate positive youth development;" while Richard Catalano and his colleagues find that there are just 15 core "constructs" of positive youth development (Catalano, Berglund, Ryan, Lonczak & Hawkins, 2004). Academic journals in the field regularly publish reports of studies testing which of these various lists of competencies best captures the process of positive youth development, and which interventions and programs most successfully foster these desired sets of characteristics among the young.

Some critics have argued that, despite its rhetoric of radical change, there is actually little that is new about the positive youth development movement. Coussée, Roets and De Bie (2009, p. 425), for example, argue that "the underlying assumptions of this seemingly positive and preventative paradigm indicate and reaffirm a view of the development of vulnerable youth as lacking, deviant and pathological," and warn that the positive youth development movement is a "tricky snake in the grass." As Kelly (2006, p. 16) points out, positive views of youth are simply the flipside of negative views of youth, and whether the one or the other is emphasized, each serves equally well to signal a particular set of institutional and ideological expectations "about whom we should, as adults, become." In many respects, it is the overall gestalt of what positive youth development represents that matters far more than its specific empirical claims or practices. Through providing a vague and generically defined but positive language of youth that everyone can feel good about and appearing to accommodate long-standing critiques of youth development theory (that it pathologizes youth and fails to consider social, cultural, political and economic contexts), positive youth development works to reassert the continuing relevance of the youth development framework as the most important conceptual model for thinking about and working with that ever expanding segment of our population that we have collectively come to define as youth.

However, though it is true that the positive youth development movement constitutes, in many ways, a continuation of the practices and theories of "old" youth development models, it would be a mistake to see it solely as a repackaging of old ideas about youth in new rhetoric. For the positive youth development movement also represents a shift in dominant conceptualizations of youth that has been driven, in large part, by neoliberal ideology and human capital theory. Positive youth development rhetoric is absolutely saturated with the language of human capital: youth are constantly referred to as "assets" and "resources." "Africa's greatest assets are its young people," claims Ahmad Ahendawi (2013), the UN Secretary-General's new Envoy for Youth, echoing statements that can be heard regularly around the world:

> European Youth is the Union's Most Valuable Resource.
> *(Chirimbu, Vasilescu & Barbu-Chirimbu, 2011)*

> Get involved and be a part of the forward planning critical to the employment, skills and life chances of UK plc's most valuable resource— our young people.
> *(AELP, 2013)*

> Youth, Not Oil, Is Nigeria's Most Valuable Resource.
> *(Wilson, 2013)*

> Youth are [Uganda's] most valuable asset, are an integral component of the development process and they provide for and safeguard the future of the nation.
>
> *(Mukwaya, 2001)*

Indeed, the notion that youth are "resources to be developed rather than … problems to be managed" has become one of the central mantras of the positive youth development field (Roth & Brooks-Gunn, 2003, p. 94). This "youth-as-asset" frame, moreover, is promoted in direct contrast to traditional deficit models of youth that portray youth and adolescence as a time of storm and stress, raging hormones and problematic behavior.

The nature of this shift in how youth is represented can be clearly seen by looking closely at one of the foundational texts of the positive youth development movement, the William T. Grant Foundation's (1988b) *The Forgotten Half: Pathways to Success for America's Youth and Young Families. The Forgotten Half* focused on the post-compulsory education experiences of "non-college bound" youth in the United States, many of whom spend years drifting in and out of employment and cycling from one temporary, low skill, low pay job to another. Traditionally, this phenomenon had been attributed to the immaturity of youth: because youth in their late teens and early 20s are focused primarily on their personal and social lives, they are unwilling and unable to make much of a commitment to work, and thus take on jobs that demand little from them (Osterman, 1980). Since it was believed that such "immaturity" was shaped by the "deeper foundation" of adolescent psychology, there was little that employers or policymakers could do (Osterman, 1980, p. 150). Erik Erikson's (1968) theory of adolescence as a "moratorium period," in which youth need freedom to withdraw from social commitments and responsibilities in order to explore and form their adult identities, is one of the clearest statements of such traditional developmentalist views of youth. *The Forgotten Half*, however, along with other reports that came out at the same time, turned such arguments on their head: youth are *not* inherently fragile or deviant or irresponsible; rather, when given the chance, youth make "responsible," "resourceful" and "resilient" workers (William T. Grant Foundation, 1988b, p. 4). The problem of youth today is that, first, widespread acceptance of deficit models of youth can "become self-fulfilling prophecies" (William T. Grant Foundation, 1988a, p. 9). Youth are resources, these reports argued, and as resources, they can be well-used or mis-used: if we don't expect much from our young, then we will not get much from our young in return (William T. Grant Foundation, 1988a, p. 9; see also National Center on Education and the Economy, 1990, p. 43). The second problem was that links between youth, schools and employers had become too weak and there was, therefore, an urgent need to build stronger ties between them. Far from needing to preserve a space for youth to develop that was sheltered from the adult world of work, the lives and learning experiences of youth should be harnessed ever more closely to the needs and interests of employers, the workplace, the market and the economy at large. The promotion of the youth-as-asset frame, then, was closely tied to a larger neoliberal project of further vocationalizing education, promoting close business–education partnerships, and reshaping schools and other institutions working with youth along corporate, business and market lines (Tannock, 2001, pp. 23–31).

A key part of the shift that has occurred with positive youth development has involved moving the image of youth from one of opposition or exclusion from mainstream society and the corporate-led economy to one of whole-hearted inclusion. As we discuss in the following chapter, this is not entirely new: the celebration of youth has long been part of capitalist society. But the rise of neoliberalism in the 1980s ushered in an intensified period of selling business to youth and youth to business—and individuals and institutions involved in the positive youth development movement were a key part of this process. The Kauffman Foundation, which brought together the Youth Development Directions Project in 1998—described by Benson et al. (2006, p. 899) as "one of the first efforts to capture the breadth and status of the field" of positive youth development—is dedicated to promoting entrepreneurship among youth, in order to realize its vision of creating "a society of economically independent individuals" (Kauffman Foundation, 2013b). Carl Schramm, who was president of the Kauffman Foundation for a decade (from 2002 to 2011), has been called the "evangelist of entrepreneurship," someone who, even in the midst of the global financial crisis of 2008–2009, spoke against calls for government regulation and economic stimulus packages in favor of letting business take care of matters on its own (Riley, 2009). Benno Schmidt, who was interim president of the Kauffman Foundation after Schramm's retirement and continues to serve as a board member, was also chairman of Edison Schools (now Edison Learning), which has been one of the largest operators of for-profit schools in the United States. In 2003, the Kauffman Foundation also launched its Kauffman Campuses Initiative, that aimed to "transform the way colleges and universities prepare students for success" by working with a group of 18 colleges and universities across the United States to take entrepreneurship education out of its traditional home in the business school and spread it across the entire campus, embedding it in all fields of study (Kauffman Foundation, 2013a).

Similarly, the International Youth Foundation (IYF), which has been one of the most prominent proponents of positive youth development globally (two of its executives, Rick Little and Karen Pittman, helped to create the Forum for Youth Investment, the President's Summit on Youth, and America's Promise—the Alliance for Youth), is essentially a global marketing organization for some of the world's largest and wealthiest corporations. According to the IYF, the foundation "was created largely to help global companies ... plan effective strategies for investing in children and youth" (Reese, Thorup & Gerson, 2002, p. 4). In 1997, the IYF adopted a growth strategy called the "Irresistible Proposition," in which it sought to "become the 'vehicle of choice' for donors" wanting to link their corporate image with the promotion of youth well-being (Reese et al., 2002, p. 14). The IYF argues that:

> not only are children and youth a non-threatening and emotionally satis-
> fying area of corporation and/or foundation engagement, but the turn of
> the millennium added to the global interest in "doing something for the
> next generation." From a corporate standpoint, it is difficult to think of
> a more attractive beneficiary population. Work on behalf of children and
> youth has a universal appeal that crosses political, religious, and ethnic
> lines. . . . IYF's emphasis on long-term youth development and its focus on
> the positive as opposed to the negative aspects of youth issues increase the
> organization's attractiveness to potential . . . partners.
>
> *(Reese et al., 2002, pp. 19–20)*

The IYF has partnered with USAID, the World Bank and corporations such as Nike, Nokia, Cisco, Microsoft, Shell, GE, Coca-Cola, Starbucks, the Gap and so on to set up youth development programs all over the world that serve as "an integral part of [each] company's brand and corporate identity" (Reese et al., 2002, p. 56). Youth are thus being embraced by corporations not just as both current and future consumers and workers, but also as a central part of their public relations strategies and brand marketing.

The flipside of this corporate embrace of youth in the positive youth development movement is a subtle but sustained critique of welfare state support for families, youth and children. Part of the appeal of focusing on positive aspects of youth is that social problems can be more easily ignored. The difference between traditional deficit models of youth and the new positive outlook, according to Benson and Saito (2000, p. 126), is that the deficit model "accents naming and reducing obstacles to positive human development (e.g., poverty, family violence, victimization, abuse, neglect, negative peer or adolescent influence)," whereas positive youth development "moves in the direction of naming and promoting core positive developmental processes, opportunities and experiences." In this model, in other words, there is no need to focus on unpleasant issues of poverty, unemployment, inequality, injustice, war or occupation and so on. As Ehrenreich (2009) observes more generally, in her critique of the promotion of "positive thinking" in the United States, dwelling on such negative matters is now said to be part of the problem. Instead, individuals and communities are supposed to embrace positivity and take responsibility for helping themselves to get ahead and thrive. Traditional ways of talking about youth, warns Benson (2003, p. 25), have been warped by:

> a culture dominated by deficit and risk thinking . . . [that] fuels the creation
> of elaborate and expensive service and program delivery infrastructures,
> creates a dependence on professional experts, encourages an ethos of fear,

and by consequence, derogates, ignores and interferes with the natural and inherent capacity of communities to be community.

As a field, positive youth development has both promoted and been influenced by scientific research and theory on resilience—that is, the study of the character-istics and conditions (resilience factors) that enable a minority of children and youth growing up in adverse circumstances to succeed where the majority do not (Damon, 2004). Although resilience research, in and of itself, has no inherent or necessary political ideology, it can clearly be attractive to anyone wanting to shift attention away from structural inequalities and injustices to center attention on the responsibilities of individuals, families and local communities for enabling children and youth to get ahead on an individual basis (Seccombe, 2002; Canavan, 2008; Hoffman, 2010). Furthermore, since welfare state entitlements for children and youth have been based on claims of their greater vulnerability and neediness, arguments that emphasize the positive strengths of youth can, whether intention-ally or not, undermine such claims and entitlements. Positive youth development, according to Damon (2004, p. 16), represents a move away from the "fragile child assumption" of earlier periods. Rather than see youth as delicate, vulnerable and in need of shelter and protection, Damon (2004, p. 15) and other positive youth development proponents argue for a return to a "more traditional view that young people are capable of bearing life's burdens without breaking."

These shifts in the positive youth development movement are usefully viewed through a framework suggested by Robert Enright and his colleagues at the University of Wisconsin-Madison more than two decades ago (Enright, Levy, Harris & Lapsley, 1987). In the 1980s, Enright and his co-investigators looked at how adolescence had been perceived in the field of developmental psychology over the preceding century. Focusing on articles published in a leading journal in the field over that time span, they found a close and consistent relationship between changes in social, political and economic conditions in the United States and shifts in accounts of adolescence made by US developmental psychologists. During periods of economic depression, Enright et al. report, "theories of adolescence emerge that portray teenagers as immature, psychologically unstable, and in need of prolonged participation in the educational system" (p. 553). During periods of war, however, a different theory of adolescence prevails. At such times, "the psychological competence of youth is emphasized, or else [it is claimed that] the extent and duration of participation in the educational system should not be as great as had been supposed" (p. 553). Enright et al. argue that shifts in scientific understanding and social regulation of youth broadly reflect changing labor power needs in US society and economy. Depending on historical context, political purpose and ideology, youth may be viewed alternatively as mature or immature, strong or weak, competent or incompetent, stable or unstable, a pivotal or unnec-essary (and even problematic) component of a nation's fighting army or labor force. We suggest that the positive youth development movement represents another such shift, in which in neoliberal society, the competence, strengths and maturity of youth are emphasized and celebrated, as grounds for pulling young people into the workforce, opening up the spheres of education and youth development to market forces and business interests, promoting the ideology of neoliberalism among the young and undermining the traditional entitlements of welfare state provision.

The Significance of Youth in Neoliberal Society

What exactly is it about the concept of youth that has led youth to becoming such an extraordinarily popular and productive social category and identity in neoliberal society? As we discuss in the following chapter, in part this is an old phenomenon of youth being used to package and promote social change—a phenomenon that has been particularly pronounced in capitalist society, with its relentless promotion of radical social, economic and technological invention and upheaval (Ewen, 1976). In this sense, it is perfectly understandable that neoliberal reformers would seek both to link neoliberal ideals and ideology with the image of youth, and to inculcate neoliberal subjectivities among the young through education, training and youth development programs that promote such concepts as youth entrepreneurship and financial literacy. Indeed, one key strand within the rapid expansion of youth policy and programming across the globe over the past few decades has been the proliferation of organizations and programs specifically oriented to providing business and enterpreneurship training for the young, as well as the growing interest of organizations that are principally concerned with business, markets and the economy (e.g., the World Bank and the World Economic Forum) in engaging directly with youth development programming, a field of practice more traditionally of interest to social welfare-oriented organizations. We argue here, however, that there are at least two further characteristics of youth that have made youth a particularly useful social category for the neoliberal project of renegotiating previous welfare and development state entitlements and expectations.

First, youth is a relational social category that is defined in relation to and combines characteristics from both childhood and adulthood. As Allison James (1986, p. 155) notes, youth is a border category that is ambiguous, betwixt and between, "neither child nor adult." The work of Enright and his colleagues, discussed above, is useful in pointing out how the childlike or adultlike characteristics of youth may be variously emphasized in different social and historical contexts, and in support of different political agendas and ideologies. But more than this, youth takes on differing significance depending on whether it is being contrasted with and expanded into its neighboring life stage categories of childhood or adulthood. As the category of youth is extended downward into childhood, the adultlike characteristics of children are emphasized: rather than being seen as vulnerable members of the population in need of welfare state support and protection, for example, children as youth ("pre-adolescents") can be seen as individually responsible for their own choices and actions, and ready and able to make their own way in the grown-up world of business, work and the capitalist market economy. Conversely, as the category of youth is extended upward into adulthood, the childlike characteristics of adults are emphasized: adults as youth ("emerging adults") are constructed as immature, still in development, not yet fully "grown up," and consequently, may be said to be less entitled to make claims on such things as a family wage job, career stability or the means to live independently. Indeed, the promotion of emerging adulthood as a normal stage of development, that is argued to be healthy for society and positively experienced by most individuals in their late teens and 20s (e.g., Arnett, 2007a, 2007b), works directly to normalize the erosion of social and economic standards of living that has taken place for large segments of younger generations under conditions of neoliberal restructuring (see Chapter 5 for further discussion).

Second, the extension of the social category of youth vertically across the life stage and horizontally across different populations across the globe typically involves promoting the youth development model as being the most relevant analytic framework for talking and thinking about what is happening in the lives of individuals in the second and third decades of their lives, while backgrounding other analytic frames that focus on issues of class, race, nation, gender or the global sweep of social, political and economic conflict and change. Something happens when we start thinking of a minimum wage worker in his or her 20s as a youth or emerging adult, rather than, for example, a member of the working class. In highlighting youth as the relevant social category, one's analytic lens tends to focus more narrowly on issues of formal and informal education, training, learning and the individualized acquisition of skills and competencies. *The Forgotten Half* report—which, as noted above, is one of the foundational documents of the positive youth development movement—was written during the late 1980s and was concerned with the growing inequalities in the United States at that time that were the direct result of the neoliberal restructuring of the Reagan era. But rather than contest such restructuring directly, the report claimed that the struggles of youth (from poor and working-class backgrounds, in particular) were caused by a mismatch between youth developmental needs and the organization of schooling in the United States. The solution, therefore, was to be found in education reform (William T. Grant Foundation, 1988a, 1988b). Although the positive youth development movement often claims to have shifted away from the individualist model of youth development of earlier periods to an "ecological model" that addresses the environmental contexts of youth development, these contexts almost never include broad social, economic and political issues and conflicts. They pertain, instead, to micro-contexts of school, family and local community (Ginwright & Cammarota, 2002; Males, 1996).

The frame of youth development also tends to depoliticize social analysis and action. Instead of addressing political and ideological conflict and difference directly, the positive youth development model offers a supposedly expert and scientific body of knowledge that provides a standardized and universal set of principles (the Five Cs or 40 assets or 15 constructs) for what we need to do to facilitate healthy youth development. The World Bank's (2006) *World Development Report 2007* on the state of the world's youth is a good illustration of this process. To fix all of the social, political and economic problems that are experienced and (according to the World Bank) caused by the mass of marginalized and excluded youth around the world, the *World Development Report 2007* suggests that we do not need to worry much about questions of ideology, political economy or relations of power between and within nations. Indeed, specifics of local history, culture, social relationships and political conflict are left almost invisible in the report. Instead, all of these issues, all over the world, can be tied to a single, universal, unilinear and standardized model of positive youth development in society. The *World Development Report 2007* thus offers readers a model consisting of three "youth lenses" (which it labels as opportunities, capabilities and second chances) and five key youth "transitions" or "dimensions" (learning, going to work, staying healthy, forming families, exercising citizenship). Taken together, these youth lenses and transitions provide a tool for assessing how societies measure up to one another, and determining which policies should be adopted to provide for healthy and progressive social development. In the World Bank's (2006, p. 46) own words, the correct social and economic policies will simply "emanate from a youth lens." If we care about youth, and want to have youth-friendly policies, we will let the youth lens tell us what to do. In the *World Development Report 2007*, this lens has been packaged for readers in accessible, immediately usable form by the World Bank, and is used to promote what turn out to be a fairly standard menu of neoliberal social and economic policy prescriptions that go far beyond what is traditionally thought of as youth policy (Sukarieh & Tannock, 2008).

Another example of how differences in social and political agendas can be subsumed and obscured under a flattening youth development umbrella may be seen in the growing interest of US and international foundations in supporting youth leadership, youth participation, youth activism and youth organizing projects, all of which have grown exponentially in the wake of positive youth development's rediscovery of the agency, contributions and capabilities of the young. While civic activism and social movement organizing have traditionally focused on transforming society, foundation support for youth activism shifts the focus to transforming individual youth. Instead of addressing the concerns typically at the heart of analysis of civic activism—for example, the politics and ideologies of particular youth leadership, activism or organizing projects, the success or failure of these projects in changing social policy and practice, the links of such projects to broader social movements, or the question of whether the constitution of these projects as "youth projects" is enabling or disabling for political action—evaluation tends to focus on how participation in such projects enables or fails to enable positive youth development to occur (see, for example, SPRA, 2003). Once the youth label is embraced, all else can fade into the background. Positive youth development—along with its linked set of concepts of youth participation, leadership, organizing and activism—can thus be easily deployed to present a façade of engagement with radical, oppositional, grassroots politics that in the end works toward little more than fostering a generic and benign set of designated youth skills, competencies and character traits.

The Neoliberal Model of Youth Around the World: Diffusion, Contestation and Hegemony

The key features of the social construction of youth in neoliberal society—the celebration of positive aspects of youth competence and capability, the promotion of human capital views of youth as vital resources and assets, and the extension of youth in chronological age range—have spread around the world, in part at least, through the direct agency of a dense network of foundations, NGOs, international organizations, corporations, governments and individual practitioners, theorists and researchers. The International Youth Foundation, for example, which was launched by the W.K. Kellogg Foundation in the United States in 1990 with the largest donation that the foundation had ever granted, has worked over the past two decades with 175 partner organizations and 54 public and private donors to fund 332 youth development programs in 86 countries around the world (IYF, 2013a, 2013b; Mawdsley & Lerner, 2000). In the year 2000, the International Youth Foundation collaborated with the World Bank, USAID, UNESCO and a group of multinational corporations (including Cisco Systems, Microsoft, Nike and Shell) to create a Global Partnership for Youth Development that sought "to study, promote and invest in good examples of tri-sector partnerships in youth development around the world" (GPYD, 2004). In 2012, the International Youth Foundation created a new umbrella organization, the Youth Livelihoods Alliance, this time with the US State Department, the Multilateral Investment Fund of the Inter-American Development Bank and another group of corporations (Blackstone, Caterpillar, Hilton, Manpower, Mastercard) to "address the global youth unemployment crisis" by funding and promoting youth entrepreneurship and skills development programs worldwide (IYF, 2013c).

The Ford Foundation presents another clear example of how this process of spreading a particular set of ideas and practices about youth and youth development works globally. Ford, which as far back as the 1960s had sponsored youth leadership programs as vehicles for channeling and containing the black power uprising in urban America of that era (Allen, 1969; Ferguson, 2007; Roelofs, 2003), has also been a major player in promoting both the principles of positive youth development as well as youth service, youth civic engagement and youth leadership programs around the world since the early 1980s (Perold, 2000; Mohamed & Wheeler, 2001). In 1999, Ford worked with the Innovation Center for Community and Youth Development (which is itself funded by the United States government and the Kellogg Foundation) to create the Youth Leadership Development Initiative (YLDI), a three-year project that "set out to explore how young people benefit from involvement in civic activism and to discover new strategies and practices that youth development organizations can learn from the field of youth activism" (SPRA, 2003, p. 3). Though the YLDI was focused on the United States, Ford funded "four international fellows from Kenya and South Africa" who "took new ideas and practices with them when they returned home" (SPRA, 2003, p. 3). As Ford Foundation President Susan Berresford explained about the foundation's approach, "we take ideas seriously, first by incubating them, second by promoting them, and third by exploring them in other countries" (quoted in Mohamed & Wheeler, 2001, p. 16). Thus, Ford has exported positive youth development principles and funded youth development programs in countries throughout Latin America (Irby, 2001; Perold, 2000); with the International Youth Foundation, World Bank, Microsoft and Nokia it sponsored the LEAP Africa Youth Leadership Programme in Nigeria, starting in 2002 (LEAP Africa, 2013); and in 2005, it helped to launch Naseej, a community youth development umbrella organization based in Jordan that is also supported by Save the Children and the Rockefeller and Open Society Foundations, and that sponsors youth development programs in eighteen different countries throughout the Arab world (Naseej, 2012).

In spreading youth development programming, policy and principles around the world, some organizations are committed to creating and sponsoring programs for youth that are specifically geared to engaging youth in the principles and practices of neoliberal ideology itself—in other words, promoting youth entrepreneurship, free market economic theory and financial literacy. Junior Achievement, for example, which has been operating in the United States since the early part of the twentieth century, and which develops youth training programs that are geared to securing young people's "commitment to the principle of market-based economics and entrepreneurship" (Junior Achievement, 2008, p. 2), launched a massive global expansion beginning in the 1990s, moving initially into the former Soviet bloc countries in Eastern Europe and Central Asia after the fall of the Berlin Wall in 1989, and subsequently into countries throughout the Arab world, following the September 11, 2001 World Trade Center and Pentagon attacks. Currently, Junior Achievement claims to work with over eight million students in one hundred countries around the world each year (Sukarieh & Tannock, 2009). However, while Junior Achievement represents one distinct brand of youth programming in the contemporary period, many globally operative youth organizations and foundations promote a wide range of other, alternative and even oppositional political ideologies and subjectivities. What links them together as a single phenomenon is their focus on promoting the social category and identity of youth as a global policy and development priority, their involvement with fostering youth participation and leadership programs of different kinds, and very often, their shared funding streams and institutional support networks. The Ford Foundation, for example, funds work that Junior Achievement does in Africa (Junior Achievement of Africa, 2013); but it also sponsors projects that are explicitly geared to promoting forms of youth activism and collective organizing that directly challenge neoliberal, free market ideology and practice (e.g., Ginwright, Noguera & Cammarota, 2006).

To say that a neoliberal model of youth has spread across the entire world is not to say that this model has been without contestation or local variation. As Edward Said (1983) writes in his essay on "travelling theory," ideas and practices are inevitably transformed as they move across space and time to become incorporated in new locations, each of which has a different history, social structure, cultural and political context. Like people of any age and life stage, young people are never simply passive dupes or empty vessels when they participate in youth programs that have been designed by other organizations and states, but actively contest, resist and rework such programming to their own ends—as we discuss further in our chapter below on youth and revolution. In Jordan, for example, youth entrepreneurship and micro-credit programs run by international NGOs such as Save the Children USA's Najah and Junior Achievement's Injaz have met with considerable resistance by young participants on the ground, who draw on their own class identities, collectivist traditions and political consciousness to question and reject the teachings these programs offer (Sukarieh, 2013). In the United States, Jessica Taft and Hava Gordon (2013) have written of how high school age youth "activists" make explicit decisions not to work with formal youth councils, as they believe that other forms of political engagement are more effective, democratic and genuinely empowering of youth. There is now a growing literature that questions the motivations, practices and impacts of the rapidly expanding number of youth leadership and youth participation programs: rather than "empowering" youth or giving youth an opportunity to genuinely "lead," such programs often work as spaces of social control and containment, seeking to inculcate in their young participants a narrowly prescribed set of legitimate practices and viewpoints, and offer little to no real opportunity to effect radical or significant social or political change (Barber, 2009; Bessant, 2004; Kennelly, 2011; Matthews, 2001). Soo Ah Kwon (2013), on the other hand, has described how youth who do participate in such formal youth programs have sometimes been able to actively and effectively pursue radical political projects, despite the provenance of many of these programs in foundation-sponsored agendas to contain and control the activities and subjectivities of low income youth of color in the contemporary United States.

While acknowledging the inevitable presence and importance of such resistance and contestation, however, there are two key areas in which the dimensions of social, political and ideological conflict over youth in the current era remain broadly misunderstood. First, much work done by youth studies researchers and practitioners continues to be based on the premise that the core problem of youth in society is that young people are treated as a problem: they are widely and unjustly pathologized, demonized and scapegoated by dominant groups and discourses, and thus the challenge for progressive, radical and critical youth practitioners, researchers and policymakers must be to promote more positive (and allegedly more accurate) views of youth instead. The introduction to a recent edited volume of essays on *Youth in Society* is typical in this regard:

> Generally youth tends to be seen as a problem: young people are beset by predominantly negative images, are seen as either a source of trouble or in trouble. In bringing together this collection one of our main goals has been to challenge this problematising perspective on youth.
>
> *(Roche, Tucker, Flynn & Thomson, 2004, p. xiii)*

The limitations of this analytic frame become apparent when both mainstream and critical approaches to youth are marked by an overt and deliberate positivity, that manifests itself in the endless generation of programs dedicated to empowering, engaging and including youth. Today, it is not just leftists, feminists and anti-racists speaking out against the pathologization of the young, but individuals of every political and ideological stripe and color. What needs to be recognized more clearly, then, is that the act of promoting youth, proclaiming their power, strength or virtue, or celebrating their innate creativity or revolutionary potential is not inherently any more progressive, critical or radical—or just or accurate—than is criticizing youth, complaining about youth, disregarding youth or focusing on their shortcomings, problems and deficits. The promotion of positive views of youth, and the call to engage and empower youth, can be driven by and embedded in a wide range of conflicting political ideologies and agendas that demand close and careful critical attention and analysis.

The second critical issue that needs to be recognized is that political and ideological conflicts concerning the position of young people in society today hinge not just on the particular ways in which young people and youth are represented, but also on the very embrace of the social category and identity of youth itself to begin with. When a group of individuals in their late 20s in Cairo or London or New York decide to reject mainstream youth programs and discourses, and organize to challenge the neoliberal, market fundamentalism that is increasing social and economic inequality in their societies, and do so by constituting themselves as a radical "youth group" and speaking in the name of "youth," then they may actually be contesting only one part of the neoliberal model of youth. Likewise, if a group of teenagers in Oakland or Lagos or Mumbai become convinced that it is their youth that forms the most significant part of their identity, more than their race or gender or class or religion or nationality, such that they opt to join a youth group—rather than a broader-based political party or community organization or social movement—and mobilize on behalf of youth rights and youth agendas, then it is possible that they, too, are embracing what is now the dominant model of youth in contemporary neoliberal society, regardless of how radical or oppositional their particular political standpoints may be. The point here is not that it is inherently wrong to embrace the social category and identity of youth—for, regardless of an individual's chronological age, there may be occasions where it is critically important to do just this. Nor, as we discuss in the following chapters, is the invocation of youth unique to neoliberal society. Rather, it is that this embrace and invocation demand critical and analytical reflection, and need to be recognized as an inevitably political, ideological and socially constructed act. Unless and until this is done, then the neoliberal model of youth, such as we have described it here, is likely to remain hegemonic in contemporary society, since it will continue—to use the words of Antonio Gramsci (1998)—to "form the terrain on which men move, acquire consciousness of their position, struggle, etc."

Youth and Neoliberalism After the Global Financial Crisis

In the wake of the global financial crisis of 2008–2009, there was much talk of the end of neoliberalism, and anticipation that global society and economy were shifting into a new, and yet to be fully determined ideological era (Rustin, 2010; Stanley, 2012). The question must be raised, therefore, about what has happened to the neoliberal model of youth that we argue developed over the three decades leading up to the crisis. At least initially, there was a widespread sense that something fundamental had shifted for youth across the world. For all the years of youth programming and policy making, and the attempted incorporation and embrace of youth by governments, corporations and aid and development organizations, there was a sense of failure. Youth seemed to be in outright rebellion all over the world, and as we discuss in our chapter on youth and revolution below, there was heady talk that it would be youth themselves who would lead the world by force and example into a brave, new post-neoliberal world. The collapse of the US economy, in particular, raised questions for young people around the world who had been participating in youth programs that had often been designed, sponsored and based on US exported principles of positive youth development, youth leadership and youth entrepreneurship. As participants in a youth entrepreneurship program run by Save the Children USA in Jordan explained:

> If we had an illusion first that in America the economy was going well, we discovered after the crisis that the foundation of the [Save the Children USA] training was an illusion. We were always taught that in the US, the economy is running because everybody is an entrepreneur and because of the lack of corruption. What we have been seeing in the news is a different story, it is a country that is as corrupt as ours, and they are running their own country as they run the rest of the world.
>
> *(quoted in Sukarieh, 2013)*

Anecdotally, there have been reports that at least some of the young people who have been participating in occupations and demonstrations, from Tahrir Square in Cairo to Zuccotti Park in New York, have participated in youth leadership and youth organizing training in foundation-sponsored youth programs. Regardless of the original intentions and aims of those funding and creating youth programs, the irony is that the possibility always remains for young participants to draw on the training they receive in these programs and use it to radically different, oppositional ends.

However, even within the space of a few short years following the global financial crisis, the sense of a radical break from the past is much less clear-cut than it had been to begin with. Neoliberalism as an ideology, political agenda and set of social and economic practices has not only survived the financial crisis intact, but in many ways, been intensified, as governments around the world accelerate projects to further roll back the welfare state, privatize the public sector and deregulate the labor market (Crouch, 2011; McNally, 2010). More than this, youth policy making and programming—and more generally, the social category and identity of youth itself—have played a central role in the post-crisis retrenchment and extension of neoliberal agendas. Not only has the neoliberal model of youth not gone away in the aftermath of the global financial crisis, but, as we argue in the following chapters of this book, it has continued to shape both the actions of business and political elites, as well as many of the oppositional actions of young people around the world who have risen up to challenge the unequal, unjust and deteriorating conditions of their communities, their work and their education. If there is to be an emergence of a new form of post-neoliberal society and economy, then the social category and identity of youth will have an important part to play: for it will, of necessity, both require and lead to a fundamental re-imagining of the nature and place of youth in global society and economy as well.

2
YOUTH AND CAPITALISM
IN HISTORY

The rise of neoliberalism over the last three decades witnessed a corresponding rise to prominence of youth as a social category, a proliferation of youth studies research, youth policy making and programming, and pronounced shifts in how youth and young people are constructed and represented in mainstream political, media and academic discourse. This does not mean, however, that any of these phenomena are entirely new. For there has been a long and close relationship between youth and the different stages of capitalism throughout history—so much so that many argue that the emergence of youth as a central social category in the modern period was directly linked with the rise of industrial capitalism itself (Gillis, 1974; Ruddick, 2003). Not only does an analysis of this history help to better understand what is new and what is continuous in the current neoliberal period; but it also provides important correctives to some of the conventional ways in which youth has been talked about in the youth studies literature more generally.

Histories of the emergence of youth in the modern period usually start somewhere toward the end of the nineteenth century, at the stage of advanced industrial capitalism. Typically, the story goes that the expansion of secondary education in North America and western Europe that began at this time, and the consequent withdrawal of youth from full-time engagement in the labor market, led to the rise of radically new conceptions of youth as a distinct social category and life stage. The rapid growth of secondary school enrollments in Europe and North America during the first half of the twentieth century—in the United States, for example, 3.9 percent of 14–17 year olds were enrolled in high school in 1890, compared to 67.3 percent in 1940 (Taylor, McMahill & Taylor, 1960, p. 11)—is commonly linked to the growing need for white-collar and skilled technical workers for expanding corporations and state bureaucracies, as well as concerns of maintaining social order in the context of the extensive social dislocations that were being caused by the processes of industrialization and urbanization that accompanied capitalist development. This story has a number of key elements. First, it is a story of radical breaks in the concept of youth over the course of history. Authors like Phillippe Ariès (1962), for example, are widely cited for their arguments that pre-modern Europe lacked a concept of youth, and that during this earlier period, individuals passed, at about the age of seven, from an initial stage of infancy directly into the community of adults (Ben-Amos, 1995; Heywood, 2010). Second, it is a story of unidirectional change in terms of the withdrawal of youth from the labor market, and the identification of youth instead with full-time participation in age-segregated institutions of formal education. Third, it is a story that focuses on changes that were experienced, first and foremost, by white, Western, middle-class and male youth—changes that are then said to have trickled down, to a greater or lesser extent, to young people of other class, race, gender, national and ethnic backgrounds.

In this chapter, we argue that beginning the story of modern youth earlier, during the development of early industrial capitalism, can help provide a more dynamic, accurate and useful understanding both of the constantly changing relationships between youth and capitalism over time and across geographical and social space, and of the shifts that occurred in the concept of youth between the pre-capitalist and capitalist eras. In the story we sketch out here, rather than a radical break between modern and pre-modern, capitalist and pre-capitalist conceptions of youth, we argue that there are clear continuities between the periods, as capitalist employers sought to build on and exploit previously existing social and economic practices and relationships. Second, instead of a unidirectional and universal removal of young people from productive work under the forces of capitalist development, we argue that there has been a continuing back and forth movement that alternatively pulls young people into the waged labor market and pushes them back out again, depending on cycles of economic expansion and contraction, technological change, the development of new markets, products and services, as well as the impact of broader social, cultural and political conflicts and changes. Third, rather than the emergence of youth in capitalist society being primarily about the experiences of white, Western, middle-class young men, we argue that changes in the construction and experience of youth throughout capitalism have powerfully though differentially impacted young people growing up across class, race, gender, regional and national contexts.

In this chapter, we first trace out the changing relationships between youth, work and capitalism from the late eighteenth century to the late twentieth century, and from the original sites of capitalist development in western Europe and North America to its subsequent expansion to the global South. We then turn to two other key parts of the history of youth in capitalism: the construction of youth as being the epitome of the affluent, consumerist subject; and the deployment of youth by political and economic elites as a social category and technology to manage and maintain social order and control in the context of the rapid and extensive dislocations that are the inevitable consequence of capitalist development anywhere. In the conclusion to the chapter, we return to the question of how best to understand what is new about youth in the contemporary neoliberal period, and what represents the continuation of a long and close relationship between youth and capitalism throughout history.

Youth, Work and Capitalism

Throughout the history of capitalism, the problem of recruiting a cheap, willing and disciplined workforce has been a key challenge and concern for employers. This was especially the case for the owners of the textile factories that were at the center of the earliest wave of industrialization in Europe and North America in the late eighteenth and early nineteenth centuries, when most adults were engaged full-time in domestic agricultural-based production, and where waged factory labor was still an unfamiliar and novel experience. To solve this problem, factory owners at the time often targeted young, single women before marriage, who were commonly seen by their parents as being at best a source of surplus labor who could contribute supplemental streams of income to their families, and who typically were already engaged in spinning and weaving activities in domestic textile production in their paternal homes. In order to recruit these women, and assuage parental concerns about finding their daughters "a secure and safe situation" away from home, some factory employers sought to model their new workplaces on forms of non-household work that were widely practiced and familiar in the pre-capitalist and pre-industrial period. For generations, young women from non-landowning families had often been sent out to work in other homes as domestic servants prior to marriage. Indeed, domestic service remained the largest employer of young women in Europe and North America throughout the nineteenth century (Berlanstein, 1992, p. 70). Some factory owners thus sought to attract young female workers by providing dormitory accommodation and paternalist supervision, offering "living conditions similar to those available to servants," and advertising that their working environments "resembled the best aspects of domestic service." "A working girl admitted to La Seauve," according to a contemporary report of a factory-dormitory near Lyon, France, "finds a family rather than a factory." One factory employer in France "hired nuns to supervise the moral conduct of his employees," while another employed "an honest family" to look after the young workers in his factory-run boardinghouse (Tilly & Scott, 1978, pp. 108–109).

This youth labor recruitment practice was widely successful during the early nineteenth century, adopted by textile factory owners throughout Europe and North America. In the United States, the most famous examples of such practice were the textile mills of Lowell, Massachusetts, where between 1830 and 1860 tens of thousands of unmarried young women and farmers' daughters were recruited to work in the mills and live in company-owned and supervised boarding houses. In one of these mills in the 1830s, for example, studied by Thomas Dublin (1981) in his history of the Lowell textile industry, 74 percent of the workforce was female and 96 percent were native-born: and over 80 percent of the factory's female employees were between the ages of 15 and 30 (see also Foner, 1977). Mary Jo Maynes (2004, 2009) argues that the recruitment of young women into European textile factories was pivotal to the development of early industrial capitalism:

> The labor of women, especially young unmarried women, was imagined in the calculations of entrepreneurs and political economists; they were the population toward which state-subsidized industrial training schools were largely directed.... Indeed, they comprised the bulk of Europe's modern factory labor force at the dawn of the factory era.... New technologies that revolutionized textile production beginning in the eighteenth century were developed with an eye toward a potential workforce that was imagined as young and feminine.
>
> (Maynes, 2004, pp. 54–55)

The recruitment of young unmarried women into factory-based textile production eventually became a self-reinforcing process: such forms of work became recognized as being an appropriate and normative experience for women before marriage; labor migration chains were created that enabled farmers' daughters to follow their older sisters, relatives and neighbors, who had gone into the mills to work before them; and wage labor push factors were added to pull factors, as the rapid growth of industrial textile mills began to undermine "the bases of economic stability in the rural countryside" by competing with and undercutting the domestic production of textiles and clothing that farmers' daughters had traditionally been engaged with at home (Dublin, 1981, p. 5).

As Thomas Dublin and others have pointed out, even though the youth labor recruitment practices and ethic of corporate paternalism that were adopted by many early textile industrialists were modeled explicitly on previously existing social and economic practices and relations, they in turn helped to create new sets of cultural identities and social relationships among the growing population of young, female textile factory workers. In particular, the experience of large numbers of young women living and working away from home in age- and gender-segregated factories and dormitories fostered a distinctive sense of age- and gender-based community and solidarity, as well as the embryonic emergence of a youth-oriented consumer culture. Working conditions in these early textile mills were grueling, with workers commonly putting in 12 to 14-hour workdays, six days a week. But in places like Lowell, Massachusetts, mill girls were still able to participate in evening concerts, seminars and reading groups, explore city life together, engage in writing poetry and fiction, and so forth:

> The central institution in the female community was the corporation boarding house. There operatives escaped from the noise, cotton dust, and relentless pace of work in the mills. Relationships among women which arose in the mills were reinforced in a more relaxed setting. The boarding house, with an average of twenty-five female boarders sleeping four to six in a bedroom, was above all a collective living situation. The boarding house was also the center for the social life of operatives. After more than twelve hours a day in the mills, women spent most of their remaining hours in their boarding houses. In this setting they ate meals, rested, talked, sewed, wrote letters, and read books and magazines. From within this circle, they found friends who accompanied them to shops, to evening lectures, or to church events. On Sundays or holidays they often went out together for walks along the canals or into the nearby countryside. The community of operatives, in sum, developed in a setting in which women worked and lived together twenty-four hours a day.
>
> *(Dublin, 1975, p. 31)*

Wages for the young female factory workers of nineteenth-century Europe and North America were meager, and often sent home to support their families. But they also helped to create a new degree of independence from the patriarchal authority of young women's family homes (Tilly & Scott, 1978, pp. 116–121); and for some young women, they provided a small discretionary income that could be spent, in part, on purchasing some of the textiles that the women were now involved in producing, as well as other material commodities, for use in what Maynes (2009) refers to as nascent, consumerist "projects of self-fashioning."

The factory model of youth labor recruitment and paternalist provision of company-sponsored dormitories was never universal in the early nineteenth-century textile industry, and it did not last. In some regions, factory owners adopted a family labor system instead, in which parents and children came to the textile mills together to work as a family unit (Schmidt, 2010); and in the second half of the nineteenth century, in places like Lowell, the tradition of local farmers' daughters working in the textile mills before marriage while living together in company boarding houses was increasingly supplanted by an alternative and lower cost labor recruitment model of hiring immigrant workers, both women and men, of all ages, who tended to live alone or with their families in privately rented accommodation (Dublin, 1981). Despite this, however, throughout the history of capitalism, the strategies and practices around youth and work that were adopted in this early period have continued to recur. First, employers (and the state) have often targeted youth, both female and male, as a distinct part of the population available for providing cheap, surplus, temporary and easy-to-discipline labor, that can be drawn upon for attracting new investment, expanding into new markets, and developing new products and services. Second, there has continually been a push and pull, back and forth dynamic of young people moving in and out of the waged labor force, depending on business cycles of economic expansion and contraction, changes in the technological and organizational forces of production, and the impacts of political, social and cultural conflict and transformation (Katz & Davey, 1978). Youth, in other words, have long functioned in the capitalist economy as a key part of what Marx referred to as the "reserve army of labor" (Allen & Ainley, 2012; Standing, 2011).

Thus, although throughout the global North, the proportion of teenage youth working in the labor market generally tended to decline over the course of the first half of the twentieth century, as their full-time participation in secondary education grew, this trend began to reverse during the second half of the century. In the United States, for example, starting in the 1940s, the proportion of teenagers and high school students working in part-time and seasonal jobs steadily increased, rising from 27 percent of male and 17 percent of female 14–17 year old high school students in 1947 to 44 percent of male and 41 percent of female 14–17 year old high school students in 1980 (Greenberger & Steinberg, 1986, pp. 15–16). This is a pattern that has been replicated in many other wealthy countries. As Price, McDonald, Bailey and Pini (2011, p. 2) write, "data from Britain, Ireland, the Netherlands, Canada and Australia, . . . show that between a third and a half of secondary school students are engaged in paid work at any one time, and around three quarters of school students will have worked for some time before completing school."

This worldwide growth in part-time, teenage student employment has been driven primarily by the rise of a low wage, low skill service economy, that began to emerge as early as the 1940s, accelerated in North America especially during the 1960s and 1970s, and subsequently has been exported to other countries around the globe (Hollingshead, 1949; MacDonald & Sirianni, 1996; Mizen, Bolton & Pole, 1999). During this period, the development of chain and franchise restaurants and retail outlets, as epitomized by the rise of McDonald's and other fastfood corporations, radically transformed the nature of work and the make-up of the workforce in the service sector. Led by innovations introduced by Ray Kroc and the McDonald brothers, service sector employers increasingly turned to a highly automated and routinized, assembly line model of service production, where work could be performed by low wage, low skill, temporary labor, rather than requiring skilled craftspeople (Cobble, 1992; Leidner, 1993; Ritzer, 1996). At the same time, the service sector was also expanding its work hours, as growing consumer demand and the large-scale entry of women into the workforce (that made weekday shopping more inaccessible and home cooking and other domestic labor more unmanageable for many families) pushed the industry toward a seven-day week, round-the-clock schedule. As a consequence of these shifts, restaurant and retail employers explicitly targeted teenage student workers for their growing workforces, who, as full-time students living at home, could be expected to work as temporary employees for low wages on part-time weekend and evening shifts (Marquardt, 1998; Reiter, 1991).

This service sector turn to a teenage and student workforce was facilitated by a number of other factors. The growth of the sector coincided with the Baby Boom expansion of the post-war population, so that there were more teenagers available to work than ever before in history (Schlosser, 2001, p. 70). The sector was increasingly shifting and expanding into suburban residential areas, making their workplaces easily accessible for part-time teenage student employees (Luxenberg, 1985). Continuing educational expansion was creating a ballooning population of secondary and post-secondary students who were willing and eager to take on part-time jobs, and to see themselves as being only temporary service sector workers (Tannock, 2003). Cultural shifts meant that the idea of student employment was becoming increasingly normative, as an accepted part of growing up, and a rite of passage, for young people of all class, race and gender and identities. Finally, political and ideological changes were also leading to the embrace of the ideal of the student worker. In the context of a perceived "generation gap" during the social unrest of the late 1960s, for example, government-sponsored inquiries and panels in the United States, and elsewhere, on the contemporary problems of youth often promoted work experience as a cure for these social ills (Greenberger & Steinberg, 1986, pp. 41–45). The 1976 National Panel on High School and Adolescent Education in the US, for example, argued that:

> Only in the last 25 years has the majority of teenagers, through high school attendance, been increasingly separated from significant contact with older adults, other than parents and teachers.... In prolonging youth's dependence, the schools, inadvertently, have become social 'aging vats' that have isolated adolescents and delayed their opportunity to learn adult roles, work habits and skills.
>
> *(quoted in Worsnop, 1990)*

Though this new service sector model of youth and student labor recruitment and employment developed initially in the United States, it has subsequently been developed in closely similar form in many other countries, and may be seen today in Canada, Australia and New Zealand, the United Kingdom, western and eastern Europe, Japan and elsewhere (see, for example, Allan, Bamber & Timo, 2005; Fantasia, 1995; Reiter, 1991; Royle, 2010; Royle & Towers, 2002).

By the end of the twentieth century, many low-end service sector employers were deliberately constructing virtually all of the jobs they offered as being explicitly youth jobs—even when these jobs were being held by individuals who were no longer teenagers and no longer in school. When a group of Borders Books and Music Store employees, most of whom were in their 20s, tried to unionize with the United Food and Commercial Workers union during the late 1990s, for example, their employer sent out the following response in its monthly newsletter:

> We have highly educated employees who consider themselves "professionals," but who are in reality working at an early level retail job. Ultimately, each person must make a choice within the modalities of the possible. If you desire an enjoyable job while you figure out what to do with your life, this is a good place to be. But if you try to make a career path out of something which can never be a well-paying job, you will be up against an impossible task because of all of the economic constraints in the retail industry.
>
> *(quoted in Slaughter, 1997, p. 3)*

As Naomi Klein (1999, p. 232) writes, service sector workers are increasingly treated as if they are not "real" workers and as if the jobs they hold are no more than "hobby" jobs:

> Most of the large employers in the service sector manage their workforce as if their clerks didn't depend on their paychecks for anything essential, such as rent or child support. Instead, retail and service employers tend to view their employees as children: students looking for summer jobs, spending money or a quick stopover on the road to a more fulfilling and better-paying career.

The nineteenth-century youth labor recruitment model that was pioneered by textile employers in Europe and North America also continues to be used in the textile, electronics and other light manufacturing industries throughout the global South today. With the growing global division of labor that developed in the 1970s and accelerated during the 1980s, multinational corporations sought to relocate manufacturing work away from high wage, unionized locations in the global North, in search of low wage, non-union sites across the global South—a shift that was epitomized by the rise of free trade and export processing zones throughout the world. The parallels with the era of early industrial capitalism are striking. First, corporations in these sites have commonly targeted mostly young, unmarried women without children from rural areas, whom they see as being a cheap, mobile, easy-to-discipline, temporary and disposable workforce, and who can be let go when they marry, have children or reach a certain age (Collins, 2003; Elson, 1995; Marchand & Runyon, 2000; Mills, 2003; Ong, 1989, 1991). As Aihwa Ong (1991) notes, factory managers commonly embrace ideologies of both youth and femininity in explaining how they recruit their ideal workforce:

> A Japanese manager claimed that factories prefer "fresh female labor [that] after some training, is highly efficient." ... Similarly, a manager in Ciudad Juarez on the Mexican border said he preferred women who were "unspoiled"—that is, young and inexperienced: "Women such as these are easier to shape to our requirement." ... In Taiwan, factories sought young

women from the remote areas said to "have a higher capacity for eating bitterness."

Second, young women are often made available for factory work by the undermining of rural economies that is caused by capitalist development and expansion itself, specifically by the commodification and seizure of agricultural lands across the global South—a process that David Harvey (2005) refers to as accumulation by dispossession. Linda Green (2003, p. 51), for example, has described the processes through which young Mayan women in rural Guatemala have been driven "into circuits of the world economy as wage workers" in *maquila* apparel factories, as traditional Mayan subsistence farming has been displaced and destabilized by the decades-long promotion of export-oriented industrial agriculture across the country. Similar phenomena have been documented throughout Latin America, and in southeast and east Asia as well (Ong, 1991). Third, both manufacturing employers and nation states have deliberately exploited previously existing social, cultural and economic practices, relationships and identities in order to recruit, discipline and retain their young, female workforces. In particular, employers and government bureaucrats have sought to draw on traditional patriarchal norms from the home and community in order to promote women's subordinate status and docility, and legitimate low rates of pay in the new industrial workplace, often identifying young, female factory workers as being "factory daughters," "working daughters," "village daughters," and so forth (Ong, 1991, pp. 286–287; see also Drori, 2000; Kim, 1997; Lynch, 1999; Mills, 2003; Wolf, 1992).

Finally, though manufacturing employers in export processing zones across the global South, like the nineteenth-century textile factories of Europe and North America before them, have sought to exploit previously existing social, cultural and economic practices and relationships, their presence has at the same time worked to create new forms of identity and relationship among their predominantly young and female factory workforces. Work in export zone factories, though it can often be highly exploitative, involving low wages, exhausting work schedules, grueling and monotonous work tasks, and sometimes brutal and arbitrary forms of shopfloor discipline, is at the same time often appealing to young rural women, as it can offer an opportunity to leave home, gain an income, and win a degree of independence and empowerment that would not otherwise easily be available to them (Mills, 2003; Ong, 1991). In many cases, factory workers live together in dormitories, where they form close relationships with their co-workers, and develop peer-oriented, age- and gender-based communities and cultures. Factory work also offers young women migrants an opportunity "to participate in new patterns of consumption linked to desired and often globally oriented standards of 'modernity'" (Mills, 2003, p. 49). As Mary Beth Mills (1997, p. 40) writes, for example, for young migrant female workers coming to work in export-oriented factories in and around the capital of Thailand, "participation in Bangkok's mass-market commodity culture is one of the most salient aspects of their time in the city." "Part of what draws young rural women into the city is an unspoken but powerful suggestion that there they can be at once beautiful, modern and mobile," writes Mills (1997, p. 43): "With an urban income they can enhance their own beauty and modernity ... [and] they can participate in the adventure, excitement and independence of modern city life," by going shopping in department stores, watching movies, visiting entertainment parks, beauty parlors and nightclubs.

Youth, Consumerism and Marketing

Indeed, the dominant construction of youth in capitalist society has been not as workers but as consumers. Youth are most commonly defined in terms of their removal from productive roles in the waged labor force, through their full-time participation in secondary level education, and the age and life stage, consequently, is generally identified as a period of non-production, leisure, play, fun and consumption (Griffin, 1993; Miles, 2000). Writing in the US context, Sarah Chinn (2009, p. 19) argues that "perhaps no quality of adolescence has more defined ... teenagers than [the] desire for fun" (see also Palladino, 1996). G. Stanley Hall's early twentieth-century monograph, *Adolescence*—which is widely seen as the founding text for the modern concept of adolescence—claimed about youth that "to have a good time is felt to be an inalienable right. The joys of life are never felt with so keen a relish; youth lives for pleasure, whether of an epicurean or an esthetic type" (quoted in Chinn, 2009, p. 20). Carles Feixa (2012, p. 39) notes that "youth and leisure are two concepts closely linked in contemporary history and social research." Feixa points, in particular, to the role of the mid-twentieth-century sociologist Talcott Parsons in cementing this link theoretically:

> For Parsons, the development of age groups was the expression of a new generational awareness that crystallized in an autonomous interclass culture focused on hedonist consumption. Youth culture—analyzed as a homogeneous whole—was produced by a generation that consumed without producing, and by remaining in educational institutions not only was moving away from work, but also from the class structure.
>
> *(Feixa, 2012, p. 40)*

In fact, the overwhelming majority of youth studies in the social sciences through the twentieth and twenty-first centuries has focused on youth as consumers, documenting and analyzing youth leisure activities, lifestyle choices, consumption habits, clothing and fashion statements, and the collective identities, relationships, practices and values of youthful peer culture, club culture and subcultural groups and scenes. Many of the internal debates in this literature have centered on the nature and significance of youth consumption: the degree to which youth are active or passive consumers, the relative importance of class, race, gender and national differences, and the question of whether youth consumption should be seen as an act of resistance or submission to the structures and forces of global capitalism (Bennett & Kahn-Harris, 2004; Best, 2009; Capuzzo, 2012; Furlong, 2009; Hebdige, 1979; Skelton & Valentine, 1997).

Typically, the rise of youth consumerism is said to have occurred in the years following the conclusion of the Second World War. It was at this point, in North America especially, that there was a rapid growth in middle-class affluence, and high school attendance became nearly a universal experience for teenage youth. Between 1950 and 1959, the proportion of 14–17 year olds enrolled in high school in the United States grew from 65.3 percent to 95.3 percent, the largest increase of any decade in history (Taylor, McMahill & Taylor, 1960, p. 11). This growing population of high school students, who were recognized as participating in strongly age-based peer group cultures that were organized around their school attendance, soon became of increasing interest to retailers and marketers. They came to see school-going teenagers as constituting a vital new market filled with profit potential, a group whose consumption habits were wonderfully "unencumbered by domestic responsibilities or restraints" and were instead "concentrated in the realms of leisure, styles, and hedonistic pleasure" (Osgerby, 2002, p. 16). According to Eugene Gilbert, who was one of the pioneers of the emergent practice of marketing specifically to teenage students:

> The high school set makes its own decisions about what to buy and where to buy it, often dragging their parents along in their wake. Thus teen-age boys have created the vogue for button-down collars, Bermuda shorts, cashmere sweaters, sport shirts, "Ivy League" jackets and loafers. And the junior miss . . . leads the way in endorsing "separates," "man-tailored" shirts, ballet slippers, and skintight "stem" skirts or ballooning layers of petticoats.
>
> *(quoted in Osgerby, 2002, p. 15)*

In a report on Gilbert and the growing commercial youth market for the *New Yorker* in 1958, Dwight MacDonald argued that "teenagers are not just children growing into adults but a sharply differentiated part of the population," who represent "the latest—perhaps the last—merchandising frontier." "American businessmen," *Life* magazine had reported in 1944, "have only recently begun to realize that teenagers make up a big and special market." By 1959, however, *Life* was reporting on how the American teenager represented "a new $10-billion power," and had "emerged as a big-time consumer in the US economy." Across the Atlantic, in the UK, market researcher Mark Abrams was likewise highlighting the development of "distinctive teenage spending for distinctive teenage ends in a distinctive teenage world" (all quotations are from Osgerby, 2008, pp. 27–35). Throughout the 1950s and 1960s, businesses thus sought to cater to this growing youth market, seeking to both anticipate and shape changes in teenage consumer tastes, and produce an ever-expanding set of commodities oriented explicitly to teenage student consumption. Cultural critics such as Grace Palladino (1996) and Dick Hebdige (1988) have argued, in fact, that the very concept of the "teenager" as we know it today was essentially invented as a marketing demographic in the post-war period, identifying a new market niche for which goods and services could be produced, targeted and sold.

This construction of youth as consumer and youth as a time of leisure, however, is based on a series of myths and negations that lie at the heart of advanced capitalism. One of the characteristics of the promotion of mass consumption and rise of a hegemonic discourse of consumerism, that have occurred over the course of the development of capitalist economy and society, is that individuals are increasingly pushed to construct their social identities through the consumption of material commodities, and taught to see themselves as consumers, first and foremost, rather than as workers or citizens (Billig, 1999; Carrier & Heyman, 1997; Fleetwood, 2008). As Steve Fleetwood (2008, pp. 32–33) notes, the dominance of the discourse of consumerism "encourages us to think in terms of consumption, consumers and consumer society, while discouraging us from thinking in terms of production, producers and productive aspects of society." Michael Billig (1999), along with others, has argued that, in many ways, the promotion of consumer society and consumer identity is necessarily based on a collective amnesia or forgetting. "There cannot be consumption without production," Billig (1999, p. 318) writes:

> However, if the commodities are to be consumed as items of pleasure and as confirmations of the identity of the consumer, then the consumers must routinely not think about the labour relations involved in the production of what they are consuming. This means forgetting about the social relations which lie behind the commodities.

What Billig is talking about here is what Karl Marx identified as the process of commodity fetishism, a process that, as Fridell (2007, p. 84) writes, "not only stems from capitalist social relations but also helps to preserve their legitimacy by obscuring the social exploitation and ecologically destructive conditions under which commodities are produced." When we come to think of ourselves primarily as consumers, and articulate our interests and identities through the act of material consumption, we can become blind both to our own interests and identities as workers (and citizens etc.) and those of others who produce the commodities we consume. This, of course, works to the benefit of corporate employers and capitalism as a social system (McNally, 2002). Youth in advanced capitalist society, in many ways, are constructed as the epitome of this process of consumerist amnesia and commodity fetishism, as they are held up by retailers, marketers, advertisers—as well as many social theorists and researchers—as the ultimate realization of the ideal of consumer society, as full-time, hedonistic, liberated and affluent consumers who do not work or produce.

Despite the dominant construction of youth as consumers, youth, as discussed above, have remained an important part of the workforce. Youth consumerism, just like adult consumerism, has always been closely linked with work and wage earning: after all, in order to consume, one has to have a disposable income. The development of youth-oriented consumer culture, which actually began well before the post-Second World War period, was closely tied to the rise of waged youth employment, during the initial stages of industrialization (Best, 2009; Chinn, 2009). Kathy Peiss's (1986) research on young women workers in New York City at the end of the nineteenth century, for example, focuses on the importance of young women workers in the development of an urban commercial leisure industry. "Young, unmarried working-class women … dominated the female labor force [in New York] in the period from 1880 to 1920," writes Peiss (1986, p. 34): "Nearly 60 percent of all women in New York aged sixteen to twenty worked in the early 1900's." These women participated extensively in a "youth-oriented, mixed-sex world of pleasure" in the city's new dance halls, amusement parks and movie houses (Peiss, 1986, p. 6); they also "used fashion to construct an image of conspicuous consumption, glamour and affluence, whether those things were within their financial reach or not" (Chinn, 2009, p. 25). As discussed earlier, similar practices could be found in the textile mills of Lowell and elsewhere in the early part of the nineteenth century.

Likewise, the explosion of interest in youth marketing in the post-Second World War period was based on a recognition that youth had rapidly growing disposable incomes available to them. In part, this was based on parental allowances that were financed not just by rising incomes but by exploding levels of consumer debt that were taken on by their families. As Angela Record (2002, p. 182) points out, during this period, "consumer debt skyrocketed 560 percent, from \$8.5 billion in 1946 to \$56.1 billion in 1960." But it was also connected with the rise in part-time student employment. In 1964, *Time* magazine, for example, reported that "today's teenager pulls down three times more money than his counterpart right after World War II"; and in 1966, *Newsweek* claimed that "rising allowances and swelling incomes from part-time and summer jobs this year will put a whopping \$12 billion into the jean pockets of the nation's high-school boys and girls" (quoted in Osgerby, 2008, p. 36). Finally, as discussed above, the growing numbers of young women working in export-oriented manufacturing throughout the global South is directly connected with the rise of consumerist practices and identities among these young workers; and, as Naomi Klein (1999) and others have pointed out, it is also directly connected with subsidizing the consumption of low price commodities by youth and adults alike in the global North.

The growth of low wage youth labor in the export processing zones of the global South points to a second myth connected to the construction of youth as consumers, which is the myth of youth affluence. The image of the affluent teen consumer that was constructed by retailers and advertisers during the post-Second World War period was always centered on the experiences of white, middle-class, Western youth, and neglected the economic struggles and poverty of youth from other class, race and ethnic backgrounds (Osgerby, 2008; Record, 2002). This middle-class bias continues to this day in contemporary global discourses of the teen consumer: ironically, at the same time that there is growing worry about youth unemployment and poverty around the world, there co-exists a strong narrative of youth leisure, well-being and affluence. Indeed, as Claire Wallace and Sijka Kovatcheva (1998, p. 160) point out, the construction of youth as hyper-consumers with discretionary incomes to spend is paradoxically based on the decline in their economic independence, and their growing inability to cover the basic costs of living: "The increasing dependency of young people upon the [parental] household and family results in their dwindling economic power at the same time as increasing participation in consumer culture is possible." The "anomaly" of consumerism for many youth, in other words, is that because they are unable to afford to live independently (i.e., to pay for basic housing, education, transportation and food costs, etc.), they are forced to live at home with their parents for extended periods of time; but as basic costs of living are then covered by their parents, they have increased amounts of income to spend on discretionary wants (Jones & Wallace, 1992, p. 117). The myth of youth affluence works to misconstrue the relationship between youth and adult work, earning and consumption as well. As Mike Males points out, adult consumerism dwarfs youth consumerism: in 1999 in the United States, for example, teenagers accounted for just 2.4 percent of all consumer spending. Once again, Males notes that adult spending on personal consumption is vastly greater than youth spending; adults, writes Males, "spend five times more on gambling alone than youth do on all items from clothing to school supplies." Finally, the myths of affluence and youth consumerism are often used to legitimate poor working conditions and low wages for young workers in both the global North and South. The idea that working youth are temporary workers, just passing through, who do not have any "real" financial needs and are using their incomes primarily to support personal consumption practice serves to justify the lack of job security, poor working conditions and low wages (Klein, 1999; Tannock, 2001, 2003).

The third and overarching myth of youth and consumerism—which is that there is something inherent about youth as a developmental stage and/or the structural position of youth in modern society to be excessively oriented to consumerism, materialism and hedonism—obscures that fact that, since the beginning of capitalism, youth have been consistently targeted by a massive and ever growing marketing and advertising industry. Business interest in fostering youth consumerism continued to grow throughout the twentieth century, and by the turn of the new millennium, the power of the teenage consumer had become a truly global preoccupation of multinational retailers and marketers. Naomi Klein, in her 1999 book, *No Logo*, writes of how "the image of the global teen floats over the planet like a euphoric corporate hallucination. These kids, we are repeatedly told, live not in a geographic place but in a global consumer loop" (Klein, 1999, p. 119). Marketer Elissa Moses's (2000, pp. 1–2) *The $100 Billion Allowance: Accessing the Global Teen Market*, is a classic example of such corporate rhetoric:

> We all live in hopeful times. The times are hopeful for the half-billion new world teens ages 15 to 19 who span the globe, and they are hopeful for marketers with dreams of expanding their market shares and building relationships with this new generation. Most teens have significant amounts of money to spend. In fact, teens spend more than $100 billion every year.... Teens inhabit every country on every continent. From Manhattan to Madras and Milan to Melbourne, teens who speak different languages ... all speak the same dialect of global brand consumption.... Marketers at the doorstep of the new millennium face a dynamic opportunity to grow by offering products and services to a global youth culture. In some sense, there is a gold rush going on. The world is getting more affluent and access to consumer goods is ubiquitous. As if overnight, a new crop of young consumers who want everything has emerged.

As Ritty Lukose (2005, p. 915) notes, "a short-hand way to mark the advent and impact of globalization is to point to the evidence of 'global' youth consuming practices." To help create and capitalize upon this global youth market, global marketers are spending an ever greater amount of time, effort, resources and money. In the United States alone, the annual advertising spend on marketing to children and youth up to the age of 18 more than doubled in a five-year period from 1992 to 1997 from $6.2 billion to $12.7 billion, and by 2004, it had reached $15 billion annually (Linn, 2004); in 1983, the annual advertising spend on child and youth marketing had been a mere $100 million (Lagorio, 2007). The strategies and technologies of marketing to children and youth have also become ever more sophisticated and pervasive: peer-to-peer marketing, teen marketing consultants, trend spotters and brand ambassadors, product placements, viral marketing, social media marketing, school sponsorship and curriculum commercialization and so forth (Buckingham, 2011; Linn, 2004; Mayo & Nairn, 2009; Quart, 2003; Schor, 2004). Youth marketing is also said to be responsible, at least in part, for expanding the age range of youth in contemporary society, particularly in terms of pushing youth downward in age into the realm of childhood, so that children are "growing up earlier" in a heavily commercialized world. In particular, the construction of the "tween," as yet another marketing demographic that became widespread in the 1990s, and that refers to individuals between the ages of 8 and 14, is emblematic of the marketing-led "erosion of childhood" (Hill, 2011, p. 349; see also Cook & Kaiser, 2004).

Global business interest in youth marketing is not just limited to selling commodities to young people, however, but focuses as well on using images and rhetorics of youth to sell products to adults. Bill Osgerby (2008, p. 46) thus notes how marketers and advertisers, over the course of the 1950s and 1960s, came to embrace youth not just as a "generational category" but as a "signifier of a newly prosperous age of freedom and fun," "a new brand of conspicuous, leisure-oriented consumption," and "the sharp end of the new consumer society" itself. Similarly, Stuart Ewen (1976) has described how capitalism, with its constant emphasis on endless change, novelty, innovation, replacement and discarding of the old, promotes "youth as an industrial ideal." "Youngness," Ewen (1976, p. 149) writes, by the midpoint of the twentieth century, had become a "desirable and salable commodity. People's anxieties over the turn in production were now focused toward a safe solution. Youth could be bought, or so the ads claimed." By the beginning of the twenty-first century, it has become axiomatic that youth sells—no matter what the product, from clothing to cars, electronics to travel, political parties to electoral campaigns, and indeed even capitalism as a whole, as an entire social, economic and ideological system (Kjeldgaard & Askegaard, 2006). Thus, when tracing the history of youth in consumer society, we find clear evidence of the double-sided nature of youth stereotyping: on the one hand, it is true that youth have been frequently demonized for (allegedly) being excessively consumerist, hedonist and materialist in their behavior; but on the other, there has also been a long tradition of embracing, celebrating, promoting and empowering youth (and images, characteristics and behaviors associated with youth) in the service of capitalist profit-making interests.

Youth and Social Control

In addition to the social construction of youth as workers and consumers, a whole further set of links between youth and capitalism exists. Some of these developed essentially as a side effect or "byproduct" of a series of social, cultural, political and economic shifts set in motion over the course of the nineteenth century by the rise of capitalism in Europe and North America (Ruddick, 2003). Changes in family structure and home life in response to the introduction of industrial wage labor—in particular, the separation of work and home, parental daytime absence, shifting responsibility for the socialization of the young, and decreasing family size—created a new sense of well-defined gaps between generations, a distinct separation of childhood from adulthood, and an understanding of youth as an extended period of transition between these increasingly segregated spheres of life, age and activity (Fasick, 1994; Kett, 1993; Smelser & Halpern, 1978; Zelizer, 1985). At the same time, the development of state, school and corporate apparatuses for the centralized social control and reproduction of large-scale populations led to the spread of standardized, rationalized, and finely age-graded distinctions in law, classification and institutional regulation that made chronological age socially, politically and economically relevant in a way it simply had not been before (Wallace & Kovatcheva, 1998). As Joseph Kett

(2003, pp. 360–361) notes, for example, the first census in the United States in 1790 "distinguished only two age groups, those under 16 and those 16 and over, and drew even this distinction only for white males." "Many Americans did not know their age," observes Kett (2003, p. 361), "and the only birthdays celebrated were those of great men, such as George Washington" (see also Chudacoff, 1989).

Other links between youth and capitalism, however, have been far more deliberately and explicitly invoked and shaped by employers, entrepreneurs, the state and other civil society actors, all working in support of their own interests and agendas, in the context of an emergent capitalist economy and society. For, in addition to the construction of youth as workers and consumers, a third major stream in the construction of youth within capitalist society has centered on concerns with the problem of social order and social control. While links between the discourse of youth and worries about social disorder are not unique to capitalist society (for example, see Eisenbichler, 2002; Goldberg & Riddy, 2004; Levi & Schmitt, 1997) these links rapidly became more salient in Europe and North America over the course of the nineteenth century.

Wherever capitalism has developed, it has always been associated with massive social and geographical dislocations: these typically include the enclosure and dispossession of land; the disruption of traditional family economies, cultural practices, social relationships and patterns of authority; and the triggering of mass migrations from the countryside to the city, and a consequent increase in urbanization. As Karl Marx and Frederick Engels (1848/1988, p. 38) famously argued in *The Communist Manifesto*:

> The bourgeoisie cannot exist without constantly revolutionizing the instruments of production, and thereby the relations of production, and with them the whole relations of society.... Constant revolutionizing of production, uninterrupted disturbance of all social conditions, everlasting uncertainty and agitation distinguish the bourgeois epoch from all earlier ones. All fixed, fast-frozen relations, with their train of ancient and venerable prejudices and opinions, are swept away, all new-formed ones become antiquated before they can ossify. All that is solid melts in air....

In the early stages of capitalist development in Europe and North America, such dislocations gave rise to two distinct sets of concerns that were directly related to youth. First, there was growing concern over the appearance in cities throughout the Western world at the time of large numbers of unsupervised, unemployed and underemployed young people—a concern widely articulated as the problem of "idle youth." "By 1865 half of the children of Manchester were neither in school nor working," write Neil Smelser and Sydney Halpern (1978, p. S296): "Youth had become a national issue," and "young people were perceived as one among many perils to social order" (see also Davies, 2007; Musgrove, 1964).

The situation was much the same in North America. As Michael Katz (1995, p. 109) writes:

> Moralism aside, contemporary complaints about idle and vagrant youths roaming the streets of town and cities reflected actual social behaviour; observers saw in nineteenth-century cities a genuine crisis of youth. In earlier times, long-standing customs had defined the expectations and duties of people throughout their life course. . . . Never had it been unclear where youngsters should live or how they should spend their time. Idleness was unimaginable.

As young people from rural areas came to the growing cities of the era to join young people who had grown up in the city in search of waged employment, together they often ended up alternating "between employment as day laborers, work in the street trade, and long periods of unemployment" (Kett, 1993, p. 608). The roving street "gangs" of young people that became part of the urban scenery of the era were at the heart of middle-class fears of the threats to social order created by rapid social and economic change (Teeter, 1995). As Joseph Kett (1993, p. 608) points out, "when the reformer Charles Loring Brace warned in 1871 about 'the dangerous classes of New York,' he meant the children and youth."

A second set of concerns of the era focused on the impact that industrialization and urbanization was having on white, male, middle-class youth. By the end of the nineteenth century, reformers were increasingly worried that the rapid social and economic changes of the era were sapping and undermining the manliness, strength and dominance of young, white, middle-class men—and that this, in turn, posed a threat to very stability of society and the economy as a whole (MacLeod, 1982; Lesko, 1996). The American psychologist G. Stanley Hall, whose 1904 book, *Adolescence*, is widely considered the founding text of the modern concept of adolescence, was only articulating fears that were widespread at the time, when he claimed that:

> Never has youth been exposed to such dangers of both perversion and arrest as in our land and day. Increasing urban life, with its temptations, prematurities, sedentary occupations, and passive stimuli, just when as active objective life is most needed; early emancipation and a lessening sense for both duty and discipline; the haste to know and do all befitting man's estate before its time; the mad rush for sudden wealth, and reckless fashions set by its gilded youth.
>
> *(Hall, 1904)*

City life, it was feared, could cause the young to grow up too quickly, succumb to a life of vice, but also fail to provide them with the strengthening regimen and active, physical life of traditional agricultural production work in the countryside. As this affected middle-class young men, a threat was thought to be posed to the ability of contemporary society to reproduce virile and potent future leaders. Thus, over the course of the nineteenth century in Europe and North America, a pervasive fear of youth as a social problem became widespread; and while this fear of youth had radically different causes and forms for youth of different class backgrounds, genders, racial and ethnic identities, it nevertheless tended to frame the treatment of all youth universally.

Such concern about youth and social (dis)order led to the extensive development of a range of institutions, ideologies and scientific discourses that used notions of youth and adolescence as a way to make sense of, control and improve both poor and working-class as well as middle-class young populations in the context of rapid social change. First and foremost among these was the rise of mass, compulsory primary and secondary education. While dominant narratives of the history of formal schooling in Europe and North America frequently link the rise of schooling to the growing demand for a skilled work-force, concerns with social order and control tended to be much more significant. As Michael Katz (1976, p. 399) and others have argued, "the cultivation of skills and intellectual abilities as ends in themselves did not have nearly as much importance in the view of early school promoters as ... [the desire] to shape behavior and attitudes, alleviate social problems, and reinforce a social structure under stress" (Green, 1990; Nasaw, 1981; Tyack, 1974). However, there were many other institutions and groups that developed around the end of the nineteenth and beginning of the twentieth centuries that were also concerned with under-standing, managing, developing and controlling youth: these included the Child Saving Movement, the nascent juvenile justice system, youth social work, youth counseling, youth psychiatry, youth religious missions and a wide range of other youth sporting, outdoors, social and political organizations (for further discussion of these, see Chapter 4) (Coussée, 2008; Platt, 1969; Knupfer, 2001; Lesko, 2001; Odem, 1995).

Together, these organizations helped to develop and spread a new scientific discourse of the proper stages of adolescent development, and a corresponding obsession with identifying, labeling and correcting problems of youthful delin-quency, deviance, delay, precocity and pathology—problems which were taken to exist anywhere that individuals failed to fit in with the new universalized, stan-dardized and normative models of adolescent developmental psychology. As a wide range of critics have by now pointed out, this universalist model of adoles-cent development was in fact modeled on the ideals of Western, white, middle-class youth identity, experience and values (Boyden, Ling & Lyers, 1998; Brown, Larson & Saraswathi, 2002; Finn, 2001; Griffin, 1993; Lesko, 1996, 2001; Nsamenang, 1999; Offer & Schonert-Reichl, 1992). Throughout the history of capitalism, then, teams of psychologists, educators, social workers and others have repeatedly taken what are often actually conflicts and differences across the divisional lines of class, race, gender and competing social and economic systems, and reframed these as individualized problems in normative adolescent development, to be corrected through the application of expert knowledge and intervention (Austin & Willard, 1998; Chinn, 2009; DeLuzio, 2007; Finn, 2001; Males, 1996, 1999). Thus have the lives of poor, working-class as well as middle-class youth been molded and remolded to fit functionally within industrial and post-industrial capitalist society by the enormous and complex structures and practices of schools, juvenile courts, youth organizations, psychological counseling and psychiatric treatment (Bowles & Gintis, 1976; Griffin, 1993; Willis, 1981).

While much of the intellectual and institutional apparatus that was constructed around the turn of the century in Europe and North America was preoccupied with the problems of youthful misbehavior, deviance, delinquency and pathology, those young people whose identities, attitudes, values and behaviors conformed to normative models of proper adolescent development were widely celebrated and embraced as models for others to follow. Negative images of youth, in other words, invariably carry with them a positive flipside (Kelly, 2006). More than this, youth stereotyping in society has always been a double-sided quality. Even G. Stanley Hall, who is now viewed by contemporary promoters of the positivity youth development model as being the outdated and misguided promoter of a deficit model of youth that dominated academic thought and social practice for almost one hundred years, actually viewed youth in a double light. Though Hall thought of adolescence as a period of "storm and stress" and "vulnerability," he also saw this life stage as a "powerful realm of energy and hope," in which the values he perceived to be missing from modern society could be found and/or created once again (Fass, 2008, p. 39; Kett, 2003). Hall's 1904 book, *Adolescence*, "counterposed the purity and vigor of youth to the fragmented, deadening, and routinized qualities of urban industrial life" (Cole, 1992, p. 214). "There is really no clue by which we can thread our way through all the mazes of culture and the distractions of modern life save by knowing the true nature and needs of childhood and adolescence," wrote Hall: "Other oracles may grow dim, but this one will never fail" (quoted in Cole, 1992, p. 214). As discussed further in Chapter 4 on youth as a revolutionary subject, youth have long been seen as a problem in contemporary society; but at the same time, they have been viewed as a potential source and inspiration for revolution and rejuvenation in society as well.

These ideologies, scientific discourses and institutions of youth and adolescent development, though they first arose in the context of Europe and North America, were subsequently exported to other parts of the world. The juvenile court, for example, which was first created in Chicago in 1899, as legal scholar Franklin Zimring (2005, p. xi) argues: "achieved a worldwide popularity larger than any other Anglo-American innovation. There are juvenile courts throughout the world, and the American model is the basic structure emulated in a vast number of legal systems in both the developed and developing world."

Similarly, the middle school concept, which was first implemented in Columbus, Ohio, in 1909, and was influenced by claims of the new scientific discourse of adolescent development that early adolescents required different forms of pedagogical and curricular provision to meet their unique developmental needs, has subsequently been adopted in countries all over the globe (Lesko, 2001; Lounsbury, 1998; Mertens, Anfara & Roney, 2009; Yahya, 2012). In general, this diffusion followed both the spread of capitalist development and the worldwide embrace of the nation-state model: it was typically triggered by broad-scale shifts in employment, education and consumption patterns, as well as new concerns with problems of social order and control that arose in the context of capitalist development; and very often, it was directly promoted and carried out by Western, and especially, American institutions (Ruddick, 2003). In Egypt, to take one example, Western models of adolescent development became widely embraced during the 1940s, in the wake of massive student and labor protests during the 1930s, that were themselves a reaction against the political and economic projects of British colonialism in the country. Through the adoption of the developmental model, "youth were recast as a problem in need of regulation and control and as a necessary object of study," and political insurgency was reframed as a problem of youthful delinquency and symptom of inner psychological turmoil (El Shakry, 2011, p. 592; see also Pursley, 2013). Similarly, Julie McLeod and Katie Wright (2008) describe how student guidance, counseling and psychological support services, which were based directly on psychological theories of adolescent developmental stages and needs, were widely adopted in schools across Australia starting in the 1930s. These reforms were motivated by "widespread fears across Europe and the Atlantic [and in Australia] about totalitarianism, propaganda and the vulnerability of poorly-educated and irrational citizens," and were directly inspired by "the traffic in ideas and personnel between the US, the UK and other Commonwealth countries"—and in particular, by a "travelling conference" sponsored by the US Carnegie Foundation that visited all the major cities of Australia in 1937 (pp. 6, 8).

Youth and Capitalism, Then and Now

"Far from being a byproduct of industrial capitalism," Sue Ruddick (2003, p. 337) and others have argued, "modern youth and childhood can be located at its literal and figurative core." Many of the features of youth in the neoliberal period that we have described in the previous chapter have long been part of the relationship between capitalism and youth. Economic and political elites have long used youth as a social concept and technology to manage and maintain social order and control, and to promote their own agendas and interests. Youth as a symbol and identity has long been used to sell products, ideologies and even capitalism itself as a social and economic system, and to promote the ideal of consumerist-based identities. Throughout the history of global capitalism, there has been an ever-changing dynamic of pulling youth in and pushing youth out of different segments of the labor force, in the context of changing social, economic and technological circumstances; these relationships between youth and work can be radically different for different groups of young people in different parts of the world at any given point in time. Finally, there has always been a double-sided aspect of youth as a social category and identity in capitalist societies, in which youth are alternatively and simultaneously celebrated and condemned, included and excluded, marginalized and empowered, enfranchised and disenfranchised. In order to understand the conditions and experiences of youth in any one location anywhere in the world, it is always essential to have an analysis of capitalism, not just as it is manifested locally, but as a global system of social and economic relationships.

Despite these continuities, however, the contemporary neoliberal period has ushered in a series of changes in the social position and significance of youth as a social category and identity worldwide. In describing the development of early links between youth and capitalism, for example, Ruddick (2003, p. 337) focuses on "the need to protect and sequester young people" in an "impressive array of public institutions that were part and parcel of the Keynesian welfare state" and that worked "to *generate* and *justify* many of the social relations associated with the rise of industrial capitalism" (italics in original). As a consequence of these developments, increasingly strong divisions were created in early capitalist societies between childhood, youth and adulthood as distinct stages of life. In the neoliberal period, as we sketched out in the previous chapter, there has been an extension of youth as a life stage both upward and downward in age, and an encroachment of youth into the periods of childhood and adulthood. There has been a dramatic, quantitative growth of youth programming, policy making and research around world, as youth has become an increasingly central social category and identity in global political, economic and development discourse, and as youth as a social category has spread horizontally to cover an ever greater range of the world's population who are in their second and third (and even fourth) decades of life. Finally, there has also been a pronounced emphasis on the positive aspect of youth identity and development, a shift that has been associated with the promotion of human capital models of youth as important resources and assets, and the breaking down of distinct and separate welfare state spaces and organizations dedicated to supporting youth development, and the full incorporation of youth into private sector-led, capitalist society and economy.

3

THE SPECTER OF YOUTH UNEMPLOYMENT

In November 2012 in the United Kingdom, UK Minister for Employment Mark Hoban held a meeting with executives from some of the world's largest and wealthiest food manufacturing companies: Mars, Heinz, Kraft, Vion, Associated British Foods, Tulip (owned by Danish Crown) and Moy Park (owned by the Brazilian conglomerate Marfrig). The UK government had recently launched a new £1 billion program called the "Youth Contract," that was supposedly dedicated to fighting youth unemployment in the country, and Hoban's agenda was to convince the food manufacturing executives to participate. The lure was a promise of cash incentives to any employer hiring a young person who was currently unemployed. "The money's there for the taking," Hoban told the executives, "so I encourage employers to snap it up before somebody else does" (Mullaney, 2012). As in other countries around the world, the state's dominant response to the social problem of youth unemployment in Britain has focused largely on providing economic subsidies to the private and voluntary sectors to provide unemployed young people with jobs, training and work experience. Since the government's Youth Contract was generally expected to have limited impact on reducing youth unemployment in Britain, and since corporations in Britain (as elsewhere around the world) were sitting on record-level cash reserves, some critics raised concern that, in the name of battling youth unemployment, the government was in actuality effectively providing corporate welfare to the already wealthy (Lansley, 2012; Williams, 2012; Work and Pensions Select Committee, 2012). Similar concerns about youth unemployment measures functioning as forms of corporate welfare have also been raised in South Africa, New Zealand and Ontario, Canada, over parallel plans and proposals to introduce youth subminimum wages or provide wage subsidies to employers who agree to hire unemployed youth (APDUSA, 2011; Crispe, 2013; Sweetman, 2013).

The larger question that Britain's Youth Contract and other such programs require us to ask is what are the political and ideological motivations that shape how youth unemployment is constructed and exploited by the state, employers and others as a social, political and economic problem? In other words, who really benefits from the particular ways in which media and policy attention are focused on the social problem of youth unemployment?

The global financial crisis that kicked off in 2008 led to an unprecedented rise in unemployment around the world. Between 2007 and the end of 2009, more than 29 million people joined the ranks of the global unemployed—and millions more were pushed out of the formal labor market altogether (ILO, 2013). While some were hit harder than others, no region, no industry or occupation, and no social group of workers was left untouched. Manufacturing, construction, finance, retail, hospitality, food service—all of these sectors saw large-scale layoffs. Though the crisis in unemployment hit the wealthy countries of the global North earliest and hardest, it spread quickly to the poorer nations of the global South as well (Forstater, 2010; Green, King & Miller-Dawkins, 2010; Hanieh, 2009). In China, 20 million of the 130 million internal migrant workers who make up the bulk of the country's manufacturing workforce were retrenched (Chan, 2010). Groups who were already marginalized in the global workforce were strongly affected: youth, older workers, women, racial and ethnic minorities, indigenous and migrant workers (Fix et al., 2009; Heidkamp, Corre & Van Horn, 2010; Humphreys, 2011; Stavropoulou & Jones, 2013). But by no means was the surge in worldwide unemployment limited to these groups only: for white, male and middle-class workers were also hit hard (Autor, 2010; UN, 2011; UNI Global Union, 2012). The causes of this rapid escalation in unemployment were not hard to identify. Financial crisis led to global recession and a collapse in economic demand, and employers around the world responded with mass layoffs and hiring freezes. Some of the world's largest multinational corporations led the way: General Motors, Hewlett Packard, Citigroup, Pepsico, Caterpillar, Corus and many, many more (BBC News, 2009; McIntyre, 2010). As government bank bailouts and declining tax revenues turned the financial crisis into a public debt crisis, government austerity programs and state spending cutbacks led to large-scale layoffs in the public sector as well (McNally, 2010).

Despite this rise in unemployment across virtually all segments of the global workforce, however, there were two striking developments that emerged in the dominant media and policy representations of and responses to the employment impacts of the global recession of 2008–2009. First, these employment impacts increasingly became framed as a problem, above all, of *youth* unemployment. There was widespread talk of the dangers of a "lost generation" of jobless young people—*generación cero* or *generación ni ni* in Spanish—who were being cut off from the rest of society by soaring rates of youth unemployment, whether in Europe, North America, Asia, Africa or Latin America (Anaro, 2011; APYouthnet, 2011; Coy, 2009, 2011; Lowrey, 2009; Salazar-Xirinachs, 2012). Youth, many claimed, had been the "hardest hit" by the global economic crisis (e.g., UN, 2012); and it was regularly reported, in those parts of the world that were suffering from the highest rates of youth unemployment (such as Greece and Spain), that "more than half of all young people … [were] now unemployed" (Peacock, 2012). The International Labour Organization put out an annual *Global Employment Trends* survey that showed unemployment rates for young people around the world that were between two and three times that for adults throughout this period (e.g., ILO, 2009, 2013).

The second striking development in all of this reporting was that the organizations that were at the forefront of raising concern about the crisis of global youth unemployment were often not grassroots community organizations or youth groups, but global business and financial elites—and often the very same financial players that had been at the heart of the global economic crisis to begin with. The *Global Youth Employment Agenda*, that was launched with a high profile, live CNBC broadcast in London in December 2010, and that seeks to "elevate youth unemployment to a high priority issue" around the world, was actually created by a US-based hedge fund called the Blackstone Group—whose CEO, Stephen Schwarzman, had previously gained a reputation, before the financial crisis, as being one of the most extreme examples of Wall Street excess and self-indulgence, as exemplified by a $3 million sixtieth birthday party that he threw for himself in New York City in early 2007 (Gross, 2007; Sender & Langley, 2007). The *Global Agenda Council on Youth Unemployment*, which likewise aims "to raise youth employment and economic opportunity to the highest policy priority level," is a project of the World Economic Forum, whose annual meeting in Davos, Switzerland, has become one of the important gatherings of global business elites in the world today, and whose membership is comprised of some of the world's largest multinational corporations and financial institutions. Individually, banks and other financial institutions around the globe have embraced youth unemployment as one of their preferred philanthropic concerns. Since 2008, for example, Barclays, a British banking and financial services corporation based in London, has run a *Building Young Futures* campaign in partnership with UNICEF, that aims "to help tackle global youth unemployment" by working with young people in countries across Africa and South Asia (UNICEF, 2012). This is the same Barclays that became one of the most vilified banking institutions within Britain for its actions and excesses during the financial crisis, and whose own internal review, launched in 2012, found that the bank's "focus on short-term return on equity and … competitive position [had] led to a vacuum in culture and values" among its management and core workforce (Cassidy, 2013; Jenkins, 2013).

There is no doubt that the lives of millions of young people around the world have been turned upside down and devastated by the recent economic crisis—and that, as a group, they have in some respects been affected more than other groups in society, not least because they were entering the job market at the moment the crisis broke. But the question needs to be asked: why, given the universal impact of the global financial crisis on rising unemployment among all social groups, were business elites so ready and willing to lead the way in focusing attention on the issue of youth unemployment in particular? What are the broader social, political and economic consequences of this youth frame for the ways in which the recent increases in global unemployment have been understood and addressed? We need, in other words, to investigate critically what Gareth and Teresa Rees (1982), in a study of youth unemployment in the United Kingdom more than three decades ago, referred to as the "ideology" of youth unemployment. Writing in the context of Thatcherite Britain in the early 1980s, Rees and Rees and their colleagues observed that, though "unemployment [in Britain] has grown for all groups and has been particularly severe in some regions and some industries among adults with the financial commitments of family responsibilities," nevertheless "young people in particular have been singled out for special governmental attention" (Atkinson & Rees, 1982, p. 2). "While no contemporary ... politician can avoid making expressions of regret about the general numbers of unemployed," noted Geoff Mungham of Britain in the early 1980s (1982, p. 29), "it is invariably the young workless who bear the brunt of a special kind of worry and frenzied concern." A similar phenomenon appears to be playing out today, but on a global rather than national scale.

Moral panics about youth unemployment and "idle youth" are not new but have recurred throughout the history of industrial capitalism (Griffin, 1993; Walker & Barton, 1986). In Europe in the 1850s and 1860s, commentators worried about the appearance of "wild tribes" of workless youth that were appearing across the continent (Mungham, 1982, p. 30); and again during the Depression years of the 1930s, political elites raised concern about the widespread "demoralization" of the young, caused by "prolonged periods of enforced idleness" (Rees & Rees, 1982, p. 17). In these previous eras, scholars have pointed out that political and economic elites focused policy attention on youth unemployment because having large numbers of unemployed youth—and, in particular, non-white, working-class and male youth—was seen as posing a serious threat to social order and stability. A study of "juvenile unemployment" in south Wales, for example, published by Gwynne Meara in 1936, observed that "enforced idleness leads ultimately to demoralization, to loss of pride in one's own person and appearance, to envy of those better placed in society, and envy leads in the last resort to social conflict" (quoted in Rees & Rees, 1982, pp. 17–18). Concern about "youth unemployment" thus has frequently served as a metaphor or euphemism for growing anxiety about the dangers of increased levels of crime, violence, unrest, rioting and general loss of control in society (Griffin, 1993; Horne, 1986; Mungham, 1982; Solomos, 1985).

Clearly, this fear is a factor in the current period as well. In one of the most over-used expressions of the global recession, media and political elites around the world have regularly referred to rising youth unemployment levels in their country or region as being a "ticking time bomb" that is set to explode at any moment—whether in South Africa or Nigeria, Pakistan or Thailand, Europe or North America, the "time bomb" rhetoric is essentially the same (Blua, 2012; Coy, 2011; Farrukh, 2012; Kaveevivitchai, 2012; Makhubu & Magome, 2012; PM News, 2013). In November 2012, former Nigerian president Olusegun Obasanjo, addressing a West African regional conference on youth employment in Dakar, warned that Nigeria "will witness a revolution" unless something was done to address youth unemployment: "I am afraid, and you know I am a General. When a General says he's afraid, that means the danger ahead is real and potent" (quoted in AllAfrica, 2012). In the Arab region, youth unemployment is widely pointed to as having been the principal trigger for the uprisings that spread from Tunisia through Egypt, Libya, Yemen, Bahrain and Syria from late 2010 onwards. In 2011, the International Monetary Fund said that it had warned Egypt of the politically destabilizing effects of its high youth unemployment rates just days ahead of the outbreak of mass political protests in Tahrir Square in Cairo (Talley, 2011). In a February 2011 article entitled "Young, Jobless and Looking for Trouble," the *Economist* warned its readers:

> We are all rightly fixated on the politics of what is going on in Egypt at the moment. But it is worth sparing a thought for the economics, too. If Russians in 1917 wanted "peace, bread and land" and ended up with totalitarianism, gulags and collective farms, Egyptians, particularly young Egyptians, want jobs.
>
> *(Schumpeter, 2011)*

In Europe, youth unemployment is seen as being behind the English riots of 2011, the Swedish riots of 2013, and the mass anti-austerity protests in Greece and Spain (Wood, 2012). When global business and political elites have gathered at Davos, Switzerland, recently for their annual World Economic Forum meeting, youth unemployment has been at the top of their agenda, being seen as "not a crisis, but a disaster," and a "cancer in society" that could lead to open rebellion and revolution across the world (Weber, 2012). Youth unemployment, then, is undoubtedly a specter that is haunting the contemporary global economy.

What we argue here, however, is that alongside this fear and anxiety, youth unemployment, as a concept and issue, has also been embraced by global elites as a political opportunity that enables them to frame unemployment as being, first and foremost, a problem of youth, and to use this problem as a way to promote business friendly agendas. This is not a new phenomenon. In the 1930s and again in the 1980s, the invocation of concern about youth unemployment was used to promote "individualistic and moralistic solutions, rather than [state] intervention into the labour market," and was "marked ... by a strong attempt to tie the education system firmly to the fluctuating needs of industry and hence capital"

(Horne, 1986, p. 24). Ironically, many of the initiatives launched in the name of unemployed youth thus at best do little to help unemployed youth, and at worst, directly attack their own and others' social and economic rights and entitlements. In order to effectively respond to the unemployment struggles of youth and others in the contemporary global economy, we argue that it is essential to do three things: one is to recognize directly the elite political and ideological interests to which the youth unemployment frame can be harnessed; a second is to address the ambiguities surrounding the ideal situation of youth with respect to being in and out of employment, and in and out of the labor market more generally; and a third is to focus on the unemployment struggles of all ages and generations together. What we do in this chapter is examine the dilemmas of measuring, framing and interpreting statistical counts of youth unemployment and labor force participation, analyze how the social problem of youth unemployment is used to promote business agendas, and finally, point to alternative visions that seek to address the employment struggles of all generations together in the contemporary global economy.

The (Mis)measurement and (Mis)framing of Youth Unemployment

In his classic book, *Damned Lies and Statistics*, Joel Best (2001) points out that "all statistics, from the best to the worst, are socially constructed." "All statistics," notes Best, "are products of choices and compromises that inevitably shape, limit and distort the outcome." In this, youth unemployment statistics are no exception. Many scholars have pointed out how statistics for youth unemployment have been particularly susceptible to changes in government counting rules and shifts in education, training and employment policy—that are themselves strongly influenced by shifting political and ideological agendas that are adapting to changing economic contexts. Over the course of the 1980s in Britain, for example, the youth unemployment rate dropped dramatically—to the point that Furlong (2006, p. 553) could claim that by "the late 1980s youth unemployment ceased to exist in the UK." This had little to do with real improvements in employment conditions for young people in the country, however, but with changes in how youth unemployment was being defined and counted. Furlong notes how a major policy shift in 1988 led to the withdrawal of official recognition of youth unemployment that "left most under 18 year-olds without access to unemployment benefits" (p. 553). Griffin (1993, p. 71) counts "no less than" 18 changes in government methods of calculating unemployment in the UK between 1979 and 1989 that reduced the overall numbers of (officially) unemployed youth. White and Smith (1994, p. 105) likewise observe that male youth unemployment in the UK "supposedly declined from 32.3% in 1983 to 6.9% in 1990, largely due to government programs that took youth out of the group counted as unemployed." In general, the emphasis in critical scholarship on the counting of youth unemployment has been on the ways in which this unemployment can be undercounted and made to disappear. The reasons for such counting maneuvers may be found in government attempts to be seen to be addressing a politically charged social problem without incurring large expenditures; but more generally, in youth's social function in capitalist society as a reserve army of labor, who are pulled in and pushed out of the labor force—both literally and symbolically—according to shifting political agendas and economic demand.

In the current global economic crisis, there seems to be a trend to use statistics and other representations to emphasize youth unemployment rather than to diminish it, but to do this in order to reframe and distract attention away from the problem of unemployment more generally. It is widely reported that youth have suffered the most from the employment fallout from the global economic crisis, and experience astronomically high levels of unemployment, particularly in regions such as the European Union and the Middle East. An article published in the International Monetary Fund's (IMF) *Finance & Development* journal in March 2012 is typical. "The recent global economic crisis took an outsized toll on young workers across the globe," writes IMF economist Hanan Morsy (2012), "since the global crisis began in 2008, young people have suffered a much sharper rise in joblessness than older workers." "Britain's Dole Queues Shrink But Young People Remain the Hardest Hit," reads a *Guardian* headline in August 2013 (Stewart, 2013); "Greek March unemployment rises, youth hardest hit," reported Reuters a couple of months earlier (Georgiopoulos & Behrakis, 2013). The proportion of young people who are claimed to be unemployed in many Arab and southern European countries is eye-watering. "More than half of young people" in Greece and Spain were said to be unemployed in 2012 and 2013 (Hadjimatheou, 2012; see also Papachristou, 2012; Nielsen, 2012; Vasagar, 2013). "In some countries of the Arab world," claimed the BBC in early 2012, "up to 90% of 16–24 year olds are unemployed" (Weber, 2012).

The problem with these kinds of claims, however, is that, as many critics have pointed out, they are simply not true (Enríquez, 2013; Hill, 2011; O'Higgins, 2012). While it may be the case that a country like Greece had a youth unemployment rate of over 50 percent in 2012, this does not mean that "over half of young people" in Greece were unemployed. This is because the youth unemployment rate doesn't measure the number of unemployed young people against the total youth population, but only against the number of young people who are actively participating (i.e., working or seeking work) in the formal labor market. Given that many young people are engaged fulltime in secondary or post-secondary education and not working or seeking work, this means that high youth unemployment rates can often involve relatively small numbers of young people. More than this, given that a common response of young people to economic downturns is to leave the job market and continue in further and higher education, an increase in the youth unemployment rate can sometimes actually reflect an increase in educational enrollment among the young, rather than an increase in the number of unemployed youth (Clark, 2011). In the UK, for example, the 16–17 year old age group was one of the groups *least* affected by the global economic crisis in terms of the increase in the total number of unemployed, but had by far the *highest* increase in the rate of unemployment, due to a jump in the number of 16 and 17 years olds choosing to remain in formal education (UKCES, 2012). In Greece and Spain, while youth unemployment rates hovered around 50 percent from 2011 to 2013, the youth unemployment ratio—which measures the proportion of unemployed youth out of the total population of young people—in 2011 was 13 percent in Greece and 19 percent in Spain; for the Eurozone as a whole, while the youth unemployment rate in 2011 was 20.8 percent, the youth unemployment ratio was 8.7 percent (Hill, 2011). At the same time that the youth unemployment rate can give an exaggerated sense of the number of unemployed young people in society, adult unemployment rates can also understate the true dimension of adult unemployment in society, as discouraged workers are not included and many unemployed adults may show up in other categories, for example, those on incapacity or disability benefits (Beatty, Fothergill & Gore, 2012; Hill, 2011).

Critics have generally used these observations to dismiss or question claims of the severity of youth unemployment in the global economic crisis. "Youth Unemployment—The Headlines Mislead" is the title of one article (Taylor, 2011); "Youth Unemployment in Europe: Less Dire By Another Measure," reads another (Morison, 2012); "Is Spain's Youth Unemployment Really as Bad as They Say?," asks a third (Egesberg, 2012). Here, we are more interested in taking these important observations in another direction. If the difference between youth and adult unemployment may be less stark than initially appears, why should we be focusing so much attention on youth unemployment, rather than unemployment in general? We need to remember, after all, that the distinction between "youth" and "adult" is somewhat arbitrary in terms of where and how we draw age-based distinctions: the idea that a 24 year old is a youth, while a 25 year old is an adult is a social construction, based on reporting conventions promoted globally by organizations such as the UN and ILO (O'Higgins, 2001). Because the social distinction between "youth" and "adult" is determined in large part by the extended and mass participation of young people in secondary and post-secondary education, it is almost by definition that we can therefore expect that, even if youth and adult unemployment ratios are similar or the same, youth unemployment rates will tend to be considerably higher than adult unemployment rates. Many of the individual, social and economic problems associated with unemployment are similar if not identical for youth and adults. In its 2010 *Global Employment Trends for Youth* report, the ILO posed itself the question "why focus on youth?" when looking at the employment impacts of the global economic crisis. It noted that youth unemployment can "incur costs to the economy, to society and to the individual and their family"; it can "compromise a person's future employment prospects"; and it can lead to "social exclusion," "a sense of uselessness and idleness," as well as increased "mental health problems" and substance abuse (ILO, 2010, p. 6). However, all of these problems also affect unemployed adults, who may also face the burden of greater family and financial responsibilities.

There is, furthermore, the issue of how "youth" and "adult" unemployment are defined in terms of age brackets. The officially recognized definition of youth in counts of youth unemployment worldwide is an individual between the ages of 15 and 24, the age range that is used by the UN and ILO. When we look at reports of youth unemployment from around the world, however, we find that often individuals in their late 20s and early 30s are also being included in contemporary counts of unemployed "youth." A 2011 article in the *New York Times* on "youth" unemployment in Europe, for example, presented profiles of three individuals: the first was an unemployed lawyer from Italy named Francesca Esposito, who was 29 years old; the second was an unemployed humanities PhD from Spain named Coral Gómez, who was 33; and the third was an unemployed marketing expert, also from Spain, named Sara Sanfulgencio, who was 28 (Donadia, 2011). A 2012 World Economic Forum report on youth unemployment in the Arab region defines youth as referring to individuals between the ages of 15 and 29 (World Economic Forum, 2012). In Africa, the African Union and many national governments define youth as the period of life stretching from age 15 to 35 (African Union, 2006). A 2013 Demos report on youth unemployment in the United States similarly refers to youth as being between 18 and 34 years of age (Ruetschlin & Draut, 2013). Again, it risks becoming something of a tautology to make strong claims about larger and larger numbers of youth as opposed to adults being affected by increasing unemployment rates, when the age range of people being defined as "youth" rather than "adult" keeps steadily shifting upwards in years.

Discussions of youth and adult unemployment index not just different age brackets but different causal relationships and temporal frameworks as well. As David Ashton (1986, p. 110) observes, in his book, *Unemployment Under Capitalism*:

> To understand fully the causes of youth unemployment we need to make a distinction between two sets of factors: those which operate in periods of relatively full employment, and those which operate in periods of high unemployment. In the former it is the fact that young people are entering the market for the first time and tend to move from one job to another which creates high levels of unemployment; in periods of high unemployment it is the fall in aggregate demand, combined with changes in the distribution of occupations, which are responsible.

In other words, the causal factors of youth unemployment tend to be most similar to those leading to adult unemployment during periods of economic recession: namely a collapse in overall economic demand. It is in periods of economic stability and growth that other issues that are particularly relevant to youth unemployment—in particular, the transition from school to work, and the fact that young people are entering the job market for the first time—take on a greater degree of significance. Thus, if we respond to the global economic crisis by focusing on the issue of youth unemployment, rather than unemployment generally, we are likely going to be focusing attention away from the crisis itself, and its proximal causes and impacts, and onto a more enduring and generic set of factors pertaining to the relative smoothness or difficulty of school-to-work transitions and youth labor market entry in different national economies around the world.

In fact, when we look closely at the ILO statistics on the employment effects of the global recession of 2007–2009, it may be surprising, given the prevailing headlines, that actually the recession had a greater impact on adult rather than youth unemployment, both globally and in all regions of the world (see Table 3.1). As a consequence, the ratio of youth to adult unemployment rates globally turns out to have *improved* during this period, from being 2.9 times the adult rate in 2007 to 2.6 times the adult rate in 2010 (Miller, 2011). In Europe—which was supposedly one of the regions of the world that suffered the worst increases in youth unemployment—the European Commission (2010) reported that the largest increase in the numbers of unemployed between 2008–2010 was among 25–34 year olds (30 percent), followed by 35–44 year olds (23.5 percent), while

TABLE 3.1 Changes in global adult and youth unemployment, 2007–2009

	Adult unemployment increase 2007–2009 (Total numbers)	Youth unemployment increase 2007–2009 (Total numbers)	Adult unemployment increase 2007–2009 (Percentage)	Youth unemployment increase 2007–2009 (Percentage)
Developed Economies and European Union	10.7 million	2.8 million	50.9	34.6
Middle East and North Africa	0.7 million	−0.1 million	10.9	− 1.6
Sub-Saharan Africa	1.3 million	0.5 million	10.2	5
Latin America and the Caribbean	1.9 million	0.8 million	18.4	10
South Asia and East Asia	6.1 million	1.7 million	19.7	6.8
World	23.7 million	5.8 million	24	8.2

(Authors' calculations based on data presented in ILO (2013) *Global Employment Trends 2013*).

18–24 and 45–54 years olds both saw increases of 18 per cent. For Europe as a whole, the overwhelming majority of the unemployed (78 percent in 2012) are not youth, but adults over the age of 24; in Greece and Spain, where youth unemployment has attracted the greatest amount of media and policy attention, the adult proportion of the total unemployed is even higher, with 86 percent of the unemployed in Greece and 84 percent of the unemployed in Spain being over the age of 24 in 2012 (Eurostat, 2013).

Some researchers have suggested that it is not the overall levels of unemployment that merit youth receiving special policy attention in the wake of the global economic crisis, but the increase in long-term youth unemployment (e.g., O'Higgins, 2012). But in countries such as the United Kingdom and the United States, it is workers over the age of 50 who have seen some of the biggest jumps in long-term unemployment (Jeszeck, 2012; Rampell, 2013; Tinsley, 2012). "An endless number of commentators lament about the prospects of a lost generation of young people and push Government to do more and more to help young people in our labour market find work," writes Matthew Oakley (2012), the director of the British think tank, Policy Exchange; but the global economic crisis, Oakley points out, "risks creating a whole different lost generation" of workers over 50 in the labor market as well. The point here is not to diminish the seriousness of youth unemployment. Youth unemployment rates were already very high across many regions of the world before the global economic crisis, and long-term consequences of youth unemployment can be severe. Rather, the issue is, first, the fact that adult unemployment also constitutes a serious problem, and second, the questionable decision to focus policy attention on youth unemployment rather than the unemployment of everyone.

When thinking about youth unemployment, it is not just how we count and measure the numbers and proportions of unemployed young people that matters, but how we interpret the significance of these statistical counts as well. It has been widely noted, for example, that one of the major impacts of the global economic crisis for youth is not just the rising rate of unemployment, but also the decline in overall labor force participation. Worldwide, the youth labor force participation rate declined from 51.9 percent in 2005 to 48.6 percent in 2011 (ILO, 2013, p. 139). In the United States, the labor force participation rate of teen-agers (aged 16 to 19) hit an all-time low of 33.5 percent in 2012 (Ayres, 2013). However, is low labor force participation among the young inherently a bad thing? Sub-Saharan Africa has consistently had the second highest youth labor force participation rate in the world, and the number of young people engaged in paid employment in the region increased by a third between 1998 and 2008 (ILO, 2010, p. 14). But this hardly provides a model of youth employment to emulate globally, as this high rate of youth labor market participation reflects a lack of educational opportunities, and the pressure of high poverty that forces many young people to work in poor conditions with limited social protections. Conversely, if much of the increase in the youth unemployment rate in the developed world has been caused by growing numbers of young people deciding to leave the labor market and continue in further and higher education, is this increase necessarily a bad thing? If the education that young people are accessing is of high quality, then we might welcome such shifts; but if this is largely a matter of warehousing young people in schools, colleges and universities, where they learn little—while amassing large amounts of tuition debt—then we might view such developments with concern. In the past, this has been a standard criticism of the education and training schemes brought in by governments to "solve" (or hide) the problem of high youth unemployment (Bynner, 2001). The key issues that need to be addressed—before we start making strong claims about statistical counts of labor force participation and unemployment rates among the young—are the content and quality of education, training and employment, as well as the opportunity for young people to make informed and healthy choices about their schooling and employment options. Though this applies to individuals of all ages, it is particularly salient for youth because of their conceptual definition as occupying a lifestage that exists between work and education, and because of their function in capitalist society as constituting a reserve army of labor.

Using the Specter of Youth Unemployment to Promote Business Agendas

After the collapse of the Greek and Spanish economies and the rise of mass protests against austerity policies in both countries, Marco Annunziata, formerly the Deutsche Bank Chief Economist and subsequently Chief Economist for General Electric, wrote an op-ed article entitled "Wasted Youth," in which he argued that "we shouldn't go blaming austerity" for youth unemployment. According to Annunziata, youth unemployment in southern Europe was "painfully high" even when the economy was booming. Declaring that "youth unemployment is one of Europe's most glaring problems," Annunziata wrote that "equally frightening is how long Europe has lived with high youth unemployment." The problem, he argued, is a combination of "rigid and distorted labor markets and education systems plagued by falling standards and a growing misalignment with the demand for skills of a rapidly changing and very competitive global economy" (Annunziata, 2012). Klaus Schwab, founder and director of the World Economic Forum, has similarly argued that, despite the global recession, youth unemployment is not new in Europe, but has been high for many years. Like Annunziata, Schwab insists that the key issue is a problem with inadequate and mismatched education and skills training, as well as inappropriate youth attitudes. "Young people," writes Schwab (2012), "will have to realize that jobs will no longer be handed to them on a plate; they will have to create them for themselves."

These statements by private sector leaders in Europe provide some sense of why business elites have been so ready and willing to focus public and policy attention on the problem of youth unemployment. It is not just the case that youth unemployment poses a potential social and political threat—though this clearly is an issue. Rather, the focus on youth provides a very effective set of opportunities for elites to be seen as responding to social and economic crisis, while at the same time continuing to actively pursue their own interests. As exemplified by Annunziata and Schwab, centering policy attention on youth unemployment provides a way of diverting attention from the global economic crisis itself, its underlying causes and the fundamental issue of the collapse of labor market demand, and onto the more enduring challenges of labor market entry experienced by young people first starting out in their working lives. Overwhelmingly, the dominant response to rising youth unemployment world-wide has been to focus critical attention on the failures of the education system to meet the needs of corporate employers, and provide students with the particular skill sets that employers wish to see when recruiting new employees. At a World Economic Forum conference on Latin America, for example, held in Puerto Vallarta, Mexico in April 2012, ManpowerGroup—one of the world's largest staffing companies—released a report detailing its analysis of the global youth unemployment problem. In the report, entitled *Wanted: Energized, Career-Driven Youth*, the company argued that:

> Today youth have difficulty in the [global] labor market because of identifiable—and remediable—deficits. They lack the skills, information and connections that will place them in entry-level, career-oriented jobs.
> *(ManpowerGroup, 2012, p. 1)*

Parallel arguments can be found all over the world. High youth unemployment levels in the Arab region, according to a report that was chaired by Queen Rania of Jordan, sponsored by the Islamic Development Bank and International Development Corporation, and carried out by McKinsey & Company, are caused by the "fact" that most Arab youth lack the right skills for the jobs that are being created regionally. "Only one third of new graduate employees are ready for the workplace when hired," the report claims, a situation that is created by "ill-equipped classrooms," "untrained teachers," "outmoded curriculums already obsolete in the modern marketplace," poor career advice, and lack of exposure "to the entre-preneurial spirit and potential of the private sector" (IDB & IFC, 2012, pp. 7, 9). "It's not that there are no jobs out there," Dominic Barton, global managing director of McKinsey & Company, argued with respect to the global economy more generally in late 2012, but "the available openings require skills that young people simply don't have"—and this is because "the world of work is currently out of sync with the world of education" (Barton, 2012).

Political and business elites around the world have thus sought to use the global economic crisis to consolidate and extend their involvement and influence over national education and training systems. In the Arab region, for example, a growing number of multinational corporations, international development organizations and Arab business leaders are now working together, in the name of fighting youth unemployment, to remold the area's education system in their own image. The World Economic Forum, the World Bank and global consulting corporations such as Booz Allen and McKinsey & Company are promoting an "e4e" (education for employment) agenda that seeks to foster increased privatization of the Arab education system—including an expanded role for for-profit, private sector education provision, as well as business advice on school curriculum and direct participation in the governance of educational institutions—an emphasis on the vocational goals of education over all other goals, and the promotion of employability and entrepreneurship training (IDB & IFC, 2012; WEF, 2012). Injaz al-Arab, a regional branch of the US-based Junior Achievement, which has been working in the Arab world since the beginning of the millennium, has expanded its work since the economic crisis began, signing Memoranda of Understandings with governments in Lebanon, Bahrain and Saudi Arabia, again to promote corporate partnerships in the education system and a business-focused curriculum (Sukarieh & Tannock, 2009). The UN, the ILO, USAID and the British Council have all been working directly with national ministries of education in Egypt, Yemen and Libya to reform school curricula in a more business-friendly direction. Multinational corporations such as ManpowerGroup, Royal Dutch Shell, Mastercard, JP Morgan, Barclays, Citigroup and Deloitte have all sponsored corporate curriculum projects in the region's schools and universities.

This same model of business-led education reform has been adopted all over the world as a core part of the response to youth unemployment. Worldwide, direct corporate partnerships with schools have proliferated, explicitly in the name of helping unemployed youth (Litow & Wyman, 2013). Some of these partnerships are organized locally: the *Economist* (2013) reported in April 2013, for example, that North Hertfordshire College in the UK had "launched a business venture with Fit4less, a low cost gym," while Bluegrass College in Kentucky had partnered with Toyota to create "a replica of a car factory, where workers and students go to classes together." Other partnerships have been developed at a national and even global level. In the United Kingdom, more than a third of employers are now involved in partnerships with schools, while 70 percent of state secondary schools are partnering with local companies through the government's Inspiring the Future initiative (Economic Voice, 2013). In the United States, the US State Department has partnered with the International Youth Foundation, the Inter-American Development Bank and a group of corporations (Blackstone, Caterpillar, Hilton, Manpower, Mastercard) to create a Youth Livelihoods Alliance, that seeks to address youth unemployment by promoting entrepreneurship, business and finance education in countries around the world, and by fostering local partnerships between the private, public and voluntary sectors (IYF, 2013c). The Alliance joins a growing collection of global initiatives that likewise seek to address youth unemployment through the vehicle of business-oriented education and close partnerships between schools, education systems and multinational corporations: the World Economic Forum's Global Agenda Council on Youth Unemployment, Making Cents International, the Global Partnership on Youth Employment, the Network for Teaching Entrepreneurship and so on. Through these combined efforts, the emphasis is to push schools around the world to focus more on promoting entrepreneurialism, financial literacy, free market ideology and skills, attitudes and knowledge that serve the needs and interests of some of the world's largest corporations. As Stephen Schwarzman, the CEO of the Blackstone Group, told CNBC at the launch of the Global Youth Employment Agenda in London in December 2010:

> At the heart of this situation is a need to close a significant skills gap. Preparing youth for employment requires training that is demand-driven to meet the needs of companies and ensure that young people are taught marketable skills. Most youth are lacking critical life skills that make them employable and more importantly, able to keep a job—things like teamwork, decision-making and time management. Underlying all solutions is the need for all institutions serving youth to advance a shared strategy that will alleviate the youth unemployment crisis and meet the employment needs of business through meaningful, long-term solutions.
>
> *(quoted in Allen, 2010)*

One of the ironies of the skills gap rhetoric is that a distinguishing feature of contemporary youth unemployment is that many young people who are unable to find jobs globally actually have relatively high levels of education. Paul Mason (2012), in his best-selling *Why It's Kicking Off Everywhere: The New Global Revolutions*, argues that the figure of the unemployed university graduate is at the heart of the current uprisings that many have collectively labeled a global youth rebellion. Indeed, concern about graduate unemployment and underemployment has been growing across both the global North and South (*Guardian*, 2012; Jeffrey, Jeffery & Jeffery, 2008; Shierholz, Sabadish & Finio, 2013). Despite this, the skills gap explanation of youth unemployment argues that young people, though they may indeed have high levels of education, are acquiring the *wrong types* of education—and that there is a problem with young people having inflated and unrealistic expectations about the world of work. In the Arab world, there is much talk today about needing to address a so-called "culture of shame," that allegedly leads young Arabs to look down on certain (low wage, low skill) private sector jobs that are available to them "as not being good enough" (Shoman, 2012). As Imed Drine (2012), of the UN's World Institute for Development Economics Research, argues, there is a "mismatch between what the labour market offers, and what young people expect:" many young Arab graduates hold on to the hope of securing public sector jobs, as they "don't trust the private sector because there are no guarantees (lay-offs without prior notice), no social security, no incentives and, above all, no enforcement of the labour laws." In the West, this issue is more commonly talked about as a problem of youth "entitlement." Andrew McAfee (2011), of MIT's Sloan School of Management, for example, complains in an article entitled, "When Entitlement Meets Unemployment," that:

> At a time of high unemployment and persistent joblessness, Millennials are asking for more concessions and perks from their employers ... [N]ew hires [at one company] told their CEO that they want to come in at 10 or later, have free food and a Pilates room, and get reimbursed for their personal trainers. This might be an extreme example, but it's not the only one.

Young jobseekers, according to McAfee (2011), need to learn to "take the first decent job that's offered," and "learn to serve," "be a good subordinate," and "give your employer more and ask less." Likewise, a survey of employers conducted in Britain on the problem of youth unemployment, entitled *Avoiding a Lost Generation*, notes that many young people have "inflated expectations in terms of both the type of work and the remuneration that they can aspire to initially," and argues that "recruitment agencies increasingly need to manage [young people's] expectations" (REC, 2010, p. 12). Thus, while there has long been talk of needing to raise the aspirations of the young—especially those from working-class and poor backgrounds who have been historically less likely to pursue higher education and professional forms of employment—there is now also a strong demand to work, directly and indirectly, to lower young people's expectations. This includes disciplining the young to study what employers would prefer them to study, take up jobs on the terms that employers offer—and also be willing to leave family and community behind to move to where jobs are available. In early 2012, for example, Anna Maria Cancelliari, Minister of the Interior for Italy, complained that youth unemployment in her country was high because young Italian men were "mummy's boys," who were frequently unwilling to leave their parental homes in search of jobs (quoted in Caon, 2012).

It is not just the young who have been singled out for censure as being principally responsible for causing youth unemployment: older generations have been widely blamed as well. For one of the most pronounced outcomes of the global economic crisis has been the resurgence of generational conflict rhetoric. Rather than focusing on the inequalities and conflicts between rich and poor, capital and labor, the global North and South, media and policy commentators have centered attention on alleged tensions between the old and the young as being at the root of the crisis—a move that begins with the decision to focus on youth unemployment rather than unemployment more generally. "One of the biggest issues of the euro crisis," writes David Böcking (2012) in *Der Spiegel*, is that "flush baby boomers in their fifties and sixties are today living prosperously at the expense of young people." "Why aren't more young people getting outraged?," Böcking asks, "it's high time the next generation took to the streets to confront their parents." Across Africa, the Middle East, Europe and North America, talk has grown of the rule of a "gerontocracy of older workers," who are "crushing" the younger generation through their determination "to cling to the better jobs as long as possible and then, when they do retire, demand impossibly rich private and public pensions that the younger generation will be forced to shoulder" (Coy, 2011; see also Campanella, 2010; Jaji, 2012; Marche, 2012). As former Italian Prime Minister Giuliano Amato put it, "the older generations have eaten the future of the younger ones" (quoted in Coy, 2011). A popular literature on generational conflict has developed: for example, Laurence Kotlikoff and Scott Burns' (2012) *The Clash of Generations*, Ed Howker and Shiv Malik's (2010) *Jilted Generation: How Britain Has Bankrupted Its Youth*, and David Willetts' (2010) *The Pinch: How the Baby Boomers Took Their Children's Future—And Why They Should Give It Back*. In the last instance, this is the same David Willetts who, in his role as UK Minister for Higher Education, saw fit to oversee the trebling of university tuition fees for students in England in December 2010. Again, the discourse of generational conflict serves to distract attention from the actions of political and economic elites that were at the heart of the global economic meltdown. "The recession didn't gut the prospects of American young people," writes Stephen Marche (2012) in a March 2012 *Esquire* article entitled "The War Against Youth," "The Baby Boomers took care of that."

The principal claim of generational conflict discourse is that older workers and citizens are benefitting from protections and privileges in the labor market and welfare state that have often been denied to young workers and citizens. But rather than argue for the extension of such protections and privileges to the young, or focus on the role that employers and the state have played in creating this two-tier labor market and welfare system in the first place, generational conflict discourse often claims that the protections and privileges enjoyed by older workers and citizens are directly costing the young, especially by preventing them from being able to get a foothold in the job market (Sears, 2014). The rhetoric thus argues for the removal or weakening of these protections and privileges, in the name of helping youth. In the United States, for example, Young America's Foundation—a group that advertises itself as "the principal outreach organization of the Conservative Movement"—recently created a "Youth Misery Index," that adds together data on youth unemployment, student debt and national debt per capita, and claims to find a "statistically significant relationship" between high levels of government spending and intervention in the economy, on the one hand, and high levels of youth misery, on the other. The solution, therefore, is for the state to cut spending, adopt austerity policies and eliminate market regulation (YAF, 2012). More generally in the United States, the concept of generational conflict and youth suffering has been used to push for cuts in pension and health care programs for seniors—in particular, Social Security and Medicare (Baer,

2012; Coy, 2011; Marche, 2012). In Europe, as Michele Tiraboschi (2012, pp. 4–5) has observed, concern about youth unemployment is being:

> "exploited" to justify—or perhaps to impose—major labour market reforms and deregulation on nation states overseen by central [European and international] institutions.... Fathers are now called to make a lot of sacrifices that are deemed to be "acceptable," for they contribute to provide their sons with better employment prospects.

In other words, in the name of supporting the interests of youth, states around Europe, often under pressure from the European Central Bank, the European Union and the IMF, are now introducing various forms of labor market deregulation, flexibilization and liberalization that are said to make employers more willing and able to offer employment to the young. Labor law reforms approved in Spain in February 2012, for example, made it easier and cheaper for employers to fire workers, restricted collective bargaining rights and extended probationary periods for new workers (Corujo, 2013; Sánchez, 2012). As Italian Minister of Labor Elsa Fornero (2013) said of the 2011–2012 labor law and pension reforms in Italy, which sought to end the idea of permanent employment, made it easier for employers to lay off workers and raised the retirement age, the goal was to "rebalance the Italian economy in favor of younger generations." This phenomenon is not limited to the global North. An ILO study in 2012 found that 40 out of 131 countries across Europe, Latin America, the Middle East and Sub-Saharan Africa had introduced changes to national labor law in the wake of the global economic crisis, the majority of which served to weaken employment protections for workers in the hopes of increasing overall employment levels (Cazes, Khatiwada & Malo, 2012; see also Clauwaert & Schömann, 2012).

Business leaders have also been vocal in calling for more direct state subsidies and wage cuts in order to "incentivize" them to hire young workers (CBI, 2011a). There have been widespread calls for lowering the minimum wage, particularly for those under the age of 21. Speaking at the World Economic Forum in Davos in January 2012, Tidjane Thiam, the CEO of Prudential—and a man whose own annual salary rose 65 percent in 2012 to reach £7.8 million—argued that "the minimum wage is the enemy of young people entering the labour market," and "a machine to destroy jobs." Young people, Thiam complained, "don't have a voice" to speak out against minimum wage policies (quoted in Reece, 2012; White, 2013). In the United Kingdom in 2012, the government froze the subminimum wages for 16–20 year olds, while raising the adult rates, for the first time since the minimum wage was introduced in 1999—a move that was backed by the Confederation of British Industry (CBI) and British Chambers of Commerce (Mulholland, 2012). As noted earlier, the UK government also introduced a youth wage subsidy—an idea that initially had been floated by the CBI itself (CBI, 2011b, 2011c). In New Zealand, a new youth subminimum wage was introduced by the government, again with strong backing from BusinessNZ, the country's principal business lobby group (Gray, 2012). In Greece, meanwhile, the age threshold for moving from a youth subminimum wage to a full, adult minimum wage was raised from 15 to 25 in 2010; this youth subminimum wage, that now covered all workers up to age 24, was then cut by almost a third in 2013 (Croucher & White, 2011; Reuters, 2013). Youth wage subsidies and subminimum wages were also proposed elsewhere, albeit without success, in South Africa, Ontario (Canada), and Washington state (US)—again, all in the name of combating youth unemployment. Ironically, the dominant policy rhetoric and practice in many countries have thus been to seek to "help" youth by reducing their wages, benefits and employment protections—along with those of their parents and grandparents as well.

If these different arguments and interventions being put forward by business and political elites made a significant difference in reducing the social problem of (youth) unemployment, then there might be a compelling reason to embrace them, even if they are so often transparently made to serve employer interests in the first instance. But there is little compelling evidence that they do significantly impact unemployment—and quite a lot of evidence that they don't. Invoking education and training as the primary solution to youth unemployment has been critiqued for decades. "Poor aggregate economic conditions and overall unemployment comprise the primary determinant of youth unemployment," as Henry Levin (1983, p. 240) once wrote of the US context in the early 1980s; therefore, "the problem of youth unemployment is unlikely to yield to an educational solution for the reason that it is not primarily an educational dilemma" (see also Ashton, 1986; Lafer, 2002; Petersen & Mortimer, 1994; Walker & Barton, 1986). Demonizing youth for allegedly poor attitudes, values and cultures that are held responsible for their unemployment has likewise long been critiqued in the youth studies literature as being both inaccurate and unjust (Griffin, 1993; MacDonald, 2011; McDermott, 1985; Te Riele, 2006; Solomos, 1985). Removing the elderly from the labor market in the name of opening up employment positions for youth, as some have suggested, may actually reduce work opportunities for the young, not increase them (Banks, Blundell, Bozio & Emmerson, 2010; Gruber, Milligan & Wise, 2009; Munnell & Wu, 2012). Claims about the negative impact of employment protection legislation (EPL) on youth employment levels, though they have long been popular with employers and policy-makers, are not well supported by research. According to the ILO (2012a, p. 24), "empirical evidence on the impact of EPL on youth unemployment is inconclusive;" while Clemens Noelke (2011, p. 26), in a review of theoretical and empirical research on the subject, found "no robust evidence whatsoever linking . . . EPL to inferior youth labour market performance" (see also Cazes, Khatiwada & Malo, 2012; Heyes & Lewis, 2012; O'Higgins, 2012). In the recent global economic crisis, as Heyes and Lewis (2012, p. 21) and others have pointed out, "young workers in countries with weak employment protections have suffered alongside those in countries where employment protection is relatively strong." The story is much the same with the relationship between the minimum wage and youth unemployment. Once again, despite the convictions of many business and political elites on the matter, theoretical and empirical research on the impact of minimum wage policies on youth employment has generally been equivocal and inconclusive, with no strong negative effects found (Croucher & White, 2011; O'Higgins, 2012). Finally, much of the flag waving around launching high profile campaigns and programs that focus specifically on reducing youth unemployment pales in comparison to the negative impacts of austerity policies and the failure to hold business and finance accountable for investing in socially desirable production and employment policies and practices. Thus, while German Chancellor Angela Merkel, for example, publicly embraced the cause of youth unemployment as being the "most pressing" problem in the EU in the summer of 2013, and began speaking of the importance of "youth guarantees" for education, training and employment, many critics in Europe and elsewhere argued that this was little more than a public relations campaign designed to distract attention from Merkel's own role in "compounding the situation [of high unemployment in Europe] by insisting that southern European economies balance their books rather than spend money on job-creating policies" (Connolly, 2013; see also Baker, 2012; Brown & Hansen, 2013; Tugwell & Petrakis, 2012).

Alternative Visions: Cross-Generational Movements of the Unemployed

The prioritization of youth unemployment has been widely accepted by groups across the political spectrum, including those on the political left. For example, the meeting of the World Social Forum in Tunisia in 2013 broadly adopted the rhetoric that youth were the most important priority for the contemporary global economy. The World Social Forum even invited the same speaker, Tarek Yusuf, Director of the Dubai Business School, who had presented at the World Economic Forum the year previously to talk about the links between youth unemployment and the Arab revolts. Yusuf emphasized the importance of education and skills building as the primary solution for youth unemployment in both forums (Albayan, 2013).

However, despite the dominance of the mainstream discourse on youth unemployment, there are important counter-narratives for addressing the employment fallout from the global economic crisis. In the United Kingdom, there has been extensive critique and organizing against the government's Youth Contract wage subsidy program and decision to freeze the youth minimum wage—a campaign that has been led by trade unions and youth and children's rights organizations. Part of this critique is that state measures to supposedly help youth are actually going to do little for them, and primarily benefit the private sector (UNISON, 2012; Unite, 2011). But groups have also organized on the principle of equal treatment and support for individuals of all life stages and age groups. The British Youth Council, Children's Rights Alliance, YWCA, UNISON and the Trades Union Congress have all argued against having a youth subminimum wage on the principle of equal pay for equal work, an opposition to age discrimination, and the fact that "many young workers [carry] out the same work as adults, [have] the same responsibilities, [pay] the same prices for goods and housing costs, and [are] financially independent" (Low Pay Commission, 2011, p. 68; BYC & CRAE, 2010). In September 2012, a group of trade unions, politicians, student and pensioner organizations came together to make a statement of common purpose under the banner headline, "Generations United for a Better Society:"

> At a time of economic crisis, there is often a tendency to look for someone to blame. This time a number of politicians, thinktanks and elements in the media have started to point the finger at pensioners by suggesting that they have escaped the austerity measures at the expense of younger generations. Not only is this factually incorrect, it is extremely divisive. Young and old in fact share a number of concerns. . . . What this artificial generational conflict tries to hide is the real division in our society between rich and poor. . . . The cohesion of our society rests on valuing all ages, recognising the different contributions they can make, and championing a welfare state that continues to provide support from the cradle to the grave.
>
> *(Gibson et al., 2012)*

Parallel arguments and campaigns have likewise developed elsewhere around the world. In the United States, Generations United—a coalition of more than a hundred organizations committed to fostering intergenerational collaboration, that was founded in the 1980s—has argued strongly that "high unemployment . . . is an issue that touches all ages," that "the generations are more alike than they are different in this area," and that "job creation is vital for the prosperity of all generations" (Generations United, 2011). In New Zealand, a coalition of trade unions, student and youth groups launched a *Same Work Same Pay* campaign in November 2012, in opposition to the government's plans to bring in a youth subminimum wage, arguing that youth rates were discriminatory and unfair, would not solve youth unemployment, and "will drive many young people into poverty," "lock older people out of work," and "drag down all other wages" (Same Work Same Pay, 2012). While the campaign was unable to block the new wage law, it has been successful in convincing many large employers in New Zealand to voluntarily commit to paying the adult minimum wages to all their employees, regardless of age—including McDonald's, Pizza Hut, KFC and Starbucks (Newstalk ZB, 2013).

Across southern Europe, there has been extensive, broad-based organizing against both the austerity measures and labor market liberalization that have been imposed by national governments and the troika of the IMF, the European

Central Bank and the European Union, often in the name of fighting youth unemployment. In Spain, the two main unions—Comisiones Obreras (CCOO) and Unión General de Trabajadores (UGT)—have led a series of mass protests and general strikes, starting in February 2010 and continuing through May Day 2013, that have seen hundreds of thousands of demonstrators marching in the streets of cities across the country (Frayer, 2012; Ross-Thomas, 2010). These have been joined by student and youth groups from the 15-M (or indignados) movement (Delclós & Viejo, 2012). Though Prime Minister Mariano Rajoy explicitly justified his 2012 labor reforms in the name of helping unemployed youth, protesters have rejected such rhetoric, organizing themselves under the slogan, "No to the Labor Reforms—Unfair to Workers, Ineffective and Useless to the Economy and for Employment" (Common Dreams, 2012; Tipaldou, 2012). As one protester observed, "it's absurd to think you're going to bring down unemployment by making it easier to fire people" (Dowsett, 2012). Older workers feared the reforms would lead to the increasing precarity of their own jobs; while youth groups such as Juventud Sin Futuro protested the continuing deterioration of young workers' workplace rights and benefits (JSF, 2013). Parallel protests, likewise led by unions, student and youth groups, have erupted across Portugal, France, Italy and Greece between 2008 and 2013 (Mason, 2012). In Italy, where Minister of Labor Elsa Fornero had been reported as telling graduates that they should learn not to be "choosy" in looking for jobs, and accept whatever employment is offered to them by employers, regardless of conditions, student protesters demonstrated under the banner, "We Are Choosy, and We Choose to Fight!" (CAU, 2012; Kington, Roberts, Connolly, Willsher & Smith, 2012).

One of the most protracted battles globally against the dominant response to youth unemployment has taken place in South Africa. In February 2010, South African Finance Minister Pravin Gordhan proposed introducing a youth wage subsidy, as a measure to address the country's severe youth unemployment problem. The proposal involved giving any South African employer that hired a young person between the ages of 18 to 29 in a low wage job a state subsidy that would cover 50 percent of that worker's wage costs for a period of two years. The measure was immediately condemned by the Congress of South African Trade Unions (COSATU) and the People's Budget Coalition, an umbrella group of trade unions, churches and NGOs, who feared that the subsidy would be "abused by employers," lead to the displacement of older workers and help to "create a permanent army of young, super-exploited workers" (Majavu, 2010). South Africa's Progressive Youth Alliance—a group that includes the ANC Youth League, the Communist Youth League and the South African Students Congress—also came out strongly against the proposal. For the next three years, the government hesitated on whether to move ahead with the wage subsidy plan. But, ironically, although the subsidy had been initially proposed by the ruling ANC Party, it was fervently embraced by the Democratic Alliance, South Africa's largest opposition party, who erected billboards and created videos and websites that demanded a

"Youth Wage Subsidy Now!," and berated South African President Jacob Zuma for his failure to act on the issue. "Surely our President cares more about the young unemployed people of South Africa than he does about the vested interests of COSATU," railed Democratic Alliance Parliamentary Leader Lindiwe Mazibuko, "While the President dithers, more and more unemployed young people are being sucked into a vortex of despair" (Munusamy, 2012). The conflict came to a head in May 2012, when a group of blue-shirted Democratic Alliance supporters tried to march on the COSATU headquarters in Braamfontein, Johannesburg, where they were confronted by a red-shirted group of COSATU supporters. Violence broke out, bricks and rocks were thrown, a number of marchers on both sides were injured, and police moved in with teargas to break up the confrontation (Golden, 2012). Bitter debates over the youth wage subsidy have continued since then: in November 2013, the South African Parliament passed a draft law that proposed to introduce a version of the youth wage subsidy proposal (SA.news.gov.za, 2013).

What the ongoing South African struggle over the youth wage subsidy has been vitally important in doing has less to do with the particular issue of the wage subsidy itself. Even the government, when it proposed the subsidy, acknowledged that it would likely have only limited impact on reducing youth unemployment levels in the country (National Treasury, 2011, p. 10). International research on the use of wage subsidies to reduce youth unemployment (and unemployment more generally) has tended to find these subsidies to be of limited effectiveness, with strong deadweight and substitution effects—meaning that employers use the subsidies to hire workers they would have hired anyway, or else hire the targeted group of (young) workers over other groups of (older) workers—although, in some cases, subsidies can have small but positive outcomes (Betcherman, Olivas & Dar, 2004; COSATU, 2012; ILO, 2011; Smith, 2006). In its 2012 report, *The Youth Employment Crisis: Time for Action*, the ILO, for example, argues that generalized wage subsidies, of the kind that have been proposed in South Africa:

> that target young people mainly on the basis of their age are unlikely to have a long-term impact on their employment and earnings.... These subsidies often contribute to labour market distortions in terms of deadweight and substitution effects, with employment lasting only as long as the subsidy is received.... An efficient monitoring system is also essential to avoid abuses associated with wage subsidies, and to achieve the policy objective of improving the employability of young workers, rather than turning them into a cheap source of labour.
>
> *(ILO, 2012b, pp. 58–59)*

What is more important, however, is that this policy struggle in South Africa has brought to the foreground the question of what Gareth and Teresa Rees (1982) have talked about as being the "ideology" of youth unemployment. This is the idea that the ways in which both the social problem of youth unemployment and the policies introduced to address this problem are framed are always shaped by the interests and agendas of groups other than young unemployed people themselves. One of the most widely repeated criticisms of the youth wage subsidy in South Africa, that has been made by trade unions, churches, social movements, student and youth groups alike, is that, in a country characterized by extreme levels of inequality, it proposes giving more money to the already wealthy. "Youth wage subsidies reinforce increased profitability and ... [are] nothing more than a subsidy to capital for cheap labour," argues the Democratic Left Front (2012), a coalition of left organizations that was formed in Johannesburg in January 2011. It is also the idea that by framing the labor market consequences of the global economic crisis as being a problem, first and foremost, of youth unemployment, and targeting employment policies specifically at alleged problems with youth— their skill deficits, excessive expectations, overly high wage demands or rigid employment protections—there is a risk of distracting attention from the broader structural issues that create unemployment, along with a wide range of other social and economic problems, for young and old together. The Democratic Left Front (2012) thus proposes, instead of a youth wage subsidy, an extended agenda for addressing unemployment in South Africa that involves: scaling down the country's carbon-intensive economy through creating one million renewable energy-climate jobs; providing a guaranteed basic living income for the unemployed; launching a public works program to address housing, health, transport and infrastructural needs; providing free basic services and education for all; and returning ownership of the land and natural resources to the people. Similarly, the Unemployed People's Movement (2012), a social movement that is based in Durban and Grahamstown, South Africa, and that works with the poor and unemployed, has strongly rejected the youth wage subsidy plan, and proposes instead as a "proper solution to the unemployment crisis" a structural reform agenda of radical land reform, nationalization of key sectors of the economy, increased levels of corporate taxation, stronger policing and sanctions for business "corruption and plundering," an extensive public works program, and accessible, high quality education for all. "The way forward," the Unemployed People's Movement (2012) insists, is for the poor, unemployed and "progressive forces" in society "to protest and ... continue to contest the battle of ideas in all forums from the streets to the newspapers." "If we cannot build our own power" and win this battle of ideas, the Movement continues, then chances are that "our future will be very bleak."

4

YOUTH AS A REVOLUTIONARY SUBJECT?

Across the political spectrum, political leaders, media commentators and social activists labeled the uprisings that spread across the world in the wake of the 2008–2009 global financial crisis a youth rebellion. Ismail Serageldin (2011), the Director of the Library of Alexandria in Egypt, when delivering the 2011 Nelson Mandela annual lecture in Johannesburg, South Africa, for example, spoke of "youth, from the Cape to Cairo and beyond" as being "the vanguard of the great global revolution of the 21st Century," and predicted that today's youth "will craft a world in their own image, idealistic, dynamic and imaginative." The *New Internationalist* dedicated its October 2012 issue to the topic of "Youth Rising," in which Jody McIntyre, a 22-year-old British activist and journalist who first came to public attention when he was forcibly dragged out of his wheelchair by police during the December 2010 student protests in London, England, writes of how "thousands of young people" around the world are "taking the lead" in a "sweeping wave of dissent" that is "pushing the boundaries" and "engaging with politics in new and forceful ways" (McIntyre, 2012). Zach Zill (2012), writing in the *International Socialist Review*, argues that:

> The year 2011 will go down in history as a year of youth revolt. Throughout the year, beginning with the Arab Spring, protests, riots and revolutions involving tens of millions of teenagers and twenty-somethings have shaken the global political order.... This [young] generation's struggle, from Cairo to New York to Santiago, has revived the traditions of mass revolutionary politics and breathed life into an international left that for decades faced nothing but defeat and retreat. In the span of one short year, all existing political assumptions have been turned on their heads.

Meanwhile, in the *Financial Times*, Martin Wolf (2011) writes of how "the world's youth is in a revolting state of mind," and warns that "Egypt is not the first developing country, nor will it be the last, to be rocked by [its] youthful majority." Wolf predicts that political leaders around the world who fail to "harness the energy" and meet the demands of the "idealistic and frustrated" young will "lose power—and rightly so." In 2012, the United States Institute of Peace—a government-funded thinktank closely connected to American military intelligence networks—published a report on the global "youth revolt," written by a professor from the Defense Resources Management Institute in Monterey, California. The report warns of the imminent threat of a global "youth upheaval" and "youth war" that constitutes "a new frontier of conflict," and is "the result of an 'action oriented quick results generation' impatient of waiting for change and taking matters into hand" (Amara, 2012). Carnegie Endowment scholar and *Foreign Policy* magazine CEO David Rothkopf has likewise observed that "when the cold war ended, we thought we were going to have a clash of civilisations. It turns out we're having a clash of generations" (quoted in Friedman, 2011). A global youth "revolution [is] in the air," writes Canadian business consultant Don Tapscott (2011), and if political leaders don't act quickly, "we run the risk of a generational conflict that could make the radicalisation of youth in Europe and North America in the 1960s pale in comparison."

The events and movements that have been widely labeled as being at the heart of this global youth rebellion include: the demonstrations and occupations against austerity politics and the impacts of economic crisis that began in Greece in December 2008, and have since spread across the countries of southern Europe, where they have become known as the movements of the indignados in Spain, the aganaktismenoi in Greece, and the Generação a Rasca in Portugal; the mass mobilizations across the Arab world that began in Tunisia in December 2010 and spread over the next year to Egypt, Yemen, Libya, Bahrain, Syria, Morocco, Saudi Arabia and Kuwait, and have been collectively dubbed as the Arab Spring; the university student protests that have been organized in Britain, Chile, France, Canada and the United States since late 2010; the Occupy movement that began in New York City in September 2011, and then spread to 95 cities in 82 countries around the world; and the mass social unrest and riots that have erupted in England in August 2011, France in August 2012, Sweden in May 2013 and Turkey and Brazil in June 2013.

This is not the first time that a youth revolt has been proclaimed by commentators across the political spectrum in similar fashion. In the late 1960s, student activists and their supporters proclaimed a student and youth-led revolution that was to change the world; while their critics, though opposing their politics, worried about a generational uprising and divide that threatened the very foundations of society. In Europe, during the first part of the twentieth century, there likewise were proclamations, predictions and fears—from both the political right and left—of a youth-led movement that would radically transform the contemporary social, political and economic order. The question that we ask in this chapter is how we should understand these recurrent claims of youth revolution. What is the significance of young people—or "youth"—for radical social change? What is the nature of youth as both an ideological symbol and political actor? How does the discursive construction of youth as a potent historical and social force relate to the actual lives of individual young people during these different eras? What we argue here is that the current discourse of a global youth revolt draws on a long and often contradictory conceptual history that has repeatedly constructed youth as a rebellious or revolutionary subject, but that the particular forms and ways in which youth today are being constructed as revolutionary and rebellious differ in systematic ways from previous eras. In other words, there are both continuities and changes in the theory and practice of youth revolt across time—and these changes are closely linked to broader changes in global capitalist politics, society and economy. To understand the significance of claims being made about global youth rebellion today, we thus need to understand both the long social history of youth as a revolutionary subject, as well as the shaping influence of contemporary neoliberal forms of social, cultural and political organization and practice.

The History of Youth as a Revolutionary Subject

The current construction of youth as a revolutionary subject is not new, but rather is the latest stage in a long history of portraying youth as rebellious, revolutionary, utopian and idealistic. In the West, this is a history that—*retrospectively*, at least—has been said to extend back for centuries. In the 1970s, a University of Vienna medieval historian named Friedrich Heer claimed to be able to find a historically significant role played by organized youth movements going back to the time of ancient Greece: the birth of Christianity, on this account, was in essence "a romantic Jewish youth movement" (Heer, 1974; quoted in Jarausch, 1975, p. 446). More recently, sociologist Jack Goldstone (2002, p. 11) has argued that youth have "played a prominent role in political violence throughout recorded history," and have been central actors in "most major revolutions," including "the English Revolution of the seventeenth century, the French revolution of the eighteenth century and most twentieth-century revolutions in developing countries." Herbert Moller (1968, pp. 237, 240), in his overview of "youth as a force in the modern world," suggests that the sixteenth-century "Protestant Reformation in west-central Europe provides an example of one of the outstanding youth movements in history," and insists that "there can be no doubt about the surge of youthful activism in several European countries in roughly the last 30 years of the eighteenth century." Richard Braungart (1984, p. 114) argues that youth movements, in which "young people, as an age group, reject the existing order, join together and attempt to redirect the course of human history," first emerged with the Young Europe movement of the early nineteenth century. It was during this period, that small and often quite marginal nationalist unification and independence movements emerged around the continent under the banner of youth: Young Germany, Young Italy, Young Russia, Young France, Young Poland, Young Ireland and so on (Braungart, 1984; Elkar, 1995; Ledeen, 1969). "Place the young at the head of the insurgent masses," urged Giuseppe Mazzini, the founder and leader of the Young Italy movement in 1831, "you do not know what strength is latent in those young bands, what magic influence the voices of the young have on the crowd" (quoted in Moller, 1968, p. 241).

It is clearly possible, then, to find early precursors of generational conflict, political engagement and social activism among the young throughout world history. But the development of organized youth and student movements is more commonly said to have begun to play a central role in global society, politics and economy in more recent times: initially, during a period that emerged in Europe in the early part of the twentieth century, and subsequently spread across the globe; and then again, in a university-centered phase that began in the United States during the mid-1960s and quickly went worldwide. Notably, these are two periods that saw a flourishing of historical writing on youth in earlier times— much of which today is probably more informative for what it reveals about the eras in which it was produced, than for the claims that it makes about its ostensible objects of study (e.g., Fishman & Solomon, 1964; Heer, 1974; Moller, 1968). Scholars in the late 1960s and early 1970s were explicitly motivated by the student movement of their own era to look back in time for earlier examples of student and youth movements; and they were often at risk both of projecting contemporary understandings of youth onto earlier periods, and mistaking previous expressions of political rhetoric for sociological and historical truth. Though social, political, military and religious revolts throughout history have sometimes been led by individuals who were relatively young in chronological age, this does not mean that they saw themselves, or were seen by others at the time as acting as "youth" (Lanza, 2012). Revolutionary political rhetoric, too, has long embraced an ideal of youth—to signify a sense of regeneration and transformation—even when few young individuals may have been directly engaged in formulating such politics. In the mid-1960s, for example, Jacob Fishman and Fredric Solomon (1964, p. 1) claimed that the student rebellion that was beginning to build up around them was "not a new phenomenon," arguing that "such modern states as Israel, Egypt, Ghana and Turkey were, in large measure, products of youth movement revolutions." It would have been more accurate, however, to argue that youth was a pivotal symbol of the nationalist ideologies that were embraced by the independence movements that led to the creation of these different states (e.g., for Turkey, see Lüküslü, 2005; Neyzi, 2001). In the current period of a perceived global youth revolt, there has similarly been a revival of interest in the literature from the late 1960s and 1970s on youth and student movements of that period—literature which, until recently, had been relatively marginalized in youth studies and related fields (e.g., Bayat, 2010).

When we look back across these periods over the last hundred years or so of (allegedly) youth-led rebellion and revolt—the early twentieth century, the late 1960s, and the current, post-crisis neoliberal era—a consistent pattern emerges. First, social and economic changes bring particular groups of young people to the forefront of public attention as constituting a new "youth movement," as these young individuals both act and are acted upon through an evolving set of identities, interests, institutions and ideologies that emerge in reaction to social change itself. Second, these interests and ideologies lead to vastly exaggerated claims of the power and promise or—depending on one's political point of view—menace of youth, claims that are made both by and about young people, and that may be put forward in complete sincerity and/or strategically, as a form of advertising or public relations exercise. Frequently, there is an articulation of surprise in reaction to this rediscovered power and dynamism of youth, as prior to each period of youth uprising, there had usually been widespread concern over the alleged apathy, passivity or debility of youth. Third, claims of the revolutionary power and impact of youth tend to obscure the central and continuing role of adults and adult-led organizations in working with and on youth in the new "youth" movements. Fourth and finally, in some instances, this leads paradoxically to the diminishing of broader social movement demands for change, reform and revolution, as what are fundamentally political, ideological, social and economic conflicts are reduced to being "merely" a youth or age or generation-related issue, in which immature and impatient youth act out of turn, or are improperly led astray by others, and consequently, do not need to be taken seriously as legitimate political actors.

Alongside this common pattern, there have also been key changes in the particular ways in which youth has been constructed, and young people have constructed themselves, as revolutionary subjects across these different periods— changes that are closely tied to shifts in the broader social, economic, political and ideological contexts of each era. In the early twentieth century in Europe, revolutionary and rebellious youth were linked closely to the formation of organized youth movements that were often run by or affiliated with schools, churches, political parties or the state; they were intimately associated with the dominant forces and causes of nationalism, imperialism and militarism; they were tied, by turn, to the spaces of nature, industry and the battlefield; and they were celebrated, in many instances, for their physical vitality and bodily vigor. In the student movements of the 1960s, by contrast, revolutionary and rebellious youth were associated with student identities, revolts were over-whelmingly linked with the space of the university, and key issues were tied, in the first instance, to the tensions created by the massification of higher education. Beyond this, there was often a strong reaction *against* nationalism, imperialism and militarism, and *against* organized political parties and formal youth organizations. In place of bodily vigor and physical energy, it was the cultural choices and creativity of the young that were celebrated. In the current neoliberal period, revolutionary youth are linked with the image of the unemployed or under-employed graduate; places of rebellion have moved to the occupation of open urban spaces; emphasis is placed on the absence of formal leadership and hierar-chical organization among youth activists; and it is the technological prowess and connectedness of the young that are celebrated as ushering in a new social and political order. In each of these eras, there has been a strong sense of global influence and sharing: but the intensity, scale and speed of global linkages have all steadily increased over time. Older forms of youth revolutionary activity and organization do not tend to disappear, but rather continue alongside the newer forms that emerge and develop in subsequent social and political eras.

The Rise of Organized Youth Movements in Early Twentieth-Century Europe

For three days in October 1913, on the slopes of the Hoher Meissner mountain near Kassel in central Germany, almost 3,000 young people, mostly from middle-class families from across Germany, Switzerland and Austria gathered for a camp out and revival festival. The goal of the gathering was to unite the many different youth movements and organizations that had developed in the three countries over the preceding decades into a single "Free German Youth" movement, that could represent "youth's demand to be recognised as an independent estate entitled to self-determination and responsibility" (Stachura, 1981, p. 33). The most famous statement to emerge from this event, known as the Meissner Formula, proclaimed that:

> Free German Youth, on their own initiative, under their own responsibility, and with deep sincerity, are determined to independently shape their own lives. For the sake of this inner freedom, they will take united action under any and all circumstances.
>
> *(quoted in Stachura, 1981, pp. 32–33)*

However, it wasn't just a demand for youthful autonomy that was articulated at Hoher Meissner: for there was also a powerful and shared sense among those pres-ent that youth had a special role to play in changing and saving the German nation and world as a whole. Hans Paasche, son of the vice-president of the Reichstag, told the young delegates that "the German house is on fire and we are the fire brigade!" (quoted in Laqueur, 1984, p. 34). Gustav Wyneken, a leader in the Wandervogel, the foremost German youth movement of the era, argued that "youth's special privilege of freedom obligates it to *uphold* freedom," that youth were "the future within the present," and that only youth would be able to save the German nation by pushing for "a new spiritualization and beautification of life." The ills that were said to afflict German society were the "destructive effects of rapid industrialization and materialism," and the "moral stupor, superficiality, thoughtlessness, and hypocrisy" of "bourgeois" social convention (quoted in Williams, 2001, pp. 172–173). Though the Hoher Meissner gathering had been called in opposition to the jingoistic patriotism that was on the rise in Germany, as elsewhere around Europe at the time, it wasn't opposed to nationalism *per se*, but was committed to putting forward a different kind of nationalist vision, in which youth would lead Germany, and indeed, "all of humanity out of the darkness into the light . . . guided by [their own] inner truthfulness" (Williams, 2001. p. 173; see also Laqueur, 1984; Stachura, 1981).

Hoher Meissner is one of the best known events and clearest articulations of the ideas associated with many of the organized youth movements that developed throughout Europe during the first decades of the twentieth century. During this period, there emerged on the continent a "cult of youth," in which the "vital" characteristics of youth—"beauty, health, purity, energy, idealism, creativity, boldness, vision," as well as rebelliousness and openness to uncertainty and transformation—were celebrated not just as "an attribute of the life-cycle but a quality to which society as a whole could aspire" (Harvey, 2005, p. 66; see also Jorgensen, 2009; Kalman, 2003). Driving and driven by this emergent ideology of youth, the era saw the rapid proliferation of formal, organized youth movements that were dedicated to nurturing these essential characteristics of youthfulness, protecting youth from the degenerative forces of modern society, and capitalizing on the inner dynamism and promise of youth to transform, regenerate and rejuvenate modern society as a whole. The most influential and earliest of these new youth movements were the back-to-nature, character-building and ostensibly non-political organizations such as the Wandervogel in Germany (established in 1901) and the Boy Scouts in the United Kingdom (established in 1908). But as the century wore on, there developed more overtly political groups, many of which were state or party affiliated. These included the Free German Youth movement (created in 1913), the Russian Young Communist League, that later became the Komsomol (1918), the Communist Youth International (1919), the Fascist Youth Vanguards in Italy (1919) and the Hitler Youth in Germany (1922)—but there were many other similar such groups in countries right across Europe.

In the aftermath of the Second World War, many of the early European youth movements became retrospectively associated in historical memory with—and thus tainted by—the subsequent rise of Nazism and fascism (Becker, 1946; Ledeen, 1969; Roseman, 1995; Stachura, 1981; Wanrooij, 1987). But these early youth organizations actually developed on all sides of the political spectrum, often producing closely mirroring rhetoric on the importance of youth, even as their official politics clashed. If Mussolini embraced youth "as the avant-garde of the fascist 'revolution'," then so too did many early twentieth-century leftist organizations promote youth as the embodiment of "authentic, uncompromising revolutionary socialism" (Passerini, 1997, p. 281; Jorgensen, 2009, p. 26). "The revoutionary proletarian youth . . . was the hottest, the purest flame of the

German revolution until now," declared Spartacist leader Karl Liebknecht in 1918, "and it will be the holiest, unquenchable flame of the revolution to come" (quoted in Jorgensen, 2009, p. 19). Indeed, one of the characteristics of this period was that youth became an object of intense political competition, as young people were organized and organized themselves under the banner of conflicting ideologies. In interwar France, for example, the Young Christian Workers, Young Communists, Young Fascists and Young Patriots competed for the allegiance of working- and middle-class French youth (Kalman, 2003; Whitney, 2009); while in Italy, the struggle over youth took place largely between the Catholic Action youth organization and the Fascists (O'Brien, 1982). By 1934, French socialist leader Léon Blum was moved to declare that "we live at a time when everyone assumes the right to speak in the name of youth, when everyone, at the same time, wants to grab hold of youth, when everyone is fighting over youth" (quoted in Whitney, 2009, p. 3).

What led to this intense ideological and institutional focus on youth in early twentieth-century Europe? In part, the sweeping social, cultural and economic changes that were being brought about by the rapid spread of industrial capitalism—large-scale urbanization, the separation of work from home, transformation of employment opportunities, and destabilization of traditional institutions of family, community and church—triggered a growing anxiety about the socialization of the young, who were so clearly growing up in a world that differed sharply from the world in which their parents and grandparents had grown up. Middle-class boys, in particular, were now spending extended periods of their lives in formal institutions of schooling, where there developed an intensive, new concern with their proper development: indeed, this is where the modern science of adolescent development first took root. At the same time, the appearance of large groups of unsupervised, underemployed and unemployed poor and working-class youth in the city streets of Europe caused alarm about the potential for social unrest, political instability and moral degeneration (Lesko, 2001; Wallace & Kovatcheva, 1998). The flipside of the celebration of the vitality of modern youth was concern about youth debility—as was articulated most influentially in G. Stanley Hall's (1904) binary representation of adolescence in his turn-of-the-century treatise on the subject. The youth organizations that developed in this period were thus simultaneously efforts to fix and save youth from modern society, as they were projects to have modern society fixed and saved by the true, internal spirit of youth. In their quest to respond to the era's anxieties about youth and social change, the organized youth movements of early twentieth-century Europe responded in different, sometimes radically opposing ways. Many, like the Boy Scouts and Wandervogel, embraced a "back to nature" ethos as part of their search for a better, stronger, more authentic foundation for modern youth and modern society, focusing their work on organized camping, hiking, woodcraft and outdoors activities (Cupers, 2008; Harvey, 2005; J. Williams, 2007). On the other hand, in much Futurist, fascist as well as socialist iconography, youth were linked directly with the new industry, machinery and technology that were transforming life in Europe at the time as the ultimate symbol of modernization and progress (Gorsuch, 2000; Harvey, 2005).

The new, intensive ideological and institutional focus on youth was also shaped, to a large degree, by the structures and forces of nationalism, imperialism and militarism in Europe during this period. As early as the mid-nineteenth century, youth had become a widely recognized symbol of the different nationalist independence, unification and republican movements that existed on the continent, and was used to represent the rise of new or "young" nations out of and against the old, continental monarchies and empires. Youth was "elevated to the status of a national principle," writes Michael Ledeen (1969, p. 137), and "distinctions between young and old nations [were] used to describe their relative vigour, creativity and virility." By the century's end, inter-imperialist rivalries and nationalist struggles for supremacy among the European powers came to be framed by a "biologistic discourse of degeneration" that viewed history as a series of "cycles of human development in which cultures, nations, races, and civilizations naturally grew, flourished, and decayed, to be supplanted by other, more vigorous organisms" (Harvey, 2005, p. 67). In such a discourse, national and imperial power was linked both symbolically and literally to the perceived purity, acuity, beauty and strength of each nation's youth—and especially, their young men (Blanch, 1979; Lesko, 2001). The creation of the Boy Scouts by Robert Baden Powell in 1908, for example, was directly linked to widespread concern at the time over the alleged moral and physical degeneration of many young men in Britain, degeneration that was thought to be caused by the squalid, unhealthy and vice-ridden environments of an increasingly urbanized society, and feared to threaten the very foundations of the British empire (Rosenthal, 1986; Springhall, 1977). Many of the early twentieth-century youth movements in Europe focused closely on developing and celebrating the physical health and strength of youth; and in the wake of the First World War, this bodily concern developed, in groups such as the Komsomol, Fascist and Hitler Youth, into a more specific celebration of the military prowess and sacrifice of youth on the battlefield itself (de Ras, 2008; Harvey, 2005; Ledeen, 1969; Tirado, 1994).

In this broad context, expansive claims were widely made in early twentieth-century Europe about the power and significance of youth for achieving radical social change. On the left, this was the period that developed the notion of youth as being the "vanguard" of the socialist and proletarian revolution (Cornell, 1982; Jorgensen, 2009; Tirado, 1994). On the right, youth were portrayed by fascist groups all over Europe as constituting a "new force [in society], ... a new knighthood, an élite alone capable of regenerating the nation and the state" (Kalman, 2003, p. 343; see also Ledeen, 1969; Passerini, 1997). Even for ostensibly non-political youth organizations such as the Wandervogel and Scouts, youth were portrayed as the saviors of the nation and society more generally. These claims for youth being a pivotal force in modern society were largely based on two key theories. The first attributed the alleged power of youth to what was widely believed at the time to be the distinctive, universal and innate characteristics of youth psychology and youth as a stage of life. Gustav Wyneken, for example, promoted a concept of "Youth Culture" that posited that youth, when freed from the constraints of adult society, was a more spiritual and idealistic life stage than other age groups, and autonomous youth, therefore, "adhered to absolute values and were inclined to realize them without compromise" (Utley, 1979, pp. 211–212). In an article entitled, "The Mission of the Young," written for *Der Anfang*, a journal that was closely linked to the Free German Youth Movement, Herbert Blumenthal argued that:

> youth lives like the lilies of the field; never again is the individual so free as in his youth. His existence is not yet determined by economic objectives, the struggle to survive, or the "seriousness of life".... [This] is where the world-historical work of young people begins—they measure all things against their highest ideals, and all things become problematic.... If young people looked at life through the eyes of maturity, things would not look good for the renewal of the world.
>
> *(quoted in Williams, 2001, p. 171)*

Though such claims clearly pertain to middle-class youth, in particular, similar claims about youth as a life stage were also made by socialists about youth of all social classes. In 1906, Vladimir Lenin paraphrased Friedrich Engels as saying "is it not natural that youth should predominate in our Party? ... We are a party of innovators, and it is always the youth that most eagerly follows the innovators" (quoted in Neumann, 2012, p. 274). Such views about the alleged idealism and openness of youth, of course, have persisted well beyond the period of early twentieth-century Europe. Thus, Robert Cornell (1982, p. x), writing in the 1980s about the early history of the Communist Youth International between 1914 and 1924, claimed that his study demonstrated "the broad historical relevance of certain qualities found, perhaps in greatest abundance, in young people: untempered idealism, a predisposition to embrace the most radical alternatives for social change, and a self-assertiveness directed against traditional adult tutelage."

The second claim for the transformative power of youth was based on an emerging theory of the social and historical significance of generations. In part, common rhetorical claims that, as Lenin put it, "the future belongs to the youth," were based on the simple if obvious recognition that any political party, ideological movement or nation state that wished to be a continued force into the future needed to continually reach out and appeal to new generations of recruits (quoted in Neumann, 2012, p. 274). In part, in the context of rapid social, economic and political change—and later, in the aftermath of the devastation of the First World War—there existed across Europe a widespread sense at this time of the fundamental datedness, limitation and failure of older generations of leaders, and a need for new thinking and new leadership (Harvey, 2005; Whitney, 2009). Political parties such as the Bolsheviks in Russia, Communists in France and Fascists in Italy, at least initially, did tend to have younger memberships and leaderships— with many in their twenties and thirties—than the parties in power they were challenging, and were thus apt to deploy a generational discourse to frame their political and ideological demands (Gorsuch, 2000; Ledeen, 1969; Whitney, 2009). More fundamentally, however, youth were seen as constituting a different and more radical type of social actor because it was believed that they had not been (or would not be) shaped or stained by the old social and ideological orders that had molded the outlook of their parents' and grandparents' generations. As Juliane Fuerst (2010) notes, many Bolshevik theorists in early twentieth-century Russia held the "utopian" conviction that "only a young person unspoiled by the experience of capitalism [would] become the 'new soviet man or woman' in possession of a true communist consciousness" (quoted in Goretti & Worley, 2012, p. 6; see also Gorsuch, 2000; Krylova, 2007; Neumann, 2012). "In Russia, as in the West, [youth] stands in the front ranks of the movement," claimed the first issue of the Komsomol's *Young Communist* magazine, because "youth . . . has not been poisoned by the prejudice and ideas of bourgeois society" (quoted in Tirado, 1994, p. 236). Indeed, in leftist political thought from this point on, the concept of youth as (a radical) generation has occupied a contradictory and unstable position, at once embraced as being pivotal to the possibility of revolutionary change, but also dismissed as a false category that obscures the continuing centrality of class (Cornell, 1982; Harvey, 2005; Neumann, 2012; Wanrooij, 1999; Whitney, 2009).

All of these claims about the social power and radical tendency of youth in early twentieth-century Europe tended to be grossly exaggerated. Only a minority of young people participated in these early youth movements, and among those who did, practices and attitudes often failed to live up to the utopian predictions and rhetoric of the era's youth ideology (Gorsuch, 2000; Krylova, 2007). Scholarly literature sometimes has drawn a distinction between youth movements of this period that truly were movements "of youth," as opposed to movements that were created and run by adults "for youth" (e.g., Harvey, 2005; Kahane, 1997). But such distinctions can be overstated, and risk setting up a misplaced quest to identify "true" and "authentic" as opposed to inauthentic instances of youth rebellion and revolution. Movements that are commonly pointed to as being the most autonomous of this period, such as the Wandervogel in Germany, were strongly shaped by both direct and indirect adult participation (Coussée, 2008). Many of the leaders of the Wandervogel, for example, were not actually young students but "young teachers in their twenties and thirties," and the movement as a whole was "dependent on the toleration . . . of the secondary school bureaucracies and the state ministries of education," not to mention the German government itself (Williams, 2001, p. 167). Young people in early twentieth-century Europe who participated in youth movements drew directly on dominant ideologies of the time—including ideologies about youth itself—worked closely with adult colleagues and mentors, and were often strongly influenced by their parents, such that those who joined leftist youth groups, for example, were more likely to come from families that also had leftist politics (Cornell, 1982; Jorgensen, 2009). As Mark Roseman (1995, p. 17) writes of early twentieth-century Germany, "the declarations of 'autonomy' on the part of the youth movement, and the much vaunted slogan 'youth is led by youth' were ... voiced so vehemently precisely because the reality was so different."

Conversely, historical scholarship on youth movements that were supposedly controlled by political parties and/or the state has generally shown that young people participating in these movements were far from passive dupes or empty vessels. Rather, these youth movements themselves became important institutional and ideological sites for struggle and contestation between different groups of young people and their adult handlers—struggles that were often framed by the discourse of youth, age and generation (Cornell, 1982; Gorsuch, 2000; Koon, 1985; Ledeen, 1969; Whitney, 2009). Throughout the 1920s, for example, the Komsomol in Russia, though clearly a state- and party-controlled organization, nonetheless "often provided an autonomous space for young people to act out their visions of communism, challenge adult authority and at times political authority ... [and] served as a specific environment for the emergence of a distinct 'Komsomol culture'" (Neumann, 2012, p. 278; see also Neumann, 2011). In their struggle for political and ideological independence from the Bolshevik Party in Russia, young leaders of the Communist Youth International in Europe, over the course of the 1920s, regularly invoked the "historic role" of youth as being "the vanguard of the revolutionary movement" (quoted in Whitney, 2009, p. 31; see also Cornell, 1982). The danger in deploying this kind of age and generation-based discourse, then as now, is not only that it obscures the actual, historical relationships between youth and adults in different social movements, but also that it can be used, paradoxically, to dismiss and undermine important political and ideological claims. In conflicts over ideology in the Social Democratic Party in early twentieth-century Germany, for example, moderates sought to dismiss radical arguments precisely because these were being linked with youth—"the Byzantine ideas are spread by those who tell young people of 14 to 18 years that they can make an independent judgement about the fundamental questions, which now concern the adult working class"—even though these conflicts were far "more related to political questions than to questions of age" (quoted in Jorgensen, 2009, p. 30).

Though many point to the early twentieth century—and more specifically, the interwar period in Europe—as constituting the heyday of organized youth movements, this form of youth organizing, rebellion and revolution has not disappeared, but has retained a global presence to the present time. Despite their initial ties with European nationalism and imperialism, early twentieth-century European youth movements strongly influenced anti-colonial and national independence struggles across the global South. Nationalist and anti-colonialist groups that followed the European model of both embracing youth as a key organizing symbol and recruiting directly among the young sprung up across both Africa (e.g.,Young Egypt (Misr al Fatat), the Jeunes Algériens, Somali Youth League and Nigerian Youth Movement) and Asia (the Young Men's Buddhist Association in Burma, Union of Malay Youth in Malaysia,Young Java, Young Turks and so on) (Anderson, 1991; Dueck, 2007; Jankowski, 1975; Neyzi, 2001). Political parties and social movements to this day often maintain dedicated youth wings, which may in turn be organized for and by young people themselves. In Cuba, following the 1959 revolution, for example, one can see a clear recurrence of much of the same rhetoric, tensions and contradictions surrounding the revolutionary significance of youth as a social actor as was present in early twentieth-century Europe. On the one hand, youth were portrayed as the heroes, martyrs and vanguards of the Cuban Revolution, and the leaders of the new Cuban society—a role that was ascribed to them on the basis of both life stage and generation (Kapcia, 2005; Luke, 2012). In a 1963 speech to Cuban students, Ché Guevara declared that "there was something more important than the social class to which the individual belongs: youth, fresh ideals, a culture which, at the point of leaving adolescence, is devoted to serving the purest of ideals" (quoted in Luke, 2012, p. 132). Three years earlier, Fidel Castro had declared that:

> Young people are the purest product of this Revolution! The most legitimate and awe-inspiring! They will be the seeds for the new fatherland because they will build a generation that will be better prepared for continuing our revolutionary effort.
>
> *(quoted in Luke, 2012, p. 133)*

However, on the other hand, only a minority of young people in Cuba ever participated in the country's principal revolutionary youth organization, the Union of Young Communists, and the revolutionary ideology of youth persistently generated a sense of "moral unease" and, at times, "moral panic" among the country's political leadership that the actual, real-world practices and attitudes of many "young people [in Cuba] were not living up to the idealised concept [of youth] they had built up" (Luke, 2012, p. 140).

The Global Student Movements of the 1960s

On December 3, 1964—a little more than 50 years after the famous Free German Youth gathering at Hoher Meissner—over 10,000 students, representing more than a third of the total student body, walked out on strike at the University of California, Berkeley, in protest of the university administration's campus policies and practices (Heirich, 1971).The mass student strike, which has been called "the mightiest and most successful single effort of any kind . . . made by an American student body in conflict with authority" in US history to that point, represented the culmination of almost three months of escalating protest by the student-led, campus-based Berkeley Free Speech Movement (Draper, 1965, p. 117; quoted in Horn, 2007). When student protests at Berkeley had begun in September 1964, over a decision by the university to ban all forms of student political outreach and activist activity along Bancroft Way on the south side of the campus, only about 200 students came out to demonstrate. But administration intransigence and heavy-handed tactics against the demonstrators—including student suspensions, expulsions and police arrests—served to inflame the Berkeley student body, leading to ever larger campus demonstrations, acts of mass civil disobedience, student sit-ins and building occupations, and eventually, the student strike. By December 8, 1964, the university had backed down, explicitly recognizing the principle of campus free speech, permitting campus political activism and outreach by students without demanding prior university approval, and dismissing all disciplinary actions that had previously been launched against students involved in the free speech movement (Cohen & Zelnik, 2002). The Berkeley Free Speech Movement, as far as those who were involved at the time were concerned, had won.

Though not the first student uprising of the era, the Berkeley Free Speech Movement was massively influential, inspiring similar student movements not just across the United States, but throughout Europe and the rest of the world as well (Feuer, 1969; Flacks, 1971; Horn, 2007). Students have, of course, participated in political activism throughout recorded history (Altbach & Peterson, 1971; Boren, 2001). But there was a dramatic spike in the scale, intensity and public and political attention paid to student movement protests around the world during the decade that lasted from the early 1960s to the early 1970s. In the United States, student movement uprisings came to define the 1960s, triggering not just an outpouring of academic literature—for example, *Students in Revolt* (Lipset & Altbach, 1969), *Protest! Student Activism in America* (Foster, 1969), *Confrontation on Campus* (Grant, 1969), *Confrontation: The Student Rebellion and the Universities* (Bell & Kristol, 1969), *Youth in Turmoil* (Douglas, 1970), *Rebellion in the University* (Lipset, 1971) and so on—but also attracting close political scrutiny. The FBI led an extensive campaign of spying on and harassing student radicals; the CIA issued a 200-page paper in 1968 entitled *Restless Youth* that reported on the activities of Students for a Democratic Society domestically, as well as the phenomenon of "youthful dissidence" in 19 other countries around the world; and in 1970, President Richard Nixon established a President's Commission on Campus Unrest to investigate the "serious situation" of nationwide "disruption" and "violence" on university campuses committed by student demonstrators (Klimke, 2009; Rosenfeld, 2012). By the late 1960s, student uprisings on the nation's university campuses had become the primary concern of the US public (Altbach & Cohen, 1990, p. 32). In the aftermath of the shooting of four student antiwar protesters at Kent State University in Ohio by the Ohio National Guard in 1970, a nationwide student strike involving 4 million students disrupted courses at almost a third of the country's 2,500 university campuses (Barker, 2008; Gitlin, 1993; Horn, 2007).

Parallel student uprisings broke out throughout the decade in Europe, Africa, Latin America and Asia, peaking with the May 1968 student-initiated general strike in France that had many convinced the country was on the brink of revolution (Christiansen & Scarlett, 2013; Horn, 2007; Weiss & Aspinall, 2012). In 1968 alone, 56 countries around the world saw significant student movement protests (Siegfried, 2006, p. 61). In many cases, student demonstrations were seen by political elites as constituting serious threats to social stability and were met by forceful, sometimes violent state repression: in Rangoon, Burma, in July 1962, over 100 student demonstrators were killed and the Rangoon University Student Union was blown up by the military; in Mexico City, Mexico, in October 1968, hundreds of student and civilian protesters were shot dead by government forces; and in October 1976, at least 46 student protesters were killed by government security forces at Thammasat University in Bangkok, Thailand (Carey, 2005; Weiss & Aspinall, 2012). The principal issues that motivated student movement protests were similar everywhere: demand for greater student rights and freedoms on campus and opposition to university discipline and police repression; support for national, racial, ethnic and religious liberation and freedom struggles; and opposition to colonialist wars and imperialist interventions in Southeast Asia, North Africa and Latin America (Altbach, 1989; Bereday, 1966; Christiansen & Scarlett, 2013; Weiss & Aspinall, 2012). Indeed, student protesters around the world explicitly saw themselves as participating in a global student rebellion, and were directly inspired by the tactics and demands made by student movements in other countries. "Paris, Berlin, Frankfurt, New York, Berkeley, Rome, Prague, Rio, Mexico City, Warsaw—those were the places of a revolt that stretched all around the globe and captured the hearts and dreams of a whole generation," reflected Daniel Cohn-Bendit, a prominent student leader in France during this period (quoted in Klimke, 2009, p. 2). As the CIA's *Restless Youth* report warned:

> [Y]outhful dissidence, involving students and nonstudents alike, is a world-wide phenomenon.... Because of the revolution in communications, the ease of travel, and the evolution of society everywhere, student behavior never again will resemble what it was when education was reserved for the elite.
>
> *(quoted in Klimke, 2009, p. 1)*

Nor was it just college and university students who were involved in student movement demonstrations, as in many countries, hundreds of thousands of high school students participated in mass student protests as well (Horn, 2007).

What led to this explosion of student protest during this period? For the most part, these were not protests over students' material interests, as tuition fees were either low or non-existent, graduate employment rates were high, and most national economies were growing. One key trigger, however, was that this was the era in which many countries were witnessing rapid growth of higher education enrollment numbers, and in the global North at least, countries were transitioning from a system of elite to mass higher education. This process was driven by demographic growth—as the baby boomers started to come of age and enter university—but more fundamentally, by the transformations of an advanced global capitalist economy that increasingly required large numbers of technical, managerial and professional white-collar workers. The quantitative change in student numbers in many countries was staggering: in France, the number of university students nearly tripled between the start and end of the 1960s; in Italy, the number nearly doubled; in Germany, the number of post-secondary students increased fivefold between 1960 and 1975; while in Mexico, university student numbers increased by a factor of ten between 1960 and 1980 (Barker, 2008). The problem was that, while enrollment numbers had swung dramatically from an elite to a mass model of higher education, bringing a larger and more diverse body of students onto university campuses, university policies and practices tended to remain firmly elitist and traditionalist. As Christopher Rootes (2013: 4865) writes, "Inadequate facilities, unreformed curricula and antiquated rules generated conflicts between students who considered themselves adults and authorities who regarded themselves as acting in loco parentis." There were other factors as well, of course, that supported the outbreak of student protest. Structural and institutional characteristics of university life played a role: universities are one of the few places that bring together large groups of young adults in concentrated spaces, and in most countries, are given greater latitudes of freedom for the expression of controversial opinion than other institutions (Altbach, 1989; Barker, 2008; Rootes, 2013). Once initial protests had broken out, a wave of student protest carried its own momentum, leading to deliberate, copycat protests in other institutions and countries (Barker, 2008). Broader social conflicts—antiwar protests, civil rights organizing, national independence struggles, and so forth—also swept up students along with other social groups.

The global student uprisings triggered expansive claims regarding the sources and larger historical significance of student and youth power, made both by students and young people themselves and their contemporary observers. Some of these were similar to arguments made about youth movements in Europe in the early twentieth century. Many claimed that there was something particular about youth as a developmental stage that made young students particularly prone to radical political behavior (Fillieule, 2013). "Within the life cycle," wrote David Matza (1961, p. 104) in the early 1960s, "the apex of rebelliousness is reached during the period of youth, before and after which rates of rebelliousness seem considerably lower." "The politics of the ideal," according to Matza (1961, p. 110), "seems peculiarly well suited to the predispositions of youthful rebelliousness" (see also Rooke, 1971). Kenneth Keniston (1971, p. 7) likewise argued in *Youth and Dissent: The Rise of a New Opposition* that social and historical change had led to "the emergence on a mass scale of a previously unrecognized stage of life, a stage that intervenes between adolescence and adulthood," that Keniston calls "the stage of youth." Youth, according to Keniston (1971, p. 9), "is a time of alternating estrangement and omnipotentiality," in which young people in their late teens and early twenties experience "feelings of isolation, unreality, absurdity, and disconnectedness from the interpersonal, social and phenomenological world," but also the sensation of "absolute freedom, of living in a world of pure possibilities, of being able to change or achieve anything." It is this individual developmental conflict, according to Keniston (1971, p. 4), that provides the "psychological basis" for social and historical conflict and change—and eventually, for the possible emergence of "a more truly liberated society."

Others argued that the student uprisings constituted evidence of the growing importance of generations and generational conflict in reshaping world history. S. N. Eisenstadt (1971, p. 170) argued that the student protests of the 1960s were characterized by "intergenerational discontinuity and conflict to an unprecedented extent" in history, as their leading elements had "become entirely dissociated from broader social or national movements, from the adult world, and do not tend to accept any adult models of association." Such generational conflict, according to Eisenstadt, was caused by the growing discontinuities between the institutions of family, education and work in contemporary society (Westby, 1976). Lewis Feuer (1969, p. viii), meanwhile, claimed in *The Conflict of Generations*, his mammoth study of student and youth movements across history, that the student movements of the 1960s were "the product of selfless, altruistic idealism combined with the resentment and aggression of one generation against another." Although student demonstrators claimed to be fighting over specific material, political or ideological grievances, their actions, according to Feuer, were in reality driven by unconscious and fundamentally irrational conflicts with their parents' generation:

> Every student movement tries to attach itself to a "carrier" movement of more major proportions—such as a peasant, labor, nationalist, racial, or anti-colonial movement. . . . Emotions arising from the students' unconscious, and deriving from the conflict of generations, impose or attach themselves to the underlying political carrier movement, and deflect it in irrational directions . . . Student movements are thus . . . among the most irrationalist in history.
>
> *(Feuer, 1969, p. 8)*

Generational theories, however, were not always as reductionist or dismissive as those offered by writers such as Eisenstadt and Feuer. Indeed, youth and student movement leaders in the 1960s themselves widely employed generational rhetoric to frame their actions and demands. "Don't trust anyone above 30," was one of the most well-known slogans of the era. "The most important political conflict in the United States today is the generational conflict," wrote Jerry Rubin, co-founder of the Youth International Party (or Yippies), as he called "on kids to leave their homes, burn down their schools and create a new society upon the ashes of the old" (Feuer, 1972, p. 176; Siegfried, 2006, p. 61). Some commentators likewise argued that generational conflict had become a primary motor of radical social change. "In the contemporary era," the American sociologist Ralph Turner (1969, p. 398) argued in the late 1960s, "the major readjustments which are being made in society no longer concern socio-economic classes but concern *age groups*" (italics in original). Generational conflict, on Turner's account, is exacerbated by social, economic and technological changes that have led to "increasing authority and independence and recognition [being] accorded to the youthful generation." Rapid technological development, for example, inverts previous generational relationships, in that "the technical expertise of the young is [now] often superior to that of the more mature." "Having gained considerable power and autonomy and comfort," writes Turner (1969, p. 398), "young people ... demand that the system be changed so as to remove the last restrictions on their assumption of an appropriate condition in society."

But a new argument that was made about the historical significance of the student movements of the 1960s was that students—or youth more generally—had become the new working class. "Today in America the class which is exploited and therefore potentially revolutionary is no longer the working class," US socialists John and Margaret Rowntree claimed in 1968, "the new proletariat is made up of 1) the masses in underdeveloped countries; 2) young people in the USA" (quoted in Wanrooij, 1999, p. 81). In France, Jerome Férrând similarly argued that youth constituted a new international revolutionary social class, a new Third Estate or proletariat, "who were nothing and became everything," and were "conscious of having goals, a role to play, and an incontestable power" (quoted in Jobs, 2009, p. 381). In Britain, leftist thinkers began to speak of university campuses as having become essential "base areas" for carrying out "revolutionary struggle" against capitalism (Halliday, 1969; quoted in Barker, 2008, p. 73). In part, these kinds of arguments were made in the context of a growing belief among some theorists—such as C. Wright Mills, Herbert Marcuse, André Gorz and others—that the traditional working class no longer had the social or historical agency ascribed to it in Marxist political theory. Other groups, including students, were thus looked to by these thinkers as new possible sources of revolutionary activity (Barker, 2008; Marcuse, 1969; Siegfried, 2006). In part, too, the theory of youth as the new working class was made in the context of the belief that a new knowledge economy was emerging, in which the proletariat would increasingly be made up not of workers engaged in material production, but those involved in knowledge production—many of whom would be university educated. As Alain Touraine wrote, in an article on the "Birth of a Student Movement" published in *Le Monde* in 1968:

> If it is true that knowledge and technical progress are the motors of the new
> society, as the accumulation of capital was the motor of the preceding

(industrial) society, does not the university then occupy the same place as the great capitalist enterprise formerly did? Thus, is not the student movement, in principle at least, of the same importance as the labor movement of the past?

(Touraine, 1968; quoted in Westby, 1976, p. 221)

Some student movement activists themselves embraced this rhetoric of students as the new and revolutionary working class, particularly in Europe and the United States (Siegfried, 2006; Westby, 1976). "What we are witnessing and participating in is an important historical phenomenon," a member of Students for a Democratic Society wrote in the late 1960s, "the revolt of the trainees of the new working class against the alienated and oppressive conditions of production and consumption within corporate capitalism" (Davidson, 2011, p. 33). "Hopefully, in the not too distant future," the writer continues, "we [Students for a Democratic Society] may be instrumental in forming a new International Union of Revolutionary Youth," and from there, "begin to build the conditions for human liberation" (Davidson, 2011, p. 51).

As was the case with the youth movements of early twentieth-century Europe, however, claims about the global student movements of the 1960s were highly exaggerated. Only a minority of students ever participated in student protests of any kind. Even at peak moments of student unrest, such as the Berkeley Free Speech Movement in 1964 or the May 1968 student uprising and general strike in Paris, France, the overwhelming majority of students were not involved. Ironically, during the period leading up to the early 1960s, the dominant concern of campus observers was not student radicalism but apathy (Flacks, 1971). For example, a report in the United States on *What College Students Think* that was published in 1960 claimed that:

In modern society, students have practically ceased to be a factor of productive unrest. They are no longer interested in changing their own lives, let alone the world ... Students are conservative rather than rebellious. They shun political non-conformism just as they reject social non-conformism.

(Goldsen, Rosenberg, Williams & Suchman, 1960, pp. 103–104)

Moreover, students who were politically active during the 1960s did not just participate in movements of the left—for many young students in this period joined politically conservative movements as well (Klatch, 1999; Lipset, 1971). As Karl Mannheim (1998, p. 194) warned in his 1927 essay on the sociological study of generations, "nothing is more false than the usual assumption uncritically shared by most students of generations, that the younger generation is "progressive" and the older generation *eo ipso* conservative."

Commentators and participants in the global student movements of the 1960s have also tended to understate the importance of adults and adult organizations in supporting and nurturing these movements. Seymour Lipset (1971, p. 3), for example, claims that "unlike the leftist youth and student movements of the 1930s which were linked to adult political parties, the dominant ones of the 1960s constituted a genuine youth rebellion." But in actuality, there are strong parallels between the two periods. The Berkeley Free Speech Movement, for example, which Lipset (1971) characterized as a "prototype" of the 1960s student movements and Feuer (1969) labeled as a "generational revolt," was, like many student protests of the era, strongly molded by adult actors. Many of the student leaders at Berkeley, including Mario Savio and Jack Weiner, had received training in the tactics of civil disobedience and collective organization by the (multi-generational) civil rights movement, and had only just returned from the Freedom Summer voter registration drive in Mississippi in the summer of 1964. Adult supporters such as Hal Draper, a leftist campus librarian, played a role in energizing and directing the movement. Berkeley's faculty, though initially divided over their stance toward the Free Speech Movement, ended up playing a decisive role in enabling the movement's success. As Cohen (2002, p. 22) writes:

> The issue of power in the educational community has not been well understood by those historians who depict the FSM [Berkeley Free Speech Movement] strictly as a *youth* revolt. Although it was surely students … who initiated the movement and applied the pressures that led to its victory, it was the words of the Berkeley Academic Senate—the faculty's representative body—that proved decisive.… Although fundamentally a student revolt, the FSM, as both its adherents and its opponents concede, would never have triumphed if unaccompanied, especially during its final phase, by a faculty revolt against the administration's position on political advocacy.

As with student demonstrators elsewhere, family background played a key role, with students who came from families with liberal and radical political views being more likely to participate in student demonstrations (Flacks, 1967; Forland, Korsvik & Christophersen, 2010; Lipset & Altbach, 1969). Similar patterns may be found in other student movement protests globally. In contradiction to Eisenstadt's (1971) claim that student radicals of the 1960s had become "entirely dissociated" from the adult world, student movement activists were strongly influenced by adult theorists and organizers of the era, from Herbert Marcuse to C. Wright Mills to Frantz Fanon. As had been the case in early twentieth-century Europe, framing the 1960s student movements as a generational revolt sometimes served to dismiss or marginalize the broader social, political and ideological argument made by student protestors. Observers such as Feuer (1969), for example, trivialized the student movements as being part of the "follies of youth," depicting youth "as a time of rebellion, … a phase, which young persons will 'grow out of'" (Hanna, 2008, p. 1543). The portrayal of youth and student movements as a "generational rebellion," argues Jessica Taft (2011, pp. 49, 69), often "implies that youth activism and youth social movements are an irrational, silly, or ill-conceived approach to politics and social change."

Despite the revolutionary rhetoric espoused by many student protesters and their supporters, the impact of student movements in most countries in the global North was quite limited. There is little evidence of any sustained and substantial social, political or economic transformation as a result of the 1960s student uprisings. Most of the more visible changes may be found with the university itself, where there were shifts in university policies toward student governance, rights and freedoms on campus, as well as the introduction of new areas of curriculum focusing on women's, ethnic and racial studies (Barker, 2008; Horn, 2007; Rootes, 2013). Other impacts of the student movements were more indirect and diffuse. The movements firmly established the idea that young students can be and often are serious and legitimate political actors in society. Many of the students who participated directly in the movements of the 1960s were themselves radicalized by their experience, and some went on to become important leaders in the labor, civil rights, women's and environmental movements in their adult lives. In countries of the global South, where student movements were involved in protests that led to radical political change, this was usually as part of broader movements that involved many other social groups as well. As Christiansen and Scarlett (2013, pp. 7–8) argue, "despite the important role that students played in the anti-authoritarian revolts" across the global South during the 1960s and 1970s, "churches and religious institutions, NGOs, radical nationalist movements, various left and right wing organizations, and ... the army" also played key roles, and "ideology, resources, familial and societal links ... took precedence over youth as a distinctive social category." The limited impact of student movements, when acting in isolation from other social movements, should not be surprising. After all, as Flacks (1971, p.99) and many others have noted, "students, acting as students, can have only limited success in realizing their goals and aspirations for social change," for "despite their increased numbers, students represent a small and special minority of the total population [and] they have few levers on power."

Though there are clear parallels between the youth movements of early twentieth-century Europe and the global student movements of the 1960s, there were important changes as well. The primary locus of youth activism shifted to the university campus, which now became a key space of social, political and ideological struggle. As Richard Flacks (1971, p. 83) observes, one of the most important lessons to come out of the Berkeley Free Speech Movement of 1964, which had quickly drawn in the involvement of political actors not directly related to the university, was that "the university had itself been transformed during the fifties and was now intimately and fundamentally connected to the major centers of power and political initiative in the larger society" (see also Draper, 1965). Rather than being affiliated with or organized by official political parties or government bodies, the 1960s student movements were driven by a strong sense of disillusionment with such groups, and were explicitly conceptualized as a preferred alternative to these older and allegedly inferior and inauthentic forms of youth movement organization. Furthermore, while the youth movements of early twentieth-century Europe had been strongly shaped by the ideologies of nationalism, imperialism and militarism, the student movements of the 1960s were organized as anti-imperialist, anti-militarist, and in the global North at least, anti-nationalist forms of protest. The proto-typical forms of youth movement activism shifted as well, centering on strategies of direct action and civil disobedience—the sit-in and the strike, for example—that were learned largely from other social movements, notably the US civil rights movement, as well as more militant parts of the labor movement. All of these shifts were driven by larger changes in global capitalist economy and society at the time: most notably the dramatic expansion of mass higher education, but also the enduring crisis of the institutions of the old left, and the rise of anti-imperialist wars and struggles from Southeast Asia to North Africa to Latin America.

While organized student movement protests had largely died down by the mid-1970s, one of their longest-lived legacies was the emphasis on youth cultural choice and creativity as a key form and site of resistance and rebellion. During the 1960s student movements, the concept of a youth counterculture that, in and of itself, posed "a definite challenge to the values and norms that are officially proclaimed and institutionalized in the larger society" attracted extensive analytic attention (Flacks, 1971, p. 17; see also Horn, 2007; O'Donnell, 2010; Siegfried, 2006). "There was a fear that the normative consensus was being threatened by the alternative values of young people," writes Gill Jones (2009, p. 49), "mainly middle-class students protesting against the Vietnam war, or hippies seen as promoting an alternative lifestyle and thus challenging the foundations of society." This interest in youth counterculture has continued, initially with the Birmingham School's focus on the importance of youth subculture and symbolic resistance in the UK during the 1970s; and subsequently, with the growing field of youth culture, subculture and post-subcultural studies. While Birmingham School analysts tended to emphasize the limited political impact of youth subcultures—viewing them as representing symbolic forms of resistance and escape, but not actual forces of social change—there has long been a countervailing tradition, that goes back to the period of the 1960s, that seeks to portray forms of youth subculture as being inherently radical and revolutionary (Blackman, 2005; Johansson & Lalander, 2012; Jones, 2009; P. Williams, 2007, 2009). By the end of the twentieth century, youth cultural or subcultural practice had often become presented in youth studies literature as the *only* form of collective youth resistance, and was the focus of a burgeoning literature on youth agency; meanwhile, critical attention to the importance of organized and active youth political movements and protests, as well as structural issues of political economy and class increasingly disappeared from view (Debies-Carl, 2013; Marchart, 2004; Taft, 2011).

Youth Rebellion in the Neoliberal Period

In late January 2011, a massive occupation began in Tahrir Square, Cairo, involving tens of thousands of demonstrators that, three weeks later, would end up forcing Egyptian President Hosni Mubarak out of office. The occupation, which had focused initially on concerns about police repression and only later expanded to call for fundamental political and economic change in Egypt, had been organized by a diverse coalition of political parties, trade unions and social movements. But very quickly, attention was drawn by the media to the participation of Egyptian youth in the Tahrir Square protest, and in particular, to a youth organization called the April Sixth Movement, that was part of the Tahrir Square organizing coalition. The April Sixth Movement was a group made up mostly of working-class and low middle-class university students from Cairo University that had been formed in the spring of 2008 in support of a textile workers' strike on April 6, in the city of Mahalla, Egypt, and since then had continued to organize sit-ins, protests and demonstrations in support of a range of issues from labor and civil rights to support for Palestine and opposition to the war in Iraq. As such, it was one of a number of student and youth groups that had become active in Egypt in the new millennium, and that included both independent organizations and groups affiliated to broader social movements, educational institutions and political parties such as the Nasserites, Revolutionary Socialists and Muslim Brotherhood. April Sixth, like many of these youth groups, relied on social media—Facebook, Twitter, internet blogging and phone texting—to communicate among its members, and at its height, boasted more than 70,000 followers on its Facebook page (this in a country of 80 million people). Movement members insisted that they were a non-political, non-ideological, autonomous and leaderless group of youth activists, who were dedicated to the strategies and principles of non-violent protest (Abul-Magd, 2012). As the Tahrir Square occupation grew in number and influence, they, along with other youth activists, gained a virtually ubiquitous media presence and became framed by the Western and Arab press alike as being the key spokespersons and leaders of the new Egyptian revolution (Kirkpatrick & Sanger, 2011; PBS, 2011; Wolman, 2011). Virtually overnight, the youth of Egypt, as elsewhere across the region in the wake of the Arab Spring, were transformed from being seen either as terrorist threats or apathetic consumers into the world's most vital agents of revolution, freedom and democracy (Sika, 2012; Staeheli & Nagel, 2012; Sukarieh, 2012). Whereas previously "young Arabs were largely passive and apolitical," asserts Rami Khouri, the director of a post-revolution UNICEF-sponsored study on Arab youth called *A Generation on the Move*, "today, they have sparked and manned one of the most important historical transformations anywhere in the world in modern history" (UNICEF, 2011). Collectively, the Arab Spring uprisings that spread from Tunisia to Egypt, Yemen, Libya, Bahrain, Syria, Morocco, Saudi Arabia and Kuwait were labeled a "youth revolt," "youth uprising," "youth quake"—or, using social media as a metonym for youth—a Facebook or Twitter revolution (Al-Momani, 2011; Beaumont, 2011). By the end of 2011, the April Sixth Movement had even been nominated for a Nobel Peace Prize. While they did not win, a young Facebook activist and journalist from Yemen, Tawakkol Karman, was awarded the prize in the context of the broad recognition of the role that young Arabs had played in the Arab Spring.

As noted at the beginning of this chapter, the Tahrir Square occupation in Egypt is just one of a number of global protests, uprisings and occupations— including all of the Arab Spring revolutions, the protests of the indignados and aganaktismenoi in southern Europe, the Occupy movement that began in New York City and later spread throughout the world, and a wide range of other student protests and urban rebellions—that have taken place in the wake of the global financial crisis of 2008–2009, and have been labeled a youth revolution with the potential to fundamentally change the current world order as we know it. A whole new set of age and generation-referenced terminology has emerged to define these groups, some created by protesters themselves and others by onlookers: the Indignant Generation, Generation Occupy, Generation 700 Euros, Generaçao a Rasca (the Desperate Generation), Juventud sin Futuro (Youth without a Future) and so on (Feixa, 2013; Sachs, 2012). These groups are distinguished not just by having a global outlook and sensibility, but also by being directly linked with one another across national borders through social media. Youth in Egypt and Tunisia communicated closely over the course of the uprisings in their respective countries over Facebook, Twitter and email (Kirkpatrick & Sanger, 2011). The protests of the aganaktismenoi (the Greek indignados) in Greece were a direct response to the actions and Facebook communications of the indignados movement in Spain (Oikonomakis & Roos, 2013; Tsaliki, 2012). The Occupy Movement that began in New York City was inspired by the protests in Europe and the Arab region, and itself was copied all over the world, spreading through a range of social media: Facebook, Twitter, YouTube, Tumblr, and other websites and listservs (Juris, 2012; Milkman, Luce & Lewis, 2013; Waldram, 2011). Student protest leaders look to and communicate with colleagues in other parts of the world to discover and develop successful movement strategies. Urban uprisings name themselves after previous occupations elsewhere, so that the Gezi Park protests in Istanbul in June 2013, for example, were labeled both "#OccupyGezi" and "Turkey's Tahrir Square."

For the most part, these uprisings are framed as having emerged in the context of widespread concern with youth political apathy and indifference (Banaji, 2008; Harris, Wyn & Younes, 2010). But there have been important precursors. There has been a resurgence of interest in the student and youth movements of the 1960s era. But more immediately, there are direct links with youth organizing efforts from the late 1990s and first decade of the new millennium. The April Sixth Movement, for example, along with other youth groups in Egypt and Tunisia, directly modeled themselves on and received training from youth movements in Serbia, Ukraine and Georgia that had participated in the color revolutions in those countries in the early 2000s. The banner used by April Sixth—a picture of a clenched fist—is even copied from the symbol of Otpor, a youth movement that was projected in the media as having played a key role in the overthrow of Slobodan Milošević in Serbia in 2000 (Abul-Magd, 2012; Joksic & Spoerri, 2011; Rosenberg, 2011). Similarly, in North America, some of the young activists who participated in the Occupy movement came out of the networks of youth leadership training and youth organizing development that had exploded across the continent since the late 1990s, and had become the focus of an extensive academic and practitioner-based literature on youth organizing (e.g., Ginwright, Noguera & Cammarota, 2006; News Taco, 2011; Uitermark & Nicholls, 2012).

The theories put forward to explain both the sources and significance of youth protest movements in the current period broadly echo those from previous eras. In part, they draw on longstanding, stereotyped views of youth as a distinctive life stage. Asef Bayat, for example, who has become one of the leading commentators on the role played by youth in the Arab Spring, has developed a theory that youth movements are motived by a desire to "claim or reclaim youthfulness":

> A youth movement is essentially about claiming youthfulness, it embodies the collective challenge whose central goal consists of defending the youth habitus, by which I mean a series of dispositions, ways of being, feeling, and carrying oneself (e.g., a greater tendency for experimentation, adventurism, idealism, autonomy, mobility and change) that are associated with the sociological fact of "being young."
>
> *(Bayat, 2012, p. 118)*

Bayat (2012, p. 135) argues that youth movements erupt when the state prevents youth from living and acting their youthfulness: however, if "moral and political authorities" are able to "accommodate youthful claims," then "young people may remain as conservative politically as any other social groups." Though somewhat esoteric in its phrasing, Bayat's theory bears strong continuity with more than a century of stereotypes of youth as being inherently idealistic and oriented to change, and of youth movements as being driven fundamentally by the essence of youth nature. In addition to such claims of inherent youth idealism, there has also been, as noted at the beginning of the chapter, a resurgence of theories that place generational conflict as being at the root of the current global uprisings (Amara, 2012; Friedman, 2011). Most commonly, contemporary versions of generational conflict theory rely less on claims about problems in youth psychology or socialization, or about the impacts of technological and occupational change—as was the case in the 1960s—and more about the alleged greed of the baby boomer generation, who are said to have indulged themselves with extravagant wages, pensions and benefits, while leaving their children to pick up the bill in the future (see Chapter 3 for further discussion).

Two of the most widespread theories used to explain the recent global "youth" rebellions, however, are relatively new and distinctive to the contemporary period. The first is an argument that places the "power of social media" at the heart of youth movement activity. In the context of repressive regimes, in particular, where there is limited space for open, public discussion, tech savvy youth are said to be able to draw on their skills and social media access to use cyberspace to discuss and organize social protest groups that subsequently surface and erupt into real space "on the street" (Austin, 2011; Halaseh, 2012; Howard & Hussain, 2011; Mason, 2012; Murphy, 2011). "Not only have cyberactivism and social-media platforms shifted the power dynamics of authoritarian Arab governments and their citizenry," claims Courtney Radsch (2012, p. 3), for example, "but it has also reconfigured power relations between the youth who make up the majority of the population and the older generation of political elites." As John Pollock (2011) argues, "the fact that regimes go to such trouble to monitor, identify, capture, beat, torture and jail young people using online tools suggests that they, at least, see the power of the new media" (see also Ross, 2012; Shah & Sardar, 2011). Some protesters and commentators argue that there is a close fit between the structures and processes of social media and new ideals about the most desirable and effective ways to organize protest and build a new type of society. As Michael Hardt and Antonio Negri (2011) write, in an article for the British newspaper, *The Guardian*:

> The uprisings spreading across north Africa and the Middle East ... [represent] original experiments that open new political possibilities well beyond the region, for freedom and democracy. . . . The organisation of the revolts resembles ... a horizontal network that has no single, central leader. . . . Outside observers have tried to designate a leader. . . . [But] what they don't understand is that the multitude is able to organise itself without a centre—that the imposition of a leader or being co-opted by a traditional organisation would undermine its power. The prevalence in the revolts of social network tools, such as Facebook, YouTube, and Twitter, are symptoms, not causes, of this organisational structure. These are the modes of expression of an intelligent population capable of using the instruments at hand to organise autonomously.

On this account, both social media and new forms of (youth) social movement activity are characterized by being leaderless, autonomous, global, open, democratic and participatory; both spread horizontally through nodal networks rather than being vertically organized; and the new youth leaders are marked not by having strong ideological commitments or party or class identities, but by their facility and engagement with new and open forms of technology, media and social interaction (Castells, 2011). Jeffrey Juris (2012, p. 260) argues that social networking media has "shaped new political subjectivities based on the network as an emerging political and cultural ideal," and proposes that recent global rebellions have been guided by a "logic of aggregation" that "involves the assembling of masses of individuals from diverse backgrounds within physical spaces." While these individuals may "forge a collective subjectivity through the process of struggle," Juris (2012, p. 266) suggests that this sense of collective subjectivity "is under the constant pressure of disaggregation into its individual components." In Paul Mason's (2012) popular narrative, a key feature of the recent youth uprisings is their fierce opposition to hierarchies and "hermetic ideologies of all forms." A central "cultural difference between modern youth protest movements and those of the past," Mason (2012) argues, is that "anyone who sounds like a career politician, anybody who attempts rhetoric, espouses an ideology, or lets their emotions overtake them is greeted with a visceral distaste." Mason (2012) claims this is because youth today "know more than their predecessors about power" and "realize, in a way previous radicals did not, that emotion-filled action, loyalty, mesmeric oratory and hierarchy all come at an overhead cost."

The second dominant framework for explaining spikes in youth rebellious activity is a theory that has been closely associated with the interests and concerns of the US security establishment, and that comes out of the field of demographics. This is the theory of the "youth bulge," which holds that there is a direct link between the proportion of young people in the overall population of a country and its level of political instability. More specifically, it has been claimed that civil unrest increases at a "critical threshold" when the number of 15–24 year olds reaches 20 percent of the total population (Fuller & Pitts, 1990; Huntington, 1996). Though youth bulge theory has existed since at least the Second World War, and was used during the 1960s to explain the rise in student movement protests during that decade (e.g., Moller, 1968), it really gained currency in the 1990s and new millennium when it was promoted by a number of scholars linked with the CIA and US State Department, who became concerned about the threat posed to US foreign policy interests by the increasingly youthful populations of many countries in the global South, especially in the Arab region and Africa. In essence, there are two core versions of youth bulge theory: one that directly links demographics with civil unrest, and a second that understands this link to be heavily mediated by social and economic conditions. Thus, a 1974 memo from the US National Security Council warned that increases in the youth proportion of the population in the global South was destabilizing because youth are "more volatile, unstable, prone to extremes, alienation, and violence than an older population" (quoted in Hendrixson, 2012, p. 2). A 2001 report by the CIA, on the other hand, warns that in regions with exploding numbers of youth—such as Africa and the Arab region—it is "the failure to adequately integrate youth populations [that] is likely to perpetuate the cycle of political instability, ethnic wars, revolutions, and anti-regime activities" (quoted in Gavin, 2007, p. 222). During the first decade of the new millennium, it was thus argued by US and other observers that the combination of an increasingly youthful population and some of the world's highest levels of youth unemployment was at the heart of growing problems with Islamic fundamentalism, political extremism and the spread of terrorist activity throughout the Arab world (Fuller, 2003; Hendrixson, 2003; Hvistendahl, 2011).

Ironically, the rise of the Arab Spring—which was entirely unpredicted by Western analysts—did little to shake youth bulge theorists. Instead, it was seamlessly adapted to explain the Arab uprisings themselves. Thus, the Arab Spring has been widely explained as being the consequence of a combination of high numbers of youth and high levels of youth unemployment (Austin, 2011; LaGraffe, 2012). "The Arab world … is facing a demographic bulge in which youth aged fifteen to twenty-nine comprise the largest proportion of the population," state Jayshree Bajoria and Ragui Assaad (2011) in a report for the US Council on Foreign Relations: "These young people, frustrated with lack of jobs, have been at the forefront of anti-government protests." Such analyses are almost inevitably anchored with the observation that the event that sparked the Arab uprisings in the first place was the actions of a 26-year-old street vendor in Tunisia, Mohamed Bouazizi, who set himself on fire after years of employment struggles were capped by police confiscating his goods and preventing him from selling on the street. Though youth bulge theory has been most closely linked with analyses of the Arab Spring protests, Paul Mason (2012) draws on the theory in his study of the recent uprisings worldwide to explain, as he puts it, "why it's kicking off everywhere." Stephen Smith (2011) also proposes, in a recent study of youth in Sub-Saharan Africa that was written in the wake of the Arab Spring, that empirical links may be found not so much between youthful populations and political extremism, religious fundamentalism and terrorism, but rather between such populations and the likelihood of democratization.

Serious limitations exist with all of the theories being used to explain youth movement uprisings in the contemporary period. Youth bulge theory has been criticized for being overly simplistic, deterministic, alarmist and prejudicial towards youth, especially non-white, male youth living in the global South. As Anne Hendrixson (2012, p. 2) and others point out:

> Youth bulge theory cannot predict war or violence in particular locations with a high level of certainty. … Fundamentally, it ignores the role of power. The youth bulge is most often personified as an angry young brown man from Africa, the Middle East or parts of Asia or Latin America. He is often portrayed as Muslim, susceptible to extremism, and sometimes driven by his very biology to unrest. This stereotype is an example of what anthropologist Nancy Scheper-Hughes calls "dangerous discourses" that over-predict individual acts of youth violence, even as they downplay the role of other

forms of violence and structural inequalities that contribute to youth poverty and powerlessness.

As Mark Sommers (2011, p. 296) observes, despite youth bulge theory being regularly used to explain unrest and violence in Sub-Saharan Africa, most African nations with youth bulge populations have not experienced recent civil conflicts, and in those that have had conflicts, most male youth never get involved with the violence (see also Gavin, 2007; Hvistendahl, 2011). If anything, Sommers (2011, p. 294) suggests, what is striking about regions such as Sub-Saharan Africa is just how "peaceful" the overwhelming majority of young people are, in spite of egregious violence, repression, inequality and injustice being regularly committed upon them by ruling elites. Youth social media theory has also been highly controversial, as many have challenged claims both of the role that social media played in the recent global uprisings and of the supposedly democratizing and empowering impacts of social media for youth movements and social movements more generally (Aday, Farrell, Lynch, Sides & Freelon, 2012; Curran, Fenton & Freedman, 2012; Fuchs, 2012). It is "important to recognise that social media are used to serve the political goals of reformers, revolutionaries, and authoritarian regimes alike," write William Youmans and Jillian York (2012, pp. 315, 317), and that there is a fundamental "mismatch between the commercial logic of [social media] platforms such as Facebook and the needs of activists using social media as public information infrastructure."

More fundamentally, the framing of recent global uprisings as being youth-led rebellions is a massive misrepresentation that obscures the central role played by a wide range of adults and adult-led organizations, protesting over issues that concern not just young people but people of all ages in society. Youth groups have certainly played a part in these global uprisings, but they have done so as part of a broad spectrum of civil society organizations. In the Arab Spring, a pivotal role has been played by trade unions, peasant movements, poor people's organizations, women's groups, political parties and Islamist and faith-based movements (Dahi, 2012; Joya, Bond, El-Amine, Hanieh & Henaway, 2012; Korany & El Mahdi, 2012; Soliman, 2011). In the protests of southern Europe, youth likewise tended to made up a minority of the individuals and groups who came out to demonstrate on the streets. According to one survey in Greece, for example, over 25 percent of the aganaktismenoi were between the ages of 25 and 34, over 27 percent were between the ages of 35 and 49, and the remainder were young students and pensioners (Tsaliki, 2010). In Spain, the protests of the indignados were supported by "more than 200 organisations including humanists, NGOs, ... ecologists, neighbour associations, youth groups, students' and teachers' organisations, Facebook groups, bloggers, mortgage defaulters, the unemployed, and [other] solidarity groups" (Hughes, 2011, p. 408; see also Delclós & Viejo, 2012; Taibo, 2013). "While many clueless reporters continue to refer to 15-M [the indignados] as a youth movement," complains one observer, "nothing could be further from the truth" (Roos, 2011). "Do not let politicians, bureaucrats and financial 'experts' feed a line of propaganda that suggests this is merely a youth movement," insists another commentator of the broad-based protests in Spain (Pangburn, 2011). Likewise, the Occupy movement in the United States and elsewhere has involved protesters of a wide range of different ages. According to one study, 63 percent of the Occupy protesters in New York City were over the age of 30 (Milkman, Luce & Lewis, 2013).

While the youth frame for talking about the recent global uprisings can be inspiring and has been embraced both by young protesters themselves and their supporters, it needs to be recognized that this frame has also been actively promoted and embraced by global elites as a way to promote their own interests and obscure broader divisions of class, race, ethnic, regional and ideological struggle that lie at the heart of these uprisings. As in previous eras, framing the current protests as being fundamentally youth protests can work to dismiss or minimize their larger social and political significance. Niall Ferguson (2011), for example, refers to the recent global cycle of protests as a "global temper tantrum" that is being led by a "mob" of "young people" who are "illogical," "self-contradictory" and poorly informed "suckers." Accounts that label the Arab Spring or Spanish indignados protests as youth movements that are being driven by youth concerns serve to render invisible the central role played by all kinds of other social movements and groups, and the direct and explicit political challenges these protests are making to the continued imposition of neoliberal ideology and austerity politics, the ongoing erosion of social democracy, and the exacerbation of wealth and power inequalities at the hands of national and global elites. It should be a telling indicator that political and business elites around the world have generally been very willing to speak out in the name of unemployed, marginalized and excluded youth—the US Department of State, for example, was quick to set up an Office of Global Youth Issues in the summer of 2011 to oversee the establishment of more than 60 Youth Councils based in US embassies and consulates around the world that are dedicated to "empowering young people as agents of change" (US Department of State, 2013). The European Union emphasized the need to focus on funding and working with youth organizations after the Arab Spring (Oxfam, 2011); and the ILO, the World Bank and the World Economic Forum rushed to create common projects with Ministries of Education and Youth in the Arab World. For so long as the focus is on youth, responses to the global protests can be more easily contained and limited to narrowly reformist measures—replacing an older generation of political leaders with younger and newer ones, tying education systems more closely to the interests of employers, whittling away the welfare state entitlements and expectations of older workers and citizens, and so on—that do little to challenge fundamental inequalities of wealth and power around the world, and indeed, as suggested in Chapter 3, can even work to maintain and extend elite agendas.

It also needs to be recognized that contemporary national and global elites, just like their predecessors in previous eras, have sought to use youth organizations to support and act upon their interests in a more direct manner. Much has been made of the links between the youth organizations in Egypt and Tunisia that played a role in the Arab Spring uprisings—the April Sixth Movement, Tamarrod, Takriz, Kefaya, Youth for Change and so on—and the youth and student groups from Eastern Europe and Central Asia that had played a role in uprisings in their countries a decade earlier—Otpor! in Serbia, Kmara in Georgia, Pora in the Ukraine, Zubr in Belarus, Kelkel in Kyrgyzstan and Mjaft in Albania (Joksic & Spoerri, 2011). But as some critics have pointed out, these earlier youth and student movements had received direct funding, training and support from US government-linked organizations such as the National Endowment for Democracy, Freedom House and USAID, as part of US efforts to extend its influence and direct the course of political change in these regions (Abul-Magd, 2012; Duda, 2010; O'Beacha'in & Polese, 2010; Traynor, 2004; Walker & Stephenson, 2010). It has also emerged that the United States has provided similar funding, training and support to both the April Sixth Movement and the Kefaya Movement in Egypt, as well as the Takriz Movement in Tunisia, again through the agency of organizations such as the National Endowment for Democracy and Freedom House (Nixon, 2011; Rowell, 2012). This does not mean that the young people participating in these different youth and student movements are passive dupes or empty vessels in the control of US foreign policy agendas, any more than was the case with young people who participated in youth and student movements and organizations that were heavily shaped by state or party interests in previous eras. But it does require us to move beyond naïve, romanticized narratives of autonomous, innate and pure forms of youth protest and rebellion.

Given that the contemporary global (youth) protest movements have only occurred recently, it is difficult to put them into full historical perspective, as it remains unclear what if any long-term impact they will have. However, already in the span of just a few years, a number of key points can be made. First, while there was a remarkable proliferation of youth protest groups in the context of the post-financial crisis global uprisings, many of these have been short-lived. In Egypt, more than 100 different youth groups were formed during and after the Tahrir Square occupation; however, more than half of these disappeared within a couple of years, as many young people joined newly established (and cross-generational) political parties instead (Khalil, 2013). Second, the role played by and ascribed to youth and youth movements in the global uprisings was strongest in the initial stages of these uprisings and has tended to decline as subsequent social and political developments have unfolded. For all the agency and power that are ascribed to youth in moments of revolutionary uprising, few young people take up positions of power or influence in the aftermath of these brief moments. This is likely due to several factors. Many young people and students occupy material, social and symbolic positions that make it relatively easy for them to quickly form highly visible protest movements, yet simultaneously difficult for them to sustain these movements (Altbach, 1989; Rootes, 2013). The student movements of the 1960s have been described as being "like fireworks displays, momentarily dazzling but then as quickly disappearing" (Barker, 2008, p. 85). Such characteristics are likely to be exacerbated by the current embrace by many young protesters of autonomous, leaderless and structureless forms of organizing (Juris, 2012; McConnell, 2011; Shah & Sardar, 2011). At the same time, the public celebration of youth as the leaders and symbols of social protest and change serves the interests of elite (and non-elite) groups in certain, revolutionary moments for a range of propaganda-related reasons. However, in the context of subsequent revolutionary advancement—or alternatively, counter-revolutionary retrenchment—the structural powerlessness of the young, combined with widespread adult discrimination against the abilities of youth as social and political actors, tends to preclude them from maintaining long-term social and political influence. In Egypt, there was a sense that the young were not trained enough in organizing and politics to be able to play a part in actually running or reforming the country, and that it was only natural that older generations and traditional leaders take over. A third and final point that can be made here is that the politics of at least some youth groups involved in the recent uprisings have proven to be highly malleable, and seem to be oriented more to responding to rather than leading the tides of social, political and ideological change that surround them. In the summer of 2013, for example, the April Sixth Movement came out on their Facebook page and publicly supported the Egyptian army's violent repression of the Muslim Brotherhood, despite an earlier stated commitment to non-violence and democracy.

While there continue to be strong parallels in the construction and framing of youth revolutionary agency across the early twentieth century, the 1960s and contemporary period, there have also been critical shifts that are linked to changes in global capitalist society and economy. Youth as a social category has continued to expand upward in age range, so that in speaking of youth one is no longer speaking just of teenagers or people in their early twenties, but individuals in their late twenties, thirties and even early forties as well. While both the youth movements of the early twentieth century and the student movements of the 1960s had a global reach, the scale, intensity and speed at which (youth) protest movements in the contemporary period have spread around the world have all increased dramatically. The centers of gravity of youth protest activity have shifted as well, both in the sense of moving from the global North to the global South, but also in their shift from university campuses in the 1960s to occupying urban spaces today. As discussed in the following chapter, both of these shifts follow from some of the central crises and contradictions of contemporary global neoliberal society and economy. Finally, although the dominant frameworks for articulating and interpreting contemporary youth protest activity come from quite different political viewpoints, both youth bulge and youth social media theories are paradoxically alike in some of their depictions of youth and youth agency. On both accounts, questions of ideology, social and economic structure and position, collective social organization and strategic, planned action are curiously ignored and made invisible, as emphasis is placed on multitudes of (young) individuals moved into action—like "loose molecules in an unstable social fluid that threaten[s] to ignite," as Robert Kaplan (1996, p. 16) memorably described his view of the situation of youth in West Africa—by the mechanical workings of demographic pressure and/or technological advance. In this, both theories are clearly shaped by the neoliberal cultural and ideological zeitgeist in which they originate, that places so much emphasis on the activities of autonomous individuals in an information-rich environment, while working simultaneously to ignore and undercut the continuing importance of social organization and collectivity.

Between Wonder and Contempt: The Revolutionary Agency of Youth

In 1973, writing critically against some of the more exaggerated claims of youth as an agent of social change that had accompanied the student protests and strikes of the 1960s, Sheila Allen (1973, p. 437) noted that in adult accounts of youth activism, there is often "a mixture of wonder, contempt, fear and romanticism," and argued strongly for the need to situate youth movements in their broader social and economic contexts. This is a "mixture" that has been observed by a number of researchers in the field of youth studies. Jessica Taft (2011, p. 68) notes that "youth, as a discursive formation, has simultaneously been linked with social change, social movements, and rebellion along with political naiveté, future (rather than present) citizenship, and apathy." Craig Jeffrey (2012b, p. 3) likewise notes that radical and rebellious youth have often been portrayed either as "ineffective dreamers" or a potent "generational force for change." Yannis Pechtelidis (2011, p. 452–453), in his analysis of media coverage of the December 2008 youth uprising in Greece, argues that youth participating in this uprising were alternatively represented as being immature and apolitical hooligans who were being "steered" by adult political actors for their own ends, or as "bearers of truth and wisdom" who "approach the world with a clear and pure view and . . . express the very best humanity has to display." In light of this binarism in representing youth revolutionary agency, there is a tendency to come down on one side or the other, so that we find excessively celebratory and overly dismissive accounts of youth as revolutionary actors. We also find attempts to differentiate between true and false, authentic and inauthentic forms of youth rebellion and social movement activity.

What we are arguing here is that it is more useful to recognize the long continuities in the construction of youth as a revolutionary actor: the repeated tendency to exaggerate and romanticize the power and autonomy of youth, while obscuring the actions of adult supporters and organizations; and the paradoxical way in which this romanticization of "youth" movements can simultaneously work to obscure, marginalize and undermine what are serious and real social, political, economic, cultural and ideological conflicts that lie at the heart of these movements. To do this is not to dismiss or write off the agency or effectiveness of the young as rebellious or revolutionary social actors. It is, rather, to insist that youth social activism is put into its broader social and economic context, and to claim that the forms and substance of youth rebellion stem not from some unchanging, universal and innate set of characteristics about youth developmental nature, generational relationships or demographic balance, but are themselves shaped and reshaped according to the culture, society, politics and economy of the day. Young people are playing and have always played a key role in revolutionary and rebellious social movements, as has youth as a symbol and ideology as well. But equally, the young have also long played a role in more conservative social movements, and the invocation of youth as symbol and ideology has been used by elites to contain and undermine social rebellion and revolution, not just inflame them. What we can say with certainty is that, in all cases, the power and autonomy of the young will inevitably be circumscribed, due to their marginalized position in social, political and economic structures of power; and their ideas and actions, potent as these may sometimes be, will be developed and carried out in conjunction with other groups, classes and movements in society as a whole.

5

EDUCATION, PROTEST, AND
THE CONTINUING EXTENSION
OF YOUTH

One of the major developments of the post-global financial crisis era has been the re-emergence of mass student protests on a global scale, which had not been seen since the early 1970s. Alongside, and indeed, as a central part of the global uprisings that included the Arab Spring, the Occupy movement and revolt of the Indignados, universities and higher education systems around the world have been subject to a wave of student occupations, demonstrations and strikes. The most high profile of these have occurred in California starting in the fall of 2009, the United Kingdom in late 2010, Chile for a period of two years that began in the spring of 2011, and Quebec, Canada, in the spring of 2012. But no part of the world has been left untouched. At the most immediate level, most of these protests have centered on the growing costs of post-secondary education for students and their families, a trend that has been driven by the escalation of tuition fees in many countries around the world, and the move to privatize higher education financing, shifting it from being a state to an individual student (or consumer) responsibility. As Peter Marcucci and Alex Usher (2012, p. 3) observe in their review of recent changes in global tuition fee policies:

> in virtually every region of the world, given increasing enrolments, rising costs and the ongoing competition for public resources from other critical public sector services, higher education institutions are being pushed to increase their income from sources such as student tuition fees, donations, faculty consulting and facility rentals.

The recent wave of student protests, however, represent much more than a battle over who should pay for higher education. At a deeper level, these protests are a response to growing structural contradictions in the relationship that post-secondary education has with society and the economy at large. For decades now, post-secondary education has been promoted by governments around the world as the most important (and increasingly, the only) vehicle for individual social mobility, promising access to good jobs and high standards of living (Altbach, Reisberg & Rumbley, 2009). Yet, at the same time, not only have many students found that their access to high quality further and higher education is restricted (for example, by their inability to pay), but also, for those students who do manage to successfully complete a post-secondary degree, many find themselves unable to obtain the high quality and high wage employment that they believed had been promised to them. In capitalist society and economy, there are simply not enough good jobs to go around for everyone. As more countries around the world move toward models of mass and universal higher education, the world's systems of post-secondary study are being pressured to deliver on promises they can't possibly keep. Individuals and nations alike are thus being pushed into an ever-escalating "educational arms race," in which they seek to obtain more, better and higher status forms of post-secondary education in order to preserve an advantage over others in the search for what is a limited supply of high quality, engaging and well-remunerated forms of work (Tomlinson, 2008).

A growing body of literature has now developed to examine these contradictions between education, society and the economy (Brown, Lauder & Ashton, 2011; Grubb & Lazerson, 2005; Lafer, 2002; Livingstone, 1999; Wolf, 2002). But what has received little attention until now are the consequences these contradictions have for the social construction of youth itself. The extension of youth as a life stage upward in age, after all, has been closely tied to the expansion of post-secondary education and the promotion of education for social mobility. Across the globe, the upward extension of youth has tended to be constructed as being highly individualized and aspirational. In other words, a normative expectation has been promoted by governments, employers and educational institutions that young people should no longer expect to be able to achieve full adult status, independence, autonomy and well-being by the conclusion of their teenage years; rather, these are deferred, as young people are expected to enter into a prolonged period of transition that can last well into their 20s and even 30s, during which they are to make sustained investments in their own education and development that, if successfully realized, are promised to lead to greater individual social mobility than would otherwise be possible (P. Brown, 2013; Furlong & Cartmel, 2007). However, if the promise of post-secondary education is undeliverable, at least for all who undertake it, and if the ideal of education for individual social mobility is inherently flawed, then the developmental functionality, desirability and justice of this extension of youth and deferral of adulthood become highly suspect. The model of an ever-escalating educational arms race suggests a possible future in which the extension of youth upward in age will continue indefinitely, with no clear upper limit. One key issue when examining the current global student protests over higher education, therefore, is whether or not these protest movements are able to develop alternative models for the future of youth, by working towards resolving the structural contradictions that exist between education, society and the economy, rather than preserving or perpetuating them.

The Expansion of Education and Extension of Youth

The expansion of education and the extension of youth as a social category have long gone hand in hand. As discussed in previous chapters, this is a process that goes back to the spread of mass secondary education, at first for middle-class and later all students, which began in Europe and North America in the nineteenth century. It is a process linked closely to the development of capitalist economy and society: technological and bureaucratic development have led to the expansion of jobs requiring higher levels of skill and knowledge, demanding longer periods of education and training and, consequently, extended periods of dependence for the young; ongoing destruction and deterioration of low skill jobs in manufacturing and the services have perpetually pushed the young from lower middle- and working-class backgrounds (back) into schooling; and governments have habitually promoted extended education for the young as a "win-win" solution for social problems and inequalities, in lieu of more politically costly labor market interventions for greater social and economic equality that would bring them into conflict with business elites (Dougherty, 1994; Katz, 1976). The account offered by Michael Katz and Ian Davey (1978) for the initial spread of adolescence as a widely recognized life stage in mid-nineteenth-century Hamilton, Ontario, thus retains its relevance for subsequent extensions of youth many decades later. In Hamilton during this period, Katz and Davey argue that the erosion of apprenticeships and other forms of traditional youth employment, combined with the proliferation of clerical jobs requiring basic literacy and numeracy skills, and the attempt by city leaders to use public schools as tools of social control to reduce poverty, crime and "immorality," together led to increased levels of school attendance across class, gender and ethnic lines, and the resulting appearance of "youth," understood as a period of "prolonged institutionalized dependency" (Katz, 1976, p. 404). Together, this combined expansion of education and extension of youth have worked paradoxically over the decades both to raise the ambitions of the young, while at the same time deferring their dreams of adult status and success.

In the post-Second World War period, this same set of factors led to the expansion of post-secondary education, again initially for middle-class students in Europe and North America, and then increasingly for students from all class backgrounds and regions. As noted in the previous chapter, it was the shift from an elite to a mass model of higher education in the 1960s that played a key part in triggering the student protest movements of that era (Rootes, 2012; Trow, 1974). This expansion continued, on a worldwide scale, over the following decades. In its 2009 *Global Education Digest*, UNESCO (2009, p. 10) reported that "the number of students pursuing tertiary education [globally] ... skyrocketed over the past 37 years, growing five-fold from 28.6 million in 1970 to 152.5 million in 2007." Participation rates for young adults (typically defined in this case as being between the ages of 18–23) in tertiary education nearly tripled globally during this period; in Europe and North America, which have the highest rates of post-secondary enrollment, over 70 percent of the 18–23-year-old age group were participating in some form of tertiary education by 2007 (UNESCO, 2009, p. 14). By the start of the twenty-first century, almost 90 percent of high school seniors in the United States said that they expected not just to enroll in post-secondary education but to attain a four-year bachelor's degree; and "college for all" was being widely promoted as a legitimate educational goal by many national policy makers (Goyette, 2008; Rosenbaum, 2011). Of course, while expectations and aspirations for post-secondary study have become increasingly universal—particularly in the global North—opportunity structures for actually being able to fulfill these expectations and aspirations have remained sharply unequal. Poor, working-class and many ethnic and racial minority youth continue to have lower rates of participation in post-secondary education; and when they do participate, are more likely to be enrolled in lower level, lower status and lower quality educational institutions than elite, middle-class and white youth (Hinton-Smith, 2012; OECD, 2012).

According to dominant narratives, post-secondary educational expansion has been driven by the shift to a post-industrial or knowledge economy, especially in the rich countries of the global North, in which most or all new jobs are said to require (or will require in the future) high levels of knowledge and skill (Brown, Lauder & Ashton, 2008). This educational expansion has, in turn, led to the further extension of youth well into the twenties and, consequently, claims that this extension therefore constitutes a functional part of post-industrial society. A recent report prepared for the government of Canada on the changing status of young adulthood in that country, for example, argues that:

> [State] policy that favours post-secondary education ... meets the needs of the knowledge economy and imposes new timetables for life. A society in which young people are encouraged to earn master's degrees will necessarily affect the age at which individuals join the full-time labour market. Knowing that this transition often represents the springboard for participation in other areas of life, such as family and housing, extending the time spent on education affects the entire life course of young people.
>
> *(Gaudet, 2007, p. 7)*

US psychologist Jeffrey Arnett (2004, p. 24) has even proposed that "economic development" and "rising education" together have led to the emergence of a new category of the life stage that he calls "emerging adulthood," and that can last through to the late 20s. Emerging adulthood, which Arnett characterizes as being based on a set of characteristics strongly linked to stereotypes of youth as a life stage—i.e., it is described as a time of identity exploration, instability, self-focused behavior and feeling "in-between"—is also portrayed by Arnett as being strongly aspirational:

> Emerging adulthood is the age of possibilities, when many different futures remain open, when little about a person's direction in life has been decided for certain. It tends to be an age of high hopes and great expectations. . . . Emerging adults look to the future and envision a well-paying, satisfying job, a loving, lifelong marriage, and happy children who are above average.
>
> *(Arnett, 2004, p.16)*

Arnett's concept of emerging adulthood has been highly influential, and now has its own dedicated scholarly society, academic journal and annual conference. This is due, in part, to Arnett's own entrepreneurial efforts on behalf of his intellectual work; but it is also due to the fact that the concept resonates with what has become a broad-based public, political and academic consensus that the period of youth, whatever we choose to call it, has been steadily extending upwards in years to take over an ever greater period of the human life stage (Côté & Bynner, 2008).

As in previous eras, however, educational expansion and youth extension over the post-war period have been driven and shaped not just by the growth in demand for skilled labor, but by the deterioration and disappearance of lower skilled jobs in manufacturing and services that the young used to be able to enter into directly out of secondary education, and earn a wage that could support themselves and their families. In the global North, the combination of deunionization, deregulation, automation and capital flight (or the threat thereof) has meant not only that such jobs no longer exist in the same numbers as before, but also when they do still exist, they often no longer support the same standard of living as had once been possible. This phenomenon is often discussed in youth studies literature as constituting the "collapse" of the youth labor market (Ashton, 1993; Furlong & Cartmel, 2007). But this phrase is something of a misnomer, as the youth labor market has not disappeared in most countries, it has been transformed. What has happened over the past decades—to borrow a term used by urban geographers to describe shifts in housing markets (e.g., Sage, Smith & Hubbard, 2012)—is more akin to the *studentification* of the (youth) labor market. By this we mean that growing proportions of the labor market are defined and shaped by individuals' participation in education as well as their possession (or lack) of formal educational credentials. One of the tacit claims of the knowledge economy rhetoric that has been embraced by governments around the world over the past decades is that jobs that don't require high levels of education don't merit decent wages and working conditions: pursuing higher levels of education is thus promoted as the appropriate way to escape such conditions. At the same time, as growing numbers of youth and young adults are spending lengthening periods of their lives moving in and out of post-secondary education, many are having to take low level jobs, often in the service and retail sector, in order to make ends meet. Employers and others have deliberately constructed these jobs as being stopgap forms of employment that, because they are filled by students and other youth on a temporary and often part-time basis, don't need to offer high wages, good working conditions or opportunities for career progression. The paradox is that the expansion of post-secondary education oriented to providing access to high skill, high wage employment has fuelled the growth of a student labor market characterized instead by low skill, low wage employment (Canny, 2002; Tannock, 2001). As one young, working-class retail worker pointed out in a study of student employment in the United States, "it's ironic that you go to school to better yourself, but while you're in school, you're at the bottom of the bottom with bad jobs, [you have] no benefits, and no help to get through" (quoted in Tannock & Flocks, 2003, p. 1).

From the beginning, there have been core contradictions and questions about the expansion of post-secondary education and consequent extension of youth. In the early 1970s, there was a proliferation of critical literature on the problem of over-education and underemployment, and the danger that the promotion of education as the route to social justice was serving to undermine more traditional social democratic commitments to social and economic equality for all (Beck, 2008; Berg, 1970; Dore, 1976; Freeman, 1976; Goldthorpe & Jackson, 2008). But much of this literature was left to the wayside, as knowledge economy and human capital theories continued to gain dominance. By the end of the twentieth century, however, problems with the model were starting to re-emerge. First, with the rise of neoliberalism and its attacks on labor unions and the welfare state, alternative routes for social mobility increasingly disappeared, so that post-secondary education became not just the most important but virtually the only set pathway to social and economic well-being. The dilemma with this is that, not only does access to post-secondary education remain strongly unequal for young people from different class, ethnic and racial backgrounds; but even if access were to be made equal for all, in most countries of the world, most jobs still do not require any kind of post-secondary diploma or degree (Livingstone, 2009; Lloyd & Payne, 2002). Second, many post-secondary graduate jobs are themselves being standardized and automated, in a process that Phillip Brown, Hugh Lauder and David Ashton (2011) refer to as "digital Taylorism," leading to the deterioration of wages and working conditions. It is no longer the case that successfully securing a job requiring a post-secondary degree can guarantee a high standard of living (Ainley & Allen, 2013). Third, there has been a massive increase in post-secondary enrollment in the global South, particularly in East Asia. Knowledge economy discourse has always been premised on the idea of a global division of labor, in which the global North monopolizes high skill employment, while the global South provides armies of low skill, low wage manual, production and assembly workers (e.g., Reich, 1991). However, while participation rates in post-secondary education in the global South remain much lower than in Europe and North America—for example, only 26 percent of 18–23 year olds in East Asia were enrolled in tertiary education in 2007—by far the largest increases in post-secondary education enrolment over the last three decades have occurred in this region. Today, the majority of the world's tertiary level students are to be found in the low and middle income countries of Latin America, Africa and Asia (UNESCO, 2009, pp. 10–15). Increasingly, workers from all over the world are competing for a limited set of high skill, post-secondary graduate jobs (Brown, Lauder & Ashton, 2011).

The consequences of this for many young people in the contemporary period is that youth is experienced not just as an extended or protracted stage of life, but also as being highly insecure, uncertain, and fraught with risk. In the youth studies literature, there is now extensive discussion of non-linear, individualized, reversible and "yo-yo" transitions, as young people in both the global North and South move back and forward between different kinds of work and education that often have unclear use or exchange value, and indeed, can entail the amassing of various kinds of debt and stigma (Cavalli & Galland, 1993; Furlong & Cartmel, 2007; Johnson-Hanks, 2002; Leccardi & Ruspini, 2006; Lloyd, 2005; Serracant, 2012). Around the world, there has been a massive proliferation of different kinds of colleges, universities, degrees and diplomas that capitalize on the aspirations of youth and present a confusing array of options for sale in an ever-expanding post-secondary educational marketplace: some of these institutions are little more than diploma mills, their programs and degrees bringing their students no definable benefits whatsoever (Cooley & Cooley, 2009). Class and race stratification within the post-secondary sector remain strong. In the United States, for example, as in many other countries, student failure, dropout and loan default rates are highest among those who come from lower-class backgrounds, and are studying at for-profit and lower status colleges and universities (Deming, Goldin & Katz, 2012; Lynch, Engle & Cruz, 2010). Students from middle-class and elite backgrounds, meanwhile, are increasingly concerned with maintaining status differentiation, as they seek to turn their economic and cultural capital into a leg up in their ascent through higher education and into the graduate labor market (Carnevale & Strohl, 2013; Mullen, 2010). This is not just a question of going to more prestigious universities, but can be reproduced at a micro-level within specific universities. A recent study of the Harvard Business School, for example, found that "even within the extremely elite confines of one of the nation's premier business schools, the ultrawealthy are segregating themselves," by forming their own exclusive student societies that are prohibitively expensive to join (Kantor, 2013a, 2013b).

The endpoint of this period of extended youth is often unclear and uncertain. In the global North, youth studies researchers have described this as a phenomenon of "frozen," "delayed" or "arrested" transitions to adulthood (Côté, 2000; Kuhar & Reiter, 2012; Wyn & Woodman, 2006), as many young people, especially from poor and working-class backgrounds, find themselves unable to attain the markers of successful adulthood—a good degree, job, home, family and community life—that their governments and societies have encouraged them to aspire toward. In the global South, researchers have likewise raised concern about the problem of "waithood," "waiting" or "time passing," in which young people, who similarly find themselves blocked from realizing what is constructed in their societies as models of successful adulthood, are forced to subsist in a prolonged state of dependency, boredom, frustration, unemployment and underemployment. Waithood is a phenomenon that has been described throughout the Arab region (Dhillon & Yousef, 2009; Honwana, 2012; Singerman, 2007), across Africa (Locke & Te Lintelo, 2012; Mains, 2007; Masquelier, 2013), and in South Asia (Jeffrey, 2010a, 2010b; Jeffrey & Young, 2012). As Alcinda Honwana (2013) writes, waithood "represents the contradictions of a modernity, in which young people's expectations are simultaneously raised by the new technologies of information and communication that connect them to global cultures, and constrained by the limited prospects and opportunities in their daily lives." While waithood is claimed to cross class boundaries, it is particularly pronounced for many urban, educated youth in the global South, whose aspirations for higher level and graduate employment have been raised by their years of extended schooling, and who find it unacceptable, shameful and irrational to work in the low wage, low skill jobs that are often the only jobs available to them locally (Mains, 2007). Craig Jeffrey locates the problem of waithood more specifically, therefore, in the changing relationships and contradictions between global education, society and economy. "One of the most unsettling paradoxes of contemporary social change in the global South," writes Jeffrey (2009, p. 182), is that "at almost the precise moment that increasing numbers of people formerly excluded from schooling have come to recognize the possibilities held out by education for individual improvement, opportunities for these groups to benefit economically from schooling are disintegrating."

The Global Eruption of Student Protest

In March 2013, Kristel Tejada, a 16-year-old university student at the University of the Philippines in Manila (UPM), committed suicide by drinking silver cleaner at her family home, after she had been forced to withdraw from the university due to her inability to pay the 10,000 pesos (about $230 US dollars) that she owed in tuition fees. Tejada had previously appealed to the university to be allowed to continue her studies and have her fees waived after her father had become unemployed and her family was no longer able to support her, but the university had turned her down. Her death triggered student protests around the capital against the problem of government cutbacks to university funding, rising tuition fees, increasing inequality and the growing commercialization of higher education. "This is a call to stand up and strike for education and justice," said UPM student council chair Mariz Zubiri, "education is a right and shouldn't be sold" (Punay, 2013; Scones, 2013). Students at the Polytechnic University of the

Philippines, the largest state university in the country—who had launched a series of walkouts, demonstrations and protests back in 2010 over a government proposal to increase undergraduate fees at their university by 2,000 percent—wore black arm bands, walked out of classes and burned furniture in solidarity during a week of "black protest" against the unaffordability of higher education for many in the country (Cruz, 2010; Mo, 2013). Only two months later, in May 2013, 354 of the 1,683 higher education institutions in the Philippines were granted permission by the national government to increase their tuition fees once again (Flores, 2013).

The protests in the Philippines are just one of a wave of student uprisings that have swept through global higher education in the wake of the financial crisis. On September 24, 2009, thousands of students at the University of California, Berkeley staged a campus walkout in protest over funding cutbacks, tuition fee increases, staff layoffs and furloughs. The walkout triggered months of strikes, demonstrations, occupations and teach-ins that spread across not just the ten campuses of the University of California, but all 23 campuses of the California State University and many of California's 112 community colleges as well (Levenson, 2011; Newfield & Lye, 2011). On November 10, 2010, 50,000 higher, further and secondary education students, staff and their families came from all over the United Kingdom to march through the streets of London in protest of funding cutbacks, tuition fee increases and the elimination of student grant support. Over the following months, thousands more participated in demonstrations and marches right across the country, and more than 40 universities had buildings occupied by student protesters. While many of these occupations were short-lived, the longest lasted for over six months (Bailey & Freedman, 2011; Power, 2012; Solomon & Palmieri, 2011). In Chile, student protests against lack of public funding for education, high university tuition and student debt levels, and growing inequalities of access to high quality post-secondary study began gradually in the spring of 2011, peaked with nationwide strikes and marches that involved hundreds of thousands of students, workers and their families in August 2011, and continued through the fall of 2013. Over this period, hundreds of schools and universities were occupied by students, mass demonstrations and marches were held regularly, and students and their supporters launched a wide range of protest tactics, including strikes, hunger strikes, collective performances, cacerolazos (pot-banging), kiss-ins, press conferences and so on (Pousadela, 2012; Salinas & Fraser, 2012; Somma, 2012). In Quebec, Canada, university and college students launched a province-wide unlimited general student strike in protest at a government proposal to raise tuition fees that lasted from March through June 2012, and involved between 170,000 and 300,000 students at different points in time. Throughout this period, the strike was accompanied by mass student and civil society demonstrations across the province, nightly solidarity marches that were accompanied by the banging of pots and pans (the "mouvement des casseroles"), as well as teach-ins, debates, press conferences and the publication of student manifestos (Ayotte-Thompson & Freeman, 2012; Choudry & Shragge, 2013; LaFrance & Sears, 2012).

California, Britain, Chile and Quebec are some of the largest and most high profile examples of the recent student protest movements, but they are far from the only ones. In 2012, students protested funding cuts and increases in tuition fees and student debt at universities not just in California, but in at least 20 other states across the United States as well (Rivera, 2012); and since 2009, over 50 countries across the globe have seen student demonstrations. Countries affected include Indonesia, Malaysia, Thailand, Vietnam, Taiwan, South Korea, India, Sri Lanka, Bangladesh, Pakistan, Armenia, and the Philippines in Asia; Spain, Italy, Portugal, Greece, Germany, Austria, Hungary, Switzerland, Denmark, Ireland, France, Belgium, the Netherlands, Croatia, Serbia, Russia, Lithuania, Latvia, Ukraine, Poland and the United Kingdom in Europe; Palestine, Lebanon and Egypt in the Middle East; South Africa, Swaziland, Tanzania, Malawi, Uganda, Nigeria, Ghana and Sudan in Africa; and Colombia, Peru, Brazil, Haiti, Chile, Canada and the United States in the Americas (see, for example, International Student Movement, 2011, 2012; zurpolitik.com, 2009). Though the particular issues and histories vary between countries, all of these protests have shared a common set of concerns (with tuition fees, student loan debt, public funding cuts and the privatization of post-secondary education), and are responses to a global restructuring of higher education that is being driven by a constellation of four key factors. First, the massive expansion in post-secondary student numbers throughout the world has led to dramatically increased costs, and state concerns about the sustainability of the sector. Second, the model of post-secondary education that has been promoted globally has been based on the individualized pursuit of social mobility for personal gain (rather than a collective project of developing the broader public good), and there has been a growing expectation, therefore, that individual students and their families, not taxpayers, should pay for these gains. Third, the continuing dominance of neoliberal ideology and its agenda of privatizing the welfare state has reinforced the effort to shift the costs of post-secondary education from the state to private individuals and corporations. Fourth, the global financial crisis and ensuing recession have presented both a push and an opportunity to rein in state budgets and restructure the post-secondary education sector (Altbach, Reisberg & Rumbley, 2009; Heller & Callender, 2013; Johnstone & Marcucci, 2010).

In the United States, in particular, where the model of high tuition fees, funding cutbacks and privatization of higher education is in many ways the most advanced, there has been an explosion recently of political, media and academic writing on the growing phenomenon of mass student debt. Total student debt in the United States surpassed the $1 trillion mark in 2012, overtaking credit card debt to become the second largest form of consumer debt in the country after home mortgages; the average university student now graduates with more than $27,000 in student loan debt, and two-thirds of graduates carry loan debt when they finish their studies (Denhart, 2013; Nelson, 2012). Many graduates find it difficult to repay their student loans: by 2013, one in seven student loan borrowers was defaulting on their debt within three years of graduation (Nasiripour & Kirkham, 2013). Debt burdens are exacerbating social inequality among post-secondary students, as default rates are highest among those who do not graduate, attend for-profit universities and come from lower socio-economic backgrounds (Cunningham & Kienzl, 2011). Researchers and social theorists in the US have begun to discuss student debt as constituting a "new paradigm of early to middle adult life," and as "being not just a mode of financing but a mode of pedagogy," one that teaches (or disciplines) students to think of their education as a private rather than public good, avoid "impractical" majors and exploratory years off, and seek higher-salary jobs in the private sector over lower-paid, public interest forms of employment (Williams, 2013, pp. 61, 68; see also McLanahan, 2011; Ross, 2013; Rothstein & Rouse, 2011; Swarthout, 2006). In 2011, activists involved with the Occupy movement launched an "Occupy Student Debt" campaign that called for tuition free higher education, zero interest student loans and a jubilee forgiveness of all current student debt (Bond, 2012). Mainstream news outlets in the United States now regularly carry stories on the nation's "student debt crisis" and the ways in which post-secondary institutions are producing "degrees of debt" for many of their graduates (e.g., Bennett, 2012; CNBC, 2013; Martin & Lehren, 2012).

Concerns over tuition fees and student debt have been heightened, both in the United States and elsewhere around the world, by the fact that the cost of post-secondary education has been growing at exactly the same time as its individual benefit—in terms of social and economic mobility—has seemed increasingly in doubt. For, in the wake of the global financial crisis, the social problem of graduate underemployment has once again regained public and political attention. In the United States, it has been estimated that as many as 48 percent of employed university graduates are working in jobs that do not require a university degree. In 2010, more than 14 percent of restaurant waitstaff, 16 percent of bartenders and 24 percent of retail sales personnel in the United States had university degrees, even though these occupations all require less than a high-school diploma (Vedder, Denhart & Robe, 2013). In the United Kingdom, a third of recent university graduates—meaning graduates who completed their university studies within the last six years—are working in jobs that do not require a university degree (MacDonald, 2013; ONS, 2012). Graduates who attended non-elite universities (and thus who are more likely to come from lower socio-economic backgrounds) are more likely to be underemployed than those who graduated from elite universities (Mosca & Wright, 2011; Vedder, Denhart & Robe, 2013). Though statistics on education-based underemployment (or over-qualification) are less readily available for other countries, concern about graduate underemployment is a worldwide phenomenon across both the global North and South (e.g., Lin, 2012; Melin, 2013). In China, more than a third of the almost 7 million university graduates that the country now produces each year report a "serious mismatch" between their academic training and their jobs (Huang, 2013). Researchers and media commentators have begun referring to China's growing numbers of young, underemployed graduates as "ant tribes," in reference to "their immense numbers" and "the fact that they often settle into crowded neighborhoods, toiling for wages that would give even low-paid factory workers pause" (Jacobs, 2010; see also Zhang, 2013). In the Middle East, high levels of graduate underemployment were widely seen as a contributing factor to the Arab Spring uprisings of 2011 (Campante & Chor, 2012).

While graduate underemployment is no doubt being exacerbated by the economic downturn that was triggered by the global financial crisis, educational scholars argue that it is also being produced by more fundamental and enduring contradictions in the relationship between education, society and the economy in the contemporary era (Brown, Lauder & Ashton, 2011; Livingstone, 1999). The promotion of post-secondary education as the ticket to individual social and economic mobility simply cannot work for everyone in what remains a deeply unequal capitalist economy and society, especially once this strategy has been adopted globally, by governments in all parts of the world. Paradoxically, the more successful educational reformers are in opening up access for young people from all social backgrounds to participate in post-secondary education, the more likely the education for social mobility strategy is to fail, at both the individual and societal levels (P. Brown, 2003, 2013). Ken Roberts (2009, p. 4) has recently argued that "underemployment is the 21st century global normality for youth in the labour market" (quoted in MacDonald, 2013). However, given the continuing embrace of the education for social mobility model by states around the world, it is likely that underemployment will remain a "global normality" not just for youth, but many adults as well. Not only do many young people work in low level jobs as they seek to move onwards and upwards through post-secondary education: significant numbers find themselves stuck in such jobs even after—or if—they graduate.

The Neoliberal Politics of Education, Social Mobility and Youth

How should we understand the broader social, political and ideological significance of the worldwide student protests of the post-global financial crisis era? This is a question that needs to be asked on at least two different levels. On an immediate level, there is the question of how successful and effective student protesters and their supporters have been in having their demands met. In this respect, the semester-long student strike in Quebec in 2012 won the most clear-cut victory of any of the student protest movements, as the strike contributed to the downfall of the Quebec Liberal government in the fall of 2012, and the immediate repeal by the incoming Parti Québécois government of both the previously proposed 82 percent university tuition fee increase and Bill 78—an inflammatory piece of legislation that the Liberals had created in a misguided attempt to end the student strike in May 2012, and that had placed broad restrictions on civil society protest rights in Quebec (Choudry & Shragge, 2013). The extensive student protest movement in Chile also saw the removal of two education ministers and ushering in of a number of concessionary moves by the government (such as increasing public funding of higher education and reducing interest rates on student loans), though the broader demands of student protesters were nowhere close to being met (Pousadela, 2012; Salinas & Fraser, 2012; Somma, 2012). For the most part, however, the gains of the student protest movements in the United States, the United Kingdom and elsewhere were limited, and consisted mostly of local, university-level victories: securing protection for protesters from legal and academic reprisals, greater transparency and student participation in campus decision making, and commitments not to cut courses or lay off staff (Levenson, 2011; Power, 2012). This general failure has led to extended discussion of the strategies that made a difference in Quebec and, to a lesser extent, Chile: for example, sustained grassroots organizing and resistance, direct action and participatory democracy, student unity, solidarity with trade unions and other civil society organizations (Hallward, 2012; Heath, 2012; Seymour, 2012). It has also led to an uneasy feeling that claims of student power may have been vastly exaggerated, and that student protest, in the current era at least, is possibly futile. As Ashok Kumar (2011, p. 135) observes in the context of the UK:

> The recent history of [the UK student] demonstrations reads like an ancient Greek tragedy. Fees are raised, students protest, nothing happens, students go home. Grants are abolished, students protest, nothing happens, students go home. With new injustices burdened upon the shoulders of incoming students, students have often mobilized but, lacking momentum and leadership, this mobilization is quickly lost and the movement falters. Like Sisyphus forever rolling his boulder up a hill, student energies are often expended without significant gains.

Even in Quebec, student victory was only temporary. In February 2013, just months after taking office, the Parti Québécois proposed a new plan of small annual tuition fee increases that were set to begin at 3 percent per year (Bradshaw & Seguin, 2013).

Debates about student leadership, organization and strategy are obviously important if student protest is to become more effective in the future. But there is another level at which the significance of the recent student movements needs to be considered that has to do not with the success of student protesters in having their demands met, but with the kinds of demands, and the rationales for these demands, that student protesters chose to make in the first place. In this respect, one of the most striking characteristics of the majority of the post-financial crisis student protest movements has been their relative conservatism. Most of the protesters' demands have not been about radically transforming the substance of current post-secondary education systems, but focused instead either on preserving and defending current systems from proposed future restructuring and/or rolling conditions in these systems back to an earlier period of welfare state post-secondary education that, in many countries, saw its heyday during the 1950s and 1960s (Newfield & Lye, 2011; Power, 2012; Pusey & Sealey-Higgins, 2013). In California, for example, student protesters rallied not only to "defend" and "save" higher education as it currently existed in the state, but also demanded that the state government recommit itself to the 1960 California Master Plan for Higher Education, that had enshrined the principle of state-provided, tuition-free post-secondary education to all state residents who were interested and capable (Bacon, 2011). This overall conservatism does not mean that there has been a uniformity of demands, politics or ideologies among student protesters—far from it. In most countries, there have been differences and divisions between those who asked for more moderate reforms—such as a freeze on tuition increases or an increase in public funding of post-secondary education—and those who sought more sweeping changes—such as the elimination of tuition fees altogether and the provision of free post-secondary education. In some countries, such as Egypt and Lebanon, protesters' interests were narrowly focused on the concerns of the current generation of students not future generations, and of middle- and upper-class students not those from the working class and poor (Ibrahim, 2012; Issa, 2010). While in other countries, such as the United Kingdom, student protesters were intent on challenging reforms that would not actually affect them directly, but future generations of students only (Power, 2012); and in places like the United Kingdom, California, Chile and Quebec, protesters were centrally motivated by concerns over the issue of guaranteed access to high quality post-secondary education not just for middle-class students, but for students from working-class and poor backgrounds as well (G. Brown, 2013).

Almost universally, however, student protesters' concerns have been focused on the issue of access to post-secondary education, and what high tuition fee regimes risk doing in terms of restricting student access. The importance of post-secondary educational access, moreover, has been framed primarily in terms of the opportunities that further and higher education can open up for individual social and economic mobility. In Chile, for example, the Confederation of Chilean Students, which spearheaded the country's student protest movement, released a public declaration explaining its decision to protest on the grounds of "the nonexistence of the right to education and the false notion that higher education is serving as a real tool and guarantee of social mobility" (quoted in Salinas & Fraser, 2012, p. 21). In the United Kingdom, both the National Union of Students (the principal student organization in the country) and the National Coalition Against Fees and Cuts (a more radical and militant organization created by students in the fall of 2010 to fight against tuition fee increases) likewise framed their opposition to fee increases primarily within the education for social mobility paradigm. As Michael Chessum (2011), a lead organizer and spokesperson for the National Coalition Against Fees and Cuts, argued:

> [The increase of tuition fees is] the biggest betrayal of young people in postwar British politics. From 2012, if you want to go to a prestigious university, you will be saddled with debts in excess of £50,000. . . . School students will now for the first time be facing a cold calculation about whether or not it is worth attending the top universities as "graduate premiums"—the amount that one can expect to earn over a lifetime as the result of doing a degree—drop below the cost of doing one in the first place. Some students will be put off university altogether.

Around the world, student protesters generally seemed to recognize that, despite the fraying of what George Caffentzis (2010) calls the "edu-deal"—that is, the promise of "higher wages and work satisfaction in exchange for workers and their families taking on the cost for higher education"—those who complete post-secondary education are still, on average, better off than those who don't. It is for this reason that they protested the threat to post-secondary educational access. But students did not tend to address the underlying contradiction that providing universal access to post-secondary education in the pursuit of social and economic mobility cannot and will not provide social and economic mobility (or even security) for everyone in a deeply unequal capitalist society and economy. By and large, the post-global financial crisis student protests were protests *for* social mobility as a legitimate and overarching political ideal, not against it (Beuret, 2011; Penny, 2010).

With some important exceptions (that are discussed below), there was remarkably little critical reflection by student protesters on the meaning and purpose of post-secondary education, or of how it should connect to the broader society and economy. Some student protesters embraced the seemingly radical demand that (post-secondary) "education is a right"—as opposed to being, for example, a consumer good (Pousadela, 2012). But the kind of education that people are claimed to have a right to, its substance, purpose and expected consequences received considerably less attention. Generally, what was intended by such claims was that *access* to post-secondary education, of whatever form, should be a right for all those who had the capability and interest. Similarly, there was extensive reference made to the idea of "public higher education," as something that should be protected and defended. But again, within the context of the student protests themselves, there was limited discussion of what exactly public higher education should mean, beyond the fact that it should be funded by the (public) state and accessible to the general public—or, at least, that portion of the general public who have the ability and interest to enroll in post-secondary education. But this leaves essential questions unanswered. One of the core arguments made by states around the world for privatizing the costs of post-secondary education and shifting these from taxpayers to individual students and their families is that individual students are the ones who disproportionately benefit from post-secondary education, in terms of their increased average earnings, opportunities and overall quality of life that come as a result of earning their degrees. In framing their protests against high tuition fees precisely in terms of the impact these fees might have on their ability to access social and economic mobility, students offered little to counter this argument. There were, of course, regular claims made for the broader public benefit of post-secondary education, and arguments that post-secondary education is and should be considered a "public good." But little was said about the exact conditions under which post-secondary education starts and stops being a public as opposed to private good (Calhoun, 2006; Marginson 2006, 2011). For example, is a world in which college and university graduates, on average, still expect to be better off than the rest of the population, and high end graduates can expect to be a lot better off, a place in which we can genuinely say that we have a "public" system of higher education that benefits everybody? The "larger enemy" of the public good in higher education, as Simon Marginson (2011, p. 19) and others have suggested, may not actually be "the economic market but the status hierarchy" that current systems of post-secondary education are centrally implicated in perpetuating (see also Tannock, 2006).

Some commentators have argued that the limitations in the demands and vision of recent student protesters reflect a deficit particular to the current generation of youth: a lack of historical memory and ideology, and an overly individualized way of looking at the world (e.g., Aitchison & Gilbert, 2012; Mason, 2012). "For all their faults," writes Paul Mason (2011), "the children of 1968 started out with something you don't find much of in [the current generation of student protesters]—a coherent vision of the kind of society they would like to create." But this critique risks removing "youth" from the social, cultural, political and economic structures in which it has been constructed and situated in contemporary capitalist society and economy. As Gavin Brown (2013, p. 419) points out, it is not just the current generation of student protesters who have tended to frame their demands within a "particular form of neoliberal social hope based around promoting individualized social mobility," but several decades of state social and educational policy as well (see also Raco, 2009). Indeed, as we argue above, the very extension of youth as a social category in contemporary society is based on the spread of this neoliberal politics of education and aspiration for social mobility across global capitalist society and economy. The problem of limitation of vision, then, is less a generational issue than a structural one. Ironically, despite the apparent disruptiveness and oppositional nature of the post-global financial crisis student protest movements, these movements, rather than being a radical rejection of the contemporary model of education in society, are better understood as both its ultimate realization and demonstration of its inherent contradictions. As Nicholas Somma (2012, p. 296) puts it, in the context of

Chile, the recent student movements can be seen as the "unintended byproduct" of neoliberal society, as "the expansion of tertiary education, . . . which took place under an educational market system during the last three decades, created both the critical mass of organized students and the frustrations and inequalities that fueled mobilization" (see also Salinas & Fraser, 2012). Similarly, Gavin Brown (2013, p. 419) argues that the student protests in the United Kingdom in 2010 both reveal and are the result of "the success of . . . policy interventions around [raising] young people's aspirations *and* the limits of the politics of aspiration" (italics in original).

Writing at the end of the 1960s about the student movements of that era, Ralph Turner (1969, p. 401) once argued that "youth are unlikely to go so far as to dismantle . . . the 'credential society', since the movement leadership will be largely recruited from those who are earning credentials that entitle them to favoured positions in bureaucracies." At the same time, Turner also suggested that "the passive, routinized, hierarchical, and continuous nature of the passage through schooling and bureaucratic employment will assuredly be a continuing target in the developing [student] movements," due to the inequalities, injustices, insecurities and alienation that this passage repeatedly generates (p. 401). Despite the radical differences between the student movements of Turner's era and the current period—in the 1960s, concerns about tuition fees, student debt, graduate unemployment and underemployment played almost no role in generating student protest—Turner's observed contradiction retains its relevance today. For the majority of the recent student protest movements are not challenging or questioning the basic vision of the education for social mobility model—that, after all, underlies the very expansion of education, extension of youth and construction of student identity in the contemporary period in the first place—but the structural obstacles they perceive to be threatening their ability to realize this vision for themselves. As Giorgio Jackson, one of the student protest leaders in Chile, explains the eruption of protest there:

> The promise of growth and expansion in higher education came without the regulatory framework that is necessary to prevent this huge gap between the expectations of students and their families that were created by expending millions in advertising and a much less promising reality.
>
> *(quoted in Salinas & Fraser, 2012, p. 37)*

The problem with this focus of protest is that, so long as student demands are stuck within the frame of access to education for individual mobility, growing numbers of young people around the world are likely to be stuck for ever lengthening periods of time in a prolonged state of precariousness, uncertainty, risk and—to use the term of youth studies researchers in the global South—waithood.

Searching for Alternative Models of Education, Youth and Society

Though the mainstream of the post-global financial crisis student protests centered on defending a politics of aspiration and social mobility, there were exceptions, counter-trends and alternative discourses. George Caffentzis (2010) has written of the global student movement as having "two souls," one that "demands free university education, reviving the dream of publicly financed 'mass scholarity', ostensibly proposing to return it to the model of the Keynesian era," and another that "is in revolt against the university itself, calling for a mass exit from it or aiming to transform the campus into a base for alternative knowledge production that is accessible to those outside its 'walls.'" This split was about more than just differences in protest tactics and funding demands, but involved attempts to rethink the very nature of higher education in contemporary society.

The most widespread of these attempts was the effort to rethink and reclaim a transformative vision of a genuinely "public" higher education. In most cases, as suggested above, invocations of saving or defending public higher education went little beyond demands for public funding and access to higher education. But there were exceptions. The *Share Our Future* manifesto that was written by CLASSE (Coalition Large de l'Association pour une Solidarité Syndicale), the most radical of the student organizations that led the student protest movement in Quebec in the spring of 2012, is a representative example. *Share Our Future* invokes a vision of building "a society that is dedicated to the public good" and creating "a different world far removed from the blind submission our present commodity-based system requires" (CLASSE, 2012, pp. 2, 3). It insists that "education is not a branch of the economy, nor is it a short-term training service," and calls instead for "an egalitarian school system that will break down hierarchies," that "we will share together," that "allows each and every one of us to blossom," and that "will lay the foundation for self-determination" and "pave the way towards freeing society as a whole" (pp. 3, 4). It links the struggles of students to broader concerns with the environment and the rights of women, immigrants and indigenous people. Yet, despite the sweeping and inspiring nature of the vision that the CLASSE manifesto puts forward, there is almost no concrete information offered of what this alternative education system would look like in practice, how it could be brought into being, or how it would have power to fundamentally transform the broader society and economy around it. CLASSE calls for the embrace of "direct democracy," in which the voices of students, academic workers and support staff play a central role in shaping educa-tion; and it also demands the abolition of tuition fees. But beyond this, the vision becomes vague and uncertain. At the same time, for example, that CLASSE calls for an egalitarian school system without hierarchies, it also raises concern that few women are able to "climb to the highest rungs of the academic ladder" (p. 4)—it thus becomes unclear whether the agenda is to get rid of hierarchy or climb it. As a number of educational researchers and theorists have argued recently, if a transformative vision of a public higher education is to be embraced and realized, there remains an extensive amount of careful, reflexive conceptual work regarding what exactly this would entail—work that, for the most part, has yet to be fully done (Calhoun, 2006; Holmwood, 2011; Marginson, 2006, 2011). It is not enough, in other words, simply to invoke the ideal of public higher education: the real challenge is how to create such an ideal model, and put substance to it.

While CLASSE and other groups seek to work within the current system of higher education to radically reform it, two other approaches turn away from the project of higher education system reform and seek out alternative methods and avenues of transformation instead. In the UK, alongside the student tuition fees protest movement that erupted in the fall of 2010, there has been a flourishing of new, free and autonomous "universities." These include the Really Open University in Leeds, the Social Science Centre in Lincoln, the Free Universities of Birmingham and Liverpool, and the Really Free School, University for Strategic Optimism, Ragged University and Tent City University in London (Pusey & Sealey-Huggins, 2013; Stanistreet, 2012; Swain, 2013). Some of these have been short-lived, and some function primarily as performance and protest groups, while others are enduring educational organizations. As Andre Pusey and Leon Sealey-Huggins (2013, pp. 447, 453), who are two founding members of the Really Open University in Leeds, argue, the creation of free, autonomous universities has been driven by a belief "that a politics simply based on resistance to cuts [in public funding of higher education] is not enough, and that it is important to go much further" and "address more fundamental questions about the form and content of education." Recognizing that "the academy has always been, in part, a striated institution of 'capture,'" and disillusioned by the "limitations of establishment politics" and the dominance of neoliberal ideology and corporate influence within the formal higher education system, those involved in creating free universities have tried to develop new, autonomous and open spaces for learning and knowledge creation that stand outside this higher education system altogether (Pusey & Sealey-Huggins, 2013, pp. 452, 453). In this effort, the free universities in the United Kingdom have linked up to share ideas and support one another nationally in a new Free University Network; and they are also connected with a global autonomous university movement that includes groups such as the transnational Edu-Factory Collective, Knowledge Liberation Front in Europe and Universidad de la Tierra (or Unitierra) in Mexico. Though the practices of free universities vary widely, many embrace alternative pedagogies, cooperative practices, open access (no fees, no admission requirements, no grades, no degrees), and the discussion of goals and strategies for radical social, economic, political and educational change.

In many ways, the contemporary project of creating autonomous universities draws on a centuries-old tradition of popular and radical adult and community education, which includes workers' study circles, miners' libraries, freedom schools, folk colleges and folk schools and so on. As such, they confront enduring dilemmas and struggles that such forms of education have always faced. As Richard Johnson (1979) observes of similar projects that proliferated in the United Kingdom in the late eighteenth and early nineteenth centuries, the attempt to develop an independent and radical form of education that is entirely separate from state provision can, on the one hand, provide vital and essential spaces for generating critical and "really useful" popular forms of knowledge and understanding; but, on the other hand, freedom and autonomy are won at the expense of forgoing public (or state) resources and support, and as such, independent and radical forms of education can be extraordinarily difficult to sustain at a local level, let along provide a universal replacement for the formal, state-supported higher education system as a whole. In the United Kingdom, most of those involved in the free university movement are also themselves students and staff in the formal higher education system itself, from which they are able to draw all sorts of resources: wages, grants, loans, free periods of time allocated for independent study, as well as a wide range of knowledge, theory, research and understanding. Autonomous universities that have been in existence for longer periods of time, such as Unitierra in Oaxaca, Mexico, have turned to philanthropic funding to support themselves (e.g., the Ford and Kellogg Foundations in the case of Unitierra), thus drawing on funds derived from corporate profiteering in the capitalist economy that many of these universities ostensibly oppose (CEDI-Unitierra, 2012). Like all forms of alternative, utopian educational spaces that operate in a deeply unequal capitalist society, resource constraints mean that autonomous universities constantly face the risk of either becoming educational luxuries that are fully accessible only to the privileged, or alternatively, becoming a second-tier level of education for the poor and marginalized that can offer only limited opportunities for students to be able to realize substantial social, political and economic improvements in both their individual and collective positions in the world (Bowles & Gintis, 1976; Delpit, 1995).

A third approach to rethinking the nature of higher education has been associated with the widely circulated writings of the radical occupationists who were a small, divisive and controversial, yet also highly influential part of the student protest movement in 2009 and 2010 in California (Connery, 2011; Newfield & Lye, 2011; Walker, 2010). The student occupationists offer some of the most trenchant critiques of the contemporary problems of higher education that can be found anywhere. In *Communiqué from an Absent Future: On the Terminus of Student Life*, for example, a group calling themselves Research and Destroy argue that "the university is bankrupt," not only financially but in its fundamental essence and purpose:

> No one knows what the university is *for* anymore. We feel this intuitively. Gone is the old project of creating a cultured and educated citizenry; gone,

too, the special advantage the degree-holder once held on the job market. These are now fantasies, spectral residues that cling to the poorly maintained halls.

(Research and Destroy, 2009, p. 1)

Like those involved in the free university movement, the occupationists see little hope in being able to radically reform the contemporary higher education system, as the system is and always has been dominated by the interests of business elites in reproducing capitalist society and economy to their benefit. "University life finally *appears* as just what it has always *been*," the Research and Destroy group write, "a machine for producing compliant producers and consumers" (p. 2; italics in original). In the midst of the California student protests, the occupationists thus parted with the rest of the student movement in refusing to make "demands" on the state or university administration. Unlike the free university creators, however, the occupationists also see little hope in being able to create effective alternative spaces for higher education in today's world: "A free university in the midst of a capitalist society is like a reading room in a prison; it serves only as a distraction from the misery of daily life" (p. 15). Instead, the occupationists present what is essentially a nihilistic call to focus student energies on destroying the contemporary higher education system entirely, and to do this by physically occupying it in order to disrupt its functioning and, eventually, shut it down:

> The university that makes us mute and dull instruments of its own reproduction must be destroyed so that we can produce our own lives. . . . This is the beginning of imagination's return. We must begin to move again, release ourselves from frozen history, from the igneous frieze of this buried life. . . . We must begin by preventing the university from functioning. We must interrupt the normal flow of bodies and things and bring work and class to a halt. We will blockade, occupy, and take what's ours.
>
> *(Research and Destroy, 2009, pp. 1, 15)*

Though radical in its rhetoric, the strategy and vision of the occupationists have to confront a number of limitations. Student occupations of university buildings have had limited effect on making any substantial impact on the everyday functioning of universities, whether in California or anywhere else, and occupations are extremely difficult to sustain for long periods of time (Fritsch, 2010). More fundamentally, there an extraordinary lack of clarity as to what occupationists expect and hope a new system of higher education will look like. Groups such as Research and Destroy (2009, p. 19) call for the "abolition of the capitalist mode of production" and "the reorganization of society according to a logic of free giving and receiving, and the immediate abolition of the wage, the value-form, compulsory labor, and exchange." But not only is it not clear how such changes are expected to happen, it is also unclear what education should and would look like in such a new society. There is almost an expectation that if energies are focused on destroying the universities of old, a new form of (higher) education will spontaneously emerge from their ashes.

In all of these alternative approaches to rethinking higher education in contemporary society, there is nothing particular about a "youth" or "student" approach. Rather, students and their supporters are drawing on different ideological perspectives that are widely shared with older, adult colleagues, whether these be traditions of the socialist, anarchist or autonomous movements. The limitations and dilemmas of each of these alternatives are ones that affect all of us, not just youth. What all of these traditions have absolutely right is the need to fundamentally rethink (higher) education and its relation to society and the economy, and develop a clear concept of an alternative model of the world we want to aim toward, in order to escape the current education impasse that has been variously referred to as the "opportunity trap" (Brown, 2003), the "collapse of the edu-deal" (Caffentzis, 2010) and the "terminus of student life" (Research and Destroy, 2009). While there remains a lack of clarity of what this would look like and how we might get there, it seems certain that it will of necessity involve separating education from the organization of political, economic and status inequality in society, and challenging directly the educational politics of social mobility and aspiration. Though the challenge and dilemma of rethinking education in society do not solely affect youth, they have particular salience for youth, whether as a social category, identity or individually lived experience. For rethinking the place of education in society and the economy, and challenging the politics and ideology of social mobility and aspiration, will also inevitably entail questioning the century-long extension of youth and its increasing prominence as a life stage in all parts of contemporary global capitalist society, and challenging the repeated and consistent deferral of adult status and dreams of the young.

CONCLUSION

In an article published in the *Journal of Youth Studies* in 2013, James Côté (2013), who has been writing on the sociology of youth for decades, calls for the development of a new "political economy perspective" for studying youth. By political economy, Côté means "a perspective that investigates the root causes and consequences of the positioning over time of the youth segment in relation to those (adults) in a given society with political and economic power," and that seeks "to imagine radical solutions to youth exploitation" (p. 2). Côté argues that such a perspective "has been largely ignored in youth studies," while the field has become "increasingly preoccupied with subjectivities" and "psychological states" (pp. 1, 12, 13). The danger of this neglect, Côté argues, is not only that youth studies tends to ignore the "material conditions" that shape the lives of young people today, but also that the field as a whole risks becoming "an 'apology' for neoliberalism," as it "risks missing the role played by neoliberalism in the current prolongations of youth, the deterioration of youth living conditions and their diminished economic prospects later in life" (pp. 1, 3). It is precisely this set of concerns and interests, laid out so articulately by Côté in his article, that motivated us to write this book. In order to understand the experiences, concerns and actions of young people today, there is a need to look not just at the structural conditions of youth in contemporary, local and national societies and economies, but at the varying social and economic positioning and significance of youth globally, across space, and historically, across time as well.

Côté's "new political economy of youth" article is useful, too, for highlighting some of the aspects that differentiate our approach from that taken by other critical youth studies scholars. For many youth studies researchers, youth tends to be approached as a clearly defined social category and identity. Drawing on the 1960s work of John and Margaret Rowntree, for example, Côté (2013) proposes that it may be both useful and possible to view youth in contemporary society as constituting a distinct social "class." The emphasis in Côté's article (although not elsewhere in Côté's work—see, for example, Côté (2014)) is thus on there being a strong line of demarcation between youth and adults, and a relationship of exploitation and opposition between the two:

> There are several common criteria associated with definitions of class that help us see how the youth segment could usefully be seen as such.... First, and most importantly, there needs to be evidence in terms of demonstrable material differences between two groups, where one group benefits from the other's exploitation and marginalisation. In this case, ... there has been a significant redistribution of wealth in many societies influenced by neoliberal economics, an important axis of which is age (i.e., sharp differences in youth–adult material conditions have emerged in many countries).
>
> *(p. 4)*

Further, the focus of Côté and other critical youth studies researchers tends to be on addressing the "stigmatization" of youth in contemporary society, and challenging widespread claims about the alleged "inferiority" and "inadequacy" of youth (p. 4). All of this work is, of course, essential; and Côté is right that there are times and places where it can be helpful to think of youth as a marginalized social class. For some writers, this issue has been framed as being a matter of intergenerational justice: from the lack of employment protections, to cutbacks in education and social welfare funding, to state failure to act on the threat posed by climate change, younger generations as a whole can be seen to be denied access to the privileges and benefits that have previously been enjoyed by older generations (Grossberg, 2001; Page, 2006; Sears, 2014).

The argument that we make in this book, however, is that one of the defining features of youth in neoliberal society is that youth is not only a subject of stigmatization but of celebration, embrace and empowerment as well. Whether positive or negative, both sides of the representation of youth can be invoked to serve the interests of political and economic elites, often to the detriment of specific groups of young people, young people as a whole, and/or youth and adults together. Indeed, this double-sided nature of youth stereotyping is part of the long history of the social construction of youth in capitalist (and other) societies, and not just limited to our current neoliberal era alone. More than this, the category of youth is, in our analysis, highly fluid and unstable, and as such, itself requires close critical analysis. It is certainly true that large groups of young people in contemporary society tend to be socially and economically marginalized relative to older adults (although social and economic inequalities among youth and among adults are probably far greater than inequalities between the two groups as a whole). Youth is also used as a social category and technology to manage and control young people (as well as adults) in the service of elite interests. But rather than assume a fixed and oppositional relationship between stable categories of youth and adults, it is this relationship that needs to be interrogated. One of the defining features of youth in the contemporary period is that it has been extended both vertically across the age ranges, downward into childhood and upward into adulthood, and horizontally across populations, such that individuals for whom the social category of youth previously held limited relevance, and who might have defined themselves in terms of class, race and ethnicity, gender, religion, nationality, region, ideology, etc., now are increasingly defined and define themselves in terms of youth. In this context, it is insufficient to embrace the category of youth (whether as exploited class or marginalized social segment or sacrificed generation) as the starting point for analysis and action. Instead, we need to ask what is at stake for whom in embracing the social category of youth as opposed to other social categories and relationships in the first place. The politics involved here are not just in how social categories and identities (of youth) are represented, but also in which social categories and identities are foregrounded and which neglected in discourse and practice, in the context of ongoing social, political and economic change and conflict.

In his article, Côté draws attention to the need to understand the "nature of youth in capitalist societies" (p. 12). We agree. To do this, it needs to be recognized that capitalism is defined at its core by constant change and upending of previous social and economic relations, inherent conflicts between social classes and other social groups, and endemic contradictions between multiple ideological formations. At different periods of time, for different groups of people, in different parts of the world, capitalism has had radically different consequences for the construction of youth as a social category and identity, and for the lived experiences of individuals in their second and third decades of life. In some eras, such as the period of welfare state capitalism, we can see the solidifying of divisions between youth and adulthood, and the sequestering of youth away from the market and economy into social welfare institutions of the school, juvenile court and youth group; while in other eras, such as the current neoliberal period, we can see the erosion of strong divisions between youth and adulthood (and youth and childhood), and the pulling of youth directly into the marketplace and economy. While young people have always functioned as a reserve army of labor in the capitalist economy, particular relationships between youth and the labor market have varied over time and place: so that youth in some settings are pulled into capitalist wage labor from positions in non-capitalist societies and economies, while in other settings, they are pulled from participation in full-time formal education into low wage service labor; at other junctures, youth are pushed back out of the waged labor market once again. While youth universally tend to be socially, politically and economically more marginal than adults, variations of income, wealth and power can be extreme between both individuals and groups of individuals in their teens and twenties (and indeed, in all decades of life) across the world; and while stereotypes of youth can be used to stigmatize, marginalize and exploit the young, so too can they be used all too effectively to stigmatize, marginalize, exploit and displace adults and the elderly as well.

Structure and Agency in Youth Studies

One of the motivations of this book is a reaction against the over-emphasis on agency and subjectivity and relative neglect of social and economic structure in much youth studies writing—what Jones (2009, p. 172) refers to as "the prevailing political correctness of stressing young people's agency." Our focus has been on the broad discourses, social and economic structures, and actions of elite actors in shaping the social category of youth and lives of young individuals in contemporary society, as these are all too often passed over and left in the background. Our view is that much more work needs to be done on analyzing all of these things. There are so many institutions working on shaping youth today: schools, corporations, the state, media in all of its different forms, foundations, NGOs of different kinds, youth groups, the courts, the military, a whole army of youth experts located in academia, government, advertising agencies, the voluntary sector, and so on. All of these need to be understood not just individually, but also in terms of how they operate within a broad and dense network of institutional actors that are linked globally around the world.

As a consequence, we have not spent as much time on looking at the experiences, ideas and actions of individual young people and groups of young people in local contexts around the world as we would have otherwise. However, the point is not to dismiss the significance of youth agency, or suggest that these things are not important. They absolutely are. But there needs to be a balanced attention to how local experiences, ideas and actions work within structural contexts. As we discussed in our chapter on youth as a revolutionary subject, young people are never empty vessels or passive dupes (any more than older adults are), even in the most top-down, hierarchical and controlled settings: there is, consequently, always a vast gulf between the official discourses of organizations, and how actual practices unfold on the ground, in real time. But at the same time, the agency of young people is itself partly produced, shaped and directed by the ideological discourses, institutional infrastructures and material resources and constraints of the multiple organizations within which individuals and groups of individuals come to develop a sense of themselves as being and acting as youthful subjects. Likewise, at a higher level of analysis, so too are the actions of individual youth groups and organizations shaped by the broader networks of funding, training and education, ideology, personal and institutional relationships, state governance and so forth, within which they are situated.

More than this, there needs to be a more developed language and analysis for talking about agency and resistance among youth. For the past several decades, much of youth studies research and writing has focused on uncovering, interpreting and celebrating instances of youth "agency" and "resistance." In large part, such an endeavor has been carried out in opposition to dominant discourses of youth as pathological, irrational, dysfunctional and deviant, such that the finding that young people are capable of rational and critical insight and action becomes important and remarkable in and of itself (Debies-Carl, 2013; P. Williams, 2007; Willis, 1981). But both agency and resistance in youth studies (as elsewhere in the social sciences) have become highly abstract, flattened, universalized and ubiquitous concepts: anything and everything can be read as an example of youthful agency and resistance. "When young rappers dress up with Rolex watches they are doing exactly what late capitalist society wants them to do, consuming and day-dreaming," write Johansson and Lalander (2012, pp. 1082–1083), "but still, their self-presentation—which also includes lyrics on police violence, racism, and oppression—may be seen as a form of resistance." At the same time, what has largely disappeared from view in much youth studies writing is attention to organized, collective, political and ideological movements of the young (and old) that seek to radically transform the social, political and economic order, as distinct from everyday instances of agency and resistance. As Adolph Reed (2000) argues, though everyday resistance (or "infrapolitics" in his words) and organized political movements are closely related, the distinction between the two is essential:

> Sure, there's infrapolitics—there always is, and there always will be; wherever there's oppression, there's resistance. . . . People don't like being oppressed or exploited, and they respond in ways that reflect that fact. . . . "Daily confrontations" are to political movements as carbon, water, and oxygen are to life on this planet. They are the raw material for movements of political change, and expressions of dissatisfaction that reflect the need for change, but their presence says nothing more about the potential for such a movement to exist, much less its actuality.

"At best," Reed (2000) argues, "those who romanticize 'everyday resistance' . . . read the evolution of political movements teleologically" by presuming "that those conditions necessarily, or even typically, lead to political action," when "they don't." "At worst, and more commonly," Reed (2000) writes, "defenders of infrapolitics treat it as politically consequential in its own right." Paradoxically, as Oliver Marchart (2004, p. 420) observes, by focusing discussion of youth agency and resistance solely on "matters of 'style'" and consumption "rather than political mobilization," youth studies researchers and theorists risk ending up with "a depoliticized account of subcultures—even as those theorists started out with the opposite intention of politicizing cultural theory" (see also Debies-Carl, 2013; Johansson & Lalander, 2012; Tuck & Yang, 2014).

The recent uprisings of the global post-financial crisis era have attracted renewed attention to the idea of youth as collective political actors. However, as we argue in our chapter on youth as a revolutionary subject, critical understandings of youth as collective political actors have thus far tended to be marred by a number of limitations: a fundamental misrepresentation of these uprisings as being youth uprisings rather than multi-generational and multi-institutional protest movements, within which youth and youth groups have played a vital role; a neglect of the role and interest of political and economic elites in positioning and framing youth as being the lead actors within these movements; a failure to situate popular representations of youth in these movements within the long and contradictory history of representing youth as revolutionary social actors; and finally, an embrace of neoliberal discourses of political mobilization that frames the relative neglect of questions of political ideology and organization, and social and economic structure and power, as constituting a new, liberatory, transformative and youthful form of social politics, rather than a basic limitation and liability.

Global and Comparative Perspectives on Youth

A further motivation for this book is to sketch out some of the ways in which the lives of young people are increasingly shaped by the structures and forces of a global capitalist economy, and the institutions and ideologies that play a central role in constructing youth as a social category and identity are truly global in nature. There has been a growing literature on global youth: however, much of this has been focused either on youth culture and youth consumption practices, or on adolescent developmental pathways and states; and much of it has been in the form of edited collections of localized studies of youth around the world (e.g., Brown, Larson & Saraswathi, 2002; Dolby & Rizvi, 2008; Jeffrey & Dyson, 2008; Nilan & Feixa, 2006). Our interest and concern are in looking at youth more broadly than simply in terms of culture and consumption. Whether looking at the discourses, practices and policies of education, work, unemployment, community organizing, civic participation and leadership, revolution, development or justice, as each of these pertain to the social construction of youth and lived experiences of young individuals, these are almost always globally formed and influenced. Very often these global connections follow the contours of political, economic, cultural and military power in global society, so that starting points are frequently to be found in the United States and elsewhere in the global North, from where discourses, practices and policies of youth spread outward. Positive youth development, for example, is a US invention that subsequently went global, just like the practices of developmental psychology, the juvenile court and the middle school before it. But global patterns of learning, communication and adoption can also progress in reverse and sideways directions—so that young (and old) activists throughout the global North have found inspiration and models for protest in the actions of demonstrators in Tahrir Square and elsewhere in the Arab Spring. Our concern in this book, in particular, has been to focus attention on the role played by elite actors in constructing and spreading discourses, practices and policies of youth around the world; and beyond this, to understand how and why youth has become increasingly central to global political and development discourse, by analyzing the role that it plays and the significance it has within contemporary global neoliberal society.

Within these global patterns and structures, there are, of course, huge variations in the construction and significance of youth across space and time that we have only gestured at throughout this book. Some of these are generated by the contradictions of capitalism itself, and the different ways that people have resisted and responded to it; and some by other social, historical, cultural and political formations. Youth studies researchers have extensively studied differences of class, gender, race and ethnicity, sexuality, religion and so forth in the construction of youth as a social category and the lived experiences of young individuals (Cieslik & Simpson, 2013; Furlong, 2009; Lesko & Talburt, 2012). But many of these studies have been done within local and national contexts: there needs to be more attention paid to global comparisons as well. A global framework can help develop better understandings not just of youth in different locales, but of the significance and nature of youth as a social category more generally. Our understanding of the relationship between youth and capitalism, or the changes in the construction and deconstruction of youth across time, or the significance of employment and labor force participation for youth, for example, can all look very different when considered across the different regions of the world, rather than solely within the contexts of a single nation state.

Effective and useful comparison, as Laura Nader (1989, p. 334) writes, "requires comparative consciousness which steers away from comparisons that are only of a dichotomous nature." For comparative frameworks are important not just for looking at how youth is constructed differently in different places for different groups of individuals. "We must also compare," Nader (1989, p. 335) argues, "to find points of convergence and commonality"—as well as to analyze how different groups of young individuals in different places are positioned with respect to one another, and to other social groups, within global discourses, policies and power structures. Neoliberal discourses that promote the ideology of global competition and national economic competitiveness, for example, position youth in different nations of the world as being in direct competition with one another—rather than focus on their shared situations and concerns of marginalization and risk with respect to political and economic elites within their own nation states. As Thomas Friedman (2004) writes, in a widely quoted column in the *New York Times*:

> When I was growing up, my parents used to say to me: "Finish your dinner—people in China are starving." I, by contrast, find myself wanting to say to my daughters: "Finish your homework—people in China and India are starving for your job."

In the wake of the global financial crisis, to take another example, youth and immigrants have increasingly been played off against one another, with immigrants being blamed for causing high levels of youth unemployment—and concern for the plight of youth being used to legitimate anti-immigrant policy and sentiment (JCWI, 2012; Tannock, 2013). Many of the immigrants in question here, of course, are themselves young and struggling, just like the native-born, to make a living and find a place for themselves in the world.

Prospects for the Politics of Youth in the Global Economy

The dominant model of youth that we have sketched out in this book, while having close links with neoliberal discourse and politics, also comes out of a long history that stretches back through the development of capitalist society and economy. The promotion and extension of youth across age ranges and social groups, the emphasis on human capital models of youth, the construction of youth as a time of individualization, aspiration and mobility—all of these are likely to continue and be intensified if, as according to current expectations, the neoliberal model of market fundamentalism, austerity politics and widening inequalities between the rich and the poor continues to hold sway in the wake of the global financial and economic crisis (Crouch, 2011; Harvey, 2009; McNally, 2010). As we have discussed throughout this book, all the signs so far are that the discourses, policies and practices of the neoliberal model of youth that have developed over the last three decades are set to remain in place into the foreseeable future. In October 2013, the World Bank hosted yet another Global Youth Summit, in collaboration with the United Nations and International Labour Organization, at its headquarters in Washington, DC, under the banner theme of "Youth Entrepreneurship: Cultivating an Innovative Spirit to Alleviate Global Youth Unemployment." The event drew together the UN Secretary General's new Envoy for Youth Ahmad Allendawi, USAID's new youth development staff, as well as youth policy experts and activists participating in the event live online from "Mexico City, Freetown, Addis Ababa, Bucharest, Juba, and many other cities around the world" (Roseen, 2013). In the words of one young, enthusiastic USAID intern, the event signaled that "the global community is at the precipice of truly elevating the youth platform on major issues in development." The message that this intern, at least, came away from the Summit with is that what most needs to be done now is for all international development organizations to "appoint a designated Youth Envoy," someone who can "work to arm young leaders not just with résumés and CVs, but with business plans and investment opportunities" (Roseen, 2013).

The argument that we put forward in this book begs to differ. If our world is to witness a fundamental change in the social standing and social construction of youth, this will require much more than designated Youth Envoys, résumés and CVs, business plans and investment opportunities. It will require much more, too, than the "youth empowerment" projects that US Secretary of State Hillary Clinton, along with so many other global elites speak so willingly about today. It will require, rather, a deep and critical analysis of the way in which youth as a social category is being produced and shaped in contemporary neoliberal society by the actions of elite institutions and individuals, and others. It will require a reflective understanding of the long history of youth in capitalist society and economy. It will also require a deep understanding and analysis of global capitalist society and economy itself, of how it works and continually seeks to reinvent itself. It will require, finally, a vision of an alternative world where new and more equitable, democratic and sustainable relationships at the heart of society, the economy, education and other cultural institutions are possible, as well as a collective self-mobilization of people, young and old, from below to make such a vision a reality. In such circumstances, it may actually come to be that not only is the situation of youth in society dramatically transformed, improved and enfranchised; but that the entire social category of youth as such becomes less important and less salient than it currently appears to be.

There are places where such an alternative politics of youth and vision of a different possible world are already being formed. Many of these have been discussed in this book: the attempts of students and academic workers across the world to imagine and create alternative models and spaces of higher education learning and practice; the protests against the inequalities and injustices of neoliberal politics that have reached from the Arab Spring to the indignados to the Occupy Movement, and that have drawn together groups from all parts of global civil society; and the cross-generational movements of the unemployed, that are calling for better and fairer models of social and economic employment and development. Others have not been discussed here, but are also vitally important: the mass organizing for climate justice, for immigrant rights, and against the use of sweatshops, against racism, war and occupation, and so on. In all of these movements, young people have an essential role to play. But so too do individuals of other ages and life stages: and the power of global civil society is likely to be felt most when it is able to move beyond simplistic labels and divisions of different age groups and generations. In many of these movements, finally, young participants are quite likely to find themselves not embraced by the youth voice, youth participation and youth empowerment forums and frameworks that are now being promoted by global elites and their representative organizations, but rather to be standing on the outside, having to fight hard and shout loud for a hearing for the alternative futures that they are struggling collectively to win.

REFERENCES

Abul-Magd, Z. (2012). Occupying Tahrir Square: The myths and the realities of the Egyptian revolution. *South Atlantic Quarterly, 111*(3), 565–572.

Aday, S., Farrell, H., Lynch, M., Sides, J., & Freelon, D. (2012). *New media and conflict after the Arab spring.* Washington, DC: United States Institute of Peace.

AELP – Association of Employment and Learning Providers. (2013). Youth employment convention. Retrieved from www.aelp.org.uk/events/details/youth-employment-convention/

African Union. (2006). *African youth charter.* Retrieved from www.africa-youth.org/charter

Ahendawi, A. (2013). Africa's greatest assets are its young people. *Africa Renewal.* Retrieved from www.un.org/africarenewal/magazine/may-2013/africa's-greatest-assets-are-its-young-people

Ainley, P., & Allen, M. (2013). Running up a down-escalator in the middle of a class structure gone pear-shaped. *Sociological Research Online, 18*(1). Retrieved from www.socresonline.org.uk/18/1/8.html

Aitchison, G., & Gilbert, J. (2012). Reflecting on the student movement. *Soundings, 50,* 32–44.

Albayan. (2013). Tarek Yusuf addressing the World Social Forum in Tunisia: Youth unemployment as cause for Arab spring. March 29th. Retrieved from www.albayan.ae/economy/capital-markets/2013-09-29-1.1968792 (In Arabic)

AllAfrica. (2012). Revolution coming, Obasanjo says – 'The danger ahead is real and potent.' *AllAfrica.* November 12th. Retrieved from http://allafrica.com/stories/201211120455.html

Allan, C., Bamber, G., & Timo, N. (2005). McJobs, student attitudes to work and employment relations in the fast-food industry. *Journal of Hospitality and Tourism Management, 12*(1), 1–11.

Allen, M., & Ainley, P. (2012). *Why young people can't get the jobs they want and the education they need.* Retrieved from www.radicaled.wordpress.com

Allen, P. (2010). Life skills are what youth need: Blackstone CEO. *CNBC.* December 2nd. Retrieved from www.cnbc.com/id/40451871

Allen, R. (1969). *Black awakening in capitalist America*. Trenton: Africa World Press.

Allen, S. (1968). Some theoretical problems in the study of youth. *Sociological Review, 16*(3), 319–331.

Allen, S. (1973). Class, culture and generation. *Sociological Review, 21*(3), 437–446.

Al-Momani, M. (2011). The Arab 'youth quake': Implications on democratization and stability. *Middle East Law and Governance, 3*(1), 159–170.

Altbach, P. (1989). Perspectives on student political activism. *Comparative Education, 25*(1), 97–110.

Altbach, P., & Cohen, R. (1990). American student activism: The post-sixties transformation. *Journal of Higher Education, 61*(1), 32–49.

Altbach, P., & Peterson, P. (1971). Before Berkeley: Historical perspectives on American student activism. *Annals of the American Academy of Political and Social Science, 395*, 1–14.

Altbach, P., Reisberg, L., & Rumbley, L. (2009). *Trends in global higher education: Tracking an academic revolution*. Paris: UNESCO.

Amara, J. (2012). The youth revolt: A new frontier of conflict. United States Institute of Peace. January 3rd. Retrieved from http://inec.usip.org/blog/2012/jan/03/youth-revolt-new-frontier-conflict

America's Promise Alliance. (2007). *The story of America's promise*. Washington, DC: America's Promise Alliance.

America's Promise Alliance. (2013). About the Alliance. Retrieved from www.americaspromise.org/About-the-Alliance.aspx

Anaro, B. (2011). Nigeria: The 'lost generation' in an excruciating economy. *All Africa*. November 29th. Retrieved from http://allafrica.com/stories/201111290896.html

Anderson, B. (1991). *Imagined communities*. London: Verso.

Annunziata, M. (2012). Wasted youth. *Vox*. May 14th. Retrieved from www.voxeu.org/article/wasted-youth

Ansell, N., Hadju, F., Robson, E., van Blerk, L., & Marandet, E. (2012). Youth policy, neoliberalism and transnational governmentality: A case study of Lesotho and Malawi. In P. Kraftl, J. Horton, & F. Tucker (Eds.), *Critical geographies of childhood and youth* (pp. 43–60). Bristol: Policy Press.

APDUSA – African People's Democratic Union of Southern Africa. (2011). The youth wage subsidy and corporate welfare. Retrieved from www.apdusa.org.za/articles/the-youth-wage-subsidity-and-corporate-welfare/

APYouthnet. (2011). The lost generation. Retrieved from http://apyouthnet.ilo.org/podcast/copy_of_apyn-podcast-2-the-lost-generation/view

Ariès, P. (1962). *Centuries of childhood*. New York: Vintage.

Arnett, J. (2000). Emerging adulthood. *American Psychologist, 55*(5), 469–480.

Arnett, J. (2004). *Emerging adulthood: The winding road from the late teens through the twenties*. Oxford: Oxford University Press.

Arnett, J. (2007a). Emerging adulthood: What is it, and what is it good for? *Child Development Perspectives, 1*(2), 68–73.

Arnett, J. (2007b). Suffering, selfish, slackers? Myths and reality about emerging adults. *Journal of Youth and Adolescence, 36*, 23–29.

Ashton, D. (1986). *Unemployment under capitalism*. Brighton: Harvester Press.

Ashton, D. (1993). Understanding change in youth labour markets: A conceptual framework. *British Journal of Education and Work, 6*(3), 3–23.

Atkinson, P., & Rees, T. (1982). Youth unemployment and state intervention. In T. Rees & P. Atkinson (Eds.), *Youth unemployment and state intervention* (pp. 1–12). London: Routledge & Kegan Paul.

Austin, J., & Willard, M. (1998). Introduction. In J. Austin & M. Willard (Eds.), *Generations of youth* (pp. 1–20). New York: NYU Press.

Austin, L. (2011). The politics of youth bulge: From Islamic activism to democratic reform in the Middle East and North Africa. *SAIS Review*, *31*(2), 81–96.

Autor, D. (2010). *The polarization of job opportunities in the US labor market*. Washington, DC: Center for American Progress.

Ayotte-Thompson, M., & Freeman, L. (2012). The Quebec student movement. *Social Policy*, fall issue, 3–6.

Ayres, S. (2013). The high cost of youth unemployment. Center for American Progress. April 5th. Retrieved from www.americanprogress.org/issues/labor/report/2013/04/05/59428/the-high-cost-of-youth-unemployment/

Bacon, D. (2011). Students, faculty occupy building to protest cuts. April 14th. Retrieved from www.peoplesworld.org/students-faculty-occupy-building-to-protest-cuts/

Baer, K. (2012). Fabricating a war between the old and the young. *Poverty Insights*. July 20th. Retrieved from www.povertyinsights.org/2012/07/20/fabricating-a-war-between-the-old-and-the-young/

Bailey, M., & Freedman, D. (Eds.) (2011). *The assault on universities*. London: Pluto.

Bajoria, J., & Assaad, R. (2011). Demographics of Arab protests. Council on Foreign Relations. February 14th. Retrieved from www.cfr.org/egypt/demographics-arab-protests/p24096

Baker, D. (2012). For Greece there is an alternative to austerity. *Guardian*. July 30th. Retrieved from www.guardian.co.uk/commentisfree/2012/jul/30/greece-alternative-austerity-argentina-imf-germany

Banaji, S. (2008). The trouble with civic: A snapshot of young people's civic and political engagements in twenty-first-century democracies. *Journal of Youth Studies*, *11*(5), 543–560.

Banks, J., Blundell, R., Bozio A., & Emmerson, C. (2010). *Releasing jobs for the young? Early retirement and youth unemployment in the United Kingdom*. IFS Working Paper. London: Institute for Fiscal Studies.

Barber, T. (2009). Participation, citizenship and well-being: Engaging with young people, making a difference. *Young*, *17*(1), 25–40.

Barker, C. (2008). Some reflections on student movements of the 1960s and early 1970s. *Revista Crítica de Ciencias Sociais*, *81*, 43–91.

Barton, D. (2012). Young people don't possess the right skills for jobs. *Telegraph*. November 7th. Retrieved from www.telegraph.co.uk/finance/jobs/youth-unemployment-competition/9659515/Young-people-dont-possess-the-right-skills-for-jobs.html

Bayat, A. (2010). Muslim youth and the claim of youthfulness. In L. Herrera & A. Bayat (Eds.), *Being young and Muslim: New cultural politics in the global South and North* (pp. 27–48). Oxford: Oxford University Press.

Bayat, A. (2012). *Life as politics: How ordinary people change the Middle East*. Amsterdam: Amsterdam University Press.

BBC News. (2009). Massive layoffs as gloom deepens. January 26th. Retrieved from http://news.bbc.co.uk/1/hi/business/7852484.stm

Beatty, C., Fothergill, S., & Gore, T. (2012). *The real level of unemployment 2012*. Sheffield: Centre for Regional Economic and Social Research.

Beaumont, P. (2011). The truth about Twitter, Facebook and the uprisings in the Arab world. *Guardian*. February 25th. Retrieved from www.theguardian.com/world/2011/feb/25/twitter-facebook-uprisings-arab-libya

Beck, J. (2008). *Meritocracy, citizenship and education.* London: Continuum.

Becker, H. (1946). *German youth: Bond or free.* Oxford: Oxford University Press.

Beehner, L. (2007). The effects of 'youth bulge' on civil conflicts. April 27th. *Council on Foreign Relations.* Retrieved from www.cfr.org/society-and-culture/effects-youth-bulge-civil-conflicts/p13093

Bell, D., & Kristol, I. (1969). *Confrontation: The student rebellion and the universities.* New York: Basic Books.

Ben-Amos, I. (1995). Adolescence as a cultural invention: Phillippe Ariès and the sociology of youth. *History of the Human Sciences, 8*(2), 69–89.

Bennett, A., & Kahn-Harris, K. (Eds.). (2004). *After subculture: Critical studies in subcultural theory and research.* New York: Palgrave.

Bennett, W. (2012). The looming crisis of student loan debt. *CNN.* December 6th. Retrieved from http://edition.cnn.com/2012/12/06/opinion/bennett-student-debt/

Benson, P. (1997). *All kids are our kids.* San Francisco: Jossey-Bass.

Benson, P. (2003). Developmental assets and asset-building community. In R. Lerner & P. Benson (Eds.), *Developmental assets and asset-building communities* (pp. 19–43). New York: Kluwer.

Benson, P., & Saito, R. (2000). The scientific foundations of youth development. In N. Jaffe (Ed.), *Youth development* (pp. 125–148). Philadelphia: Public/Private Ventures.

Benson, P., Scales, P., Hamilton, S., & Sesma, A. (2006). Positive youth development. In W. Damon & R. Lerner (Eds.), *Handbook of child psychology, Vol. 1* (pp. 894–941). 6th edn. New York: John Wiley.

Bereday, G. (1966). Student unrest on four continents: Montreal, Ibadan, Warsaw and Rangoon. *Comparative Education Review, 10*(2), 188–204.

Berg, I. (1970). *Education and jobs: The great training robbery.* New York: Praeger.

Berlanstein, L. (1992). *The industrial revolution and work in nineteenth-century Europe.* London: Routledge.

Bessant, J. (2004). Mixed messages: Youth participation and democratic practice. *Australian Journal of Political Science, 39*(2), 387–404.

Best, A. (2009). Young people and consumption. In A. Furlong (Ed.), *Handbook of youth and young adulthood* (pp. 255–262). New York: Routledge.

Best, J. (2001). *Damned lies and statistics.* Berkeley: University of California Press.

Betcherman, G., Olivas, K., & Dar, A. (2004). *Impacts of active labor market programs: New evidence from evaluations with particular attention to developing and transition countries.* Washington, DC: World Bank.

Beuret, N. (2011). Hope against hope: A necessary betrayal. Retrieved from http://libcom.org/news/hope-against-hope-necessary-betrayal-15122010

Billig, M. (1999). Commodity fetishism and repression: Reflections on Marx, Freud and the psychology of consumer capitalism. *Theory & Psychology, 9*(3), 313–329.

Blackman, S. (2005). Youth subcultural theory. *Journal of Youth Studies, 8*(1), 1–20.

Blanch, M. (1979). Imperialism, nationalism and organized youth. In J. Clarke, C. Critcher, & R. Johnson (Eds.), *Working-class culture* (pp. 103–120). London: Hutchinson.

Blua, A. (2012). 'An economic time bomb': The world's unemployed youth. *The Atlantic.* Retrieved from www.theatlantic.com/international/archive/2012/12/an-economic-time-bomb-the-worlds-unemployed-youth/266412/

Böcking, D. (2012). 'Trust no one over 30!': Euro crisis morphs into generational conflict. *Der Spiegel.* September 8th. Retrieved from www.spiegel.de/international/europe/commentary-why-the-euro-crisis-is-also-a-generational-conflict-a-849165.html

Bond, S. (2012). Student debt gains Occupy's attention. *Financial Times*. April 25th. Retrieved from www.ft.com/cms/s/0/cca61b68-8efb-11e1-aa12-00144feab49a. html#axzz2lqxve6IP

Boren, M. (2001). *Student resistance: A history of the unruly subject*. New York: Routledge.

Bourdieu, P. (1984). La jeunesse n'est qu'un mot. Interview with Anne-Marie Metailie. In *Questions de sociologie* (pp. 143–154). Paris: Editions de Minuit.

Bowles, S., & Gintis, H. (1976). *Schooling in capitalist America*. New York: Basic Books.

Boyden, J., Ling, B., & Myers, W. (1998). *What works for working children*. Stockholm: Unicef.

Bradshaw, J., & Séguin, R. (2013). Quebec to raise university tuition fees despite strong opposition. *Globe and Mail*. February 25th. Retrieved from www.theglobeandmail. com/news/national/education/quebec-to-raise-university-tuition-fees-despite-strong-opposition/article9018652/

Braungart, R. (1984). Historical generations and generation units: A global pattern of youth movements. *Journal of Political and Military Sociology, 12*, 113–135.

Brown, B., Larson, R., & Saraswathi, T.S. (Eds.). (2002). *The world's youth: Adolescence in eight regions of the globe*. Cambridge: Cambridge University Press.

Brown, G. (2013). The revolt of aspirations: Contesting neoliberal social hope. *ACME. 12*(3), 419–430.

Brown, P. (2003). The opportunity trap: Education and employment in a global economy. *European Educational Research Journal, 2*(1), 141–179.

Brown, P. (2013). Education, opportunity and the prospects for social mobility. *British Journal of Sociology of Education, 34*(5), 678–700.

Brown, P., Lauder, H., & Ashton, D. (2008). Education, globalisation and the future of the knowledge economy. *European Educational Research Journal, 7*(2), 131–156.

Brown, P., Lauder, H., & Ashton, D. (2011). *The global auction: The broken promises of education, jobs and incomes*. Oxford: Oxford University Press.

Brown, S., & Hansen, H. (2013). Merkel opponent derides jobless summit as cynical ploy. *Reuters*. July 2nd. Retrieved from www.reuters.com/article/2013/07/02/us-europe-unemployment-germany-idUSBRE9610SR20130702

Bucholtz, M. (2002). Youth and cultural practice. *Annual Review of Anthropology, 31*, 525–552.

Buckingham, D. (2011). *The material child: Growing up in consumer culture*. Cambridge: Polity Press.

BYC & CRAE – British Youth Council & Children's Rights Alliance of England. (2010). Response to Low Pay Commission consultation on the national minimum wage. September 10th. Retrieved from www.byc.org.uk/media/16136/Consultation%20 Response.%20Low%20Pay%20Commission%20on%20the%20National%20 Minimum%20Wage.%2010%20September%202010.pdf

Bynner, J. (2001). British youth transitions in comparative perspective. *Journal of Youth Studies, 4*(1), 5–23.

Caffentzis, G. (2010). University struggles at the end of the edu-deal. *Mute*. April 15th. Retrieved from www.metamute.org/editorial/articles/university-struggles-end-edu-deal

Calhoun, C. (2006). The university and the public good. *Thesis Eleven, 84*, 7–43.

Campanella, E. (2010). Beware Italy's intergenerational conflict. *Guardian*. July 14th. Retrieved from www.theguardian.com/commentisfree/2010/jul/14/italy-gerontocracy-intergenerational-conflict

Campante, F., & Chor, D. (2012). Why was the Arab world poised for revolution? Schooling, economic opportunities and the Arab spring. *Journal of Economic Perspectives, 26*(2), 167–188.

Canavan, J. (2008). Resilience. *Child Care in Practice*, *14*(1), 1–7.

Canny, A. (2002). Flexible labour? The growth of student employment in the UK. *Journal of Education and Work*, *15*(3), 277–301.

Caon, V. (2012). Italy's rigid labour market won't flex to Mario Monti's reforms. *Guardian*. 13th March. Retrieved from www.guardian.co.uk/commentisfree/2012/mar/13/italy-labour-market-mario-monti-reform

Capuzzo, P. (2012). Youth and consumption. In F. Trentmann (Ed.), *Oxford handbook of the history of consumption*. Oxford: Oxford University Press.

Carey, E. (2005). *Plaza of sacrifices: Gender, power and terror in 1968 Mexico*. Albuquerque: University of New Mexico Press.

Carnevale, A., & Strohl, J. (2013). *Separate & unequal: How higher education reinforces the intergenerational reproduction of white privilege*. Washington, DC: Georgetown Public Policy Institute.

Carrier, J., & Heyman, J. (1997). Consumption and political economy. *Journal of the Royal Anthropological Institute*, *3*(2), 355–373.

Cassidy, J. (2013). Why do banks go rogue: Bad culture or lax regulation? *New Yorker*. April 5th. Retrieved from www.newyorker.com/online/blogs/johncassidy/2013/04/why-do-banks-go-rogue-bad-culture-or-bad-regulation.html

Castells, M. (2011). *Networks of outrage and hope: Social movements in the internet age*. Cambridge: Polity Press.

Catalano, R., Berglund, L., Ryan, J., Lonczak, H., & Hawkins, D. (2004). Positive youth development in the United States. *Annals of the American Academy of Political and Social Science*, *591*, 98–124.

CAU – Collettivo Autorganizzato Universitario. (2012). We are choosy: We choose to fight! Retrieved from http://caunapoli.org/index.php?option=com_content&view=article&id=1207:choosy-fornero-profumo-napoli&catid=43:iniziative&Itemid=89

Cavalli, A., & Galland, O. (Eds.). (1993). *L'allongement de la jeunesse*. Poitiers: Actes Sud-Observatoire du Changement Social.

Cazes, S., Khatiwada, S., & Malo, M.A. (2012). Employment protection and industrial relations: Recent trends and labour market impact. In *World of work report 2012* (pp. 35–58). Geneva: ILO.

CBI – Confederation of British Industry. (2011a). Making the first year count. Retrieved from www.cbi.org.uk/campaigns/getting-the-uk-working/making-the-first-year-count-improving-the-position-of-young-people-in-the-jobs-market/

CBI. (2011b). *Action for jobs: How to get the UK working*. London: CBI.

CBI. (2011c). CBI responds to government's youth unemployment package. Retrieved from www.cbi.org.uk/media-centre/press-releases/2011/11/cbi-responds-to-governments-youth-unemployment-package/

CEDI-Unitierra. (2012). Center for Intercultural Encounters and Dialogue. Retrieved from www.mirovni-institut.si/labour/cied.html

Chan, K. (2010). The global financial crisis and migrant workers in China. *International Journal of Urban and Regional Research*, *34*(3), 659–677.

Chessum, M. (2011). Tuition fees go-ahead marks the betrayal of a generation. *Guardian*. July 13th. Retrieved from www.theguardian.com/commentisfree/2011/jul/13/tuition-fees-privatisation-education

Chinn, S. (2009). *Inventing modern adolescence: The children of immigrants in turn-of-the-century America*. New Brunswick: Rutgers University Press.

Chirimbu, S., Vasilescu, R., & Barbu-Chirimbu, A. (2011). European youth is the Union's most valuable resource. Retrieved from http://papers.ssrn.com/sol3/papers.cfm?abstract_id=1850888

Choudry, A., & Shragge, E. (2013). The 2012 student strike: Many lessons were learned and taught. *Social Policy*, spring issue, 11–14.

Christiansen, S., & Scarlett, Z. (Eds.). (2013). *The Third World in the global 1960s*. New York: Berghahn.

Chudacoff, H. (1989). *How old are you? Age consciousness in American culture*. Princeton: Princeton University Press.

Cieslik, M., & Simpson, D. (2013). *Key concepts in youth studies*. London: Sage.

Clark, D. (2011. Do recessions keep students in school? The impact of youth unemployment on enrolment in post-compulsory education in England. *Economica*, *78*(311), 523–545.

Clarke, G. (2005). Defending ski-jumpers: A critique of theories of youth subcultures. In K. Gelder (Ed.), *The subcultures reader* (pp. 169–174). 2nd edn. London: Routledge.

Clarke, J., Hall, S., Jefferson, T., & Roberts, B. (1975). Subculture, cultures and class. In S. Hall & T. Jefferson (Eds.), *Resistance through rituals* (pp. 9–74). Milton Keynes: Open University Press.

CLASSE. (2012). *Share our future: The CLASSE manifesto*. Retrieved from www.stopthehike.ca/2012/07/share-our-future-the-classe-manifesto/

Clauwaert, S., & Schömann, I. (2012). *The crisis and national labour law reforms: A mapping exercise*. European Trade Union Institute Working Paper 2012.04. Brussels: ETUI.

Clinton, H. (2012). Town hall with Tunisian youth. February 25th. Retrieved from www.state.gov/secretary/rm/2012/02/184656.htm

CNBC. (2013). *The college debt crisis – Special report*. Retrieved from www.cnbc.com/id/40682477

Cobble, D.S. (1991). *Dishing it out: Waitresses and their unions in the twentieth century*. Urbana: University of Illinois Press.

Cohen, P., & Ainley, P. (2000). In the country of the blind? Youth studies and cultural studies in Britain. *Journal of Youth Studies*, *3*(1), 79–95.

Cohen, R. (2002). The many meanings of the FSM. In R. Cohen & R. Zelnik (Eds.), *The free speech movement: Reflections on Berkeley in the 1960s* (pp. 1–53). Berkeley: University of California Press.

Cohen, R., & Zelnik, R. (Eds.). (2002). *The free speech movement: Reflections on Berkeley in the 1960s*. Berkeley: University of California Press.

Cole, T. (1992). *The journey of life*. Cambridge: Cambridge University Press.

Collins, J. (2003). *Threads: Gender, labor and power in the global apparel industry*. Chicago: University of Chicago Press.

Comaroff, J., & Comaroff, J. (2005). Reflections on youth, from the past to the postcolony. In A. Honnana & F. De Boeck (Eds.), *Makers and breakers: Children and youth in postcolonial Africa* (pp. 267–281). Oxford: James Currey.

Common Dreams. (2012). Massive crowds as Spaniards protest stripping of labor rights. February 19th. Retrieved from https://www.commondreams.org/headline/2012/02/19-1

Cook, D., & Kaiser, S. (2004). Betwixt and be tween: Age ambiguity and the sexualization of the female consuming subject. *Journal of Consumer Culture*, *4*(2), 203–227.

Cooley, A., & Cooley, A. (2009). From diploma mills to for-profit colleges and universities. *Southern California Interdisciplinary Law Journal*, *505*, 505–526.

Connery, C. (2011). Marches through the institutions: University activism in the sixties and present. *Representations, 116*, 88–106.

Connolly, K. (2013). Angela Merkel: Youth unemployment is most pressing problem facing Europe. *Guardian*, July 2nd. Retrieved from www.guardian.co.uk/world/2013/jul/02/angela-merkel-youth-unemployment-europe

Cornell, R. (1982). *Revolutionary vanguard: The early years of the Communist Youth International, 1914–1924*. Toronto: University of Toronto Press.

Corujo, B.S. (2013). Crisis and labour market in Spain. Presentation at Labour Law Research Network Conference, June 13th, Pompeu Fabra University, Barcelona, Spain.

COSATU. (2012). *The youth wage subsidy in South Africa: Response of the Congress of South African Trade Unions*. Johannesburg: COSATU.

Côté, J. (2000). *Arrested adulthood: The changing nature of maturity and identity*. New York: New York University Press.

Côté, J. (2013). Towards a new political economy of youth. *Journal of Youth Studies*. DOI: 10.1080/13676261.2013.836592.

Côté, J. (2014). *Youth studies: Fundamental issues and debates*. New York: Palgrave Macmillan.

Côté, J., & Bynner, J. (2008). Changes in the transition to adulthood in the UK and Canada: The role of structure and agency in emerging adulthood. *Journal of Youth Studies, 11*(3), 251–268.

Coussée, F. (2008). *A century of youth work policy*. Gent: Academia Press.

Coussée, F., Roets, G., & De Bie, M. (2009). Empowering the powerful: Challenging hidden processes of marginalization in youth work policy and practice in Belgium. *Critical Social Policy, 29*(3), 421–442.

Coy, P. (2009). The lost generation. *Bloomberg Businessweek*. October 8th. Retrieved from http://businessweek.com/magazine/content/09_42/b4151032038302.htm

Coy, P. (2011). The youth unemployment bomb. *Bloomberg Businessweek*. February 2nd. Retrieved from www.businessweek.com/magazine/content/11_07/b4215058743638.htm

Crispe, I. (2013). Union slams Foodstuffs over youth wage. *3News*. May 1st. Retrieved from www.3news.co.nz/Union-slams-Foodstuffs-over-youth-wage/tabid/423/articleID/296157/Default.aspx

Crouch, C. (2011). *The strange non-death of neoliberalism*. Cambridge: Polity Press.

Croucher, R., & White, G. (2011). The impact of minimum wages on the youth labour market: An international literature review for the Low Pay Commission. Retrieved from www.lowpay.gov.uk/lowpay/research/pdf/CroucherWhiteFinal.pdf

Cruz, T. (2010). Students protest 2000-percent tuition fee hike in Philippines' biggest state university. *Asian Correspondent.com*. March 19th. Retrieved from http://asiancorrespondent.com/30045/students-protest-2000-percent-tuition-fee-hike-in-philippines-biggest-state-university/

Cultural Anthropology. (2011). Virtual issue: Youth. Retrieved from www.culanth.org/?q=node/396

Cunningham, A., & Kienzl, G. (2011). *Delinquency: The untold story of student loan borrowing*. Washington, DC: Institute for Higher Education Policy.

Cupers, K. (2008). Governing through nature: Camps and youth movements in interwar Germany and the United States. *Cultural Geographies, 15*, 173–205.

Curran, J., Fenton, N., & Freedman, D. (Eds.). (2012). *Misunderstanding the internet*. New York: Routledge.

Dahi, O. (2012). The political economy of the Egyptian and Arab revolt. *IDS Bulletin*, *43*(1), 47–53.

Damon, W. (2004). What is positive youth development? *Annals of the American Academy of Political and Social Science*, *591*, 13–24.

Damon, W., & Gregory, A. (2003). Bringing in a new era in the field of youth development. In R. Lerner, F. Jacobs, & D. Wertlieb (Eds.), *Handbook of applied developmental science, Vol. 1* (pp. 407–420). Thousand Oaks, CA: Sage.

Davidson, C. (Ed.). (2011). *Revolutionary youth and the new working class*. Pittsburgh: Changemaker Publications.

Davies, A. (2007). *The gangs of Manchester: The story of the Scuttlers, Britain's first youth cult*. Preston: Milo Books.

Debies-Carl, J. (2013). Are the kids alright? A critique and agenda for taking youth cultures seriously. *Social Science Information*, *52*(1), 110–133.

Delclós, C., & Viejo, R. (2012). Beyond the indignation: Spain's Indignados and the political agenda. *Policy & Practice*, 15. Retrieved from www.developmenteducationreview.com/issue15-perspectives4?page=2

Delpit, L. (1995). *Other people's children: Cultural conflict in the classroom*. New York: New Press.

Deluzio, C. (2007) *Female adolescence in American scientific thought, 1830–1930*. Baltimore: Johns Hopkins Press.

Deming, D., Goldin, C., & Katz, L. (2012). The for-profit postsecondary school sector: Nimble critters or agile predators? *Journal of Economic Perspectives*, *26*(1), 139–164.

Democratic Left Front. (2012). South African youth wage subsidy a false solution. *Pambazuka News*. June 14th. Retrieved from http://pambazuka.org/en/category/features/82929

Denhart, C. (2013). How the $1.2 trillion college debt crisis is crippling students, parents and the economy. *Forbes*. August 7th. Retrieved from www.forbes.com/sites/specialfeatures/2013/08/07/how-the-college-debt-is-crippling-students-parents-and-the-economy/

De Ras, M. (2008). *Body, feminity and nationalism: Girls in the German youth movement 1900–1934*. London: Routledge.

Dhillon, N., & Yousef, T. (2009). *Generation in waiting: The unfulfilled promise of young people in the Middle East*. Washington, DC: Brookings Institution Press.

Dolby, N., & Rizvi, F. (Eds.). (2008). *Youth moves: Identities and education in global perspective*. New York: Routledge.

Donadia, R. (2011). Europe's young grow agitated over future prospects. *New York Times*. January 1st. Retrieved from www.nytimes.com/2011/01/02/world/europe/02youth.html?pagewanted=all&_r=0

Dore, R. (1976). *The diploma disease*. Berkeley: University of California Press.

Doswett, S. (2012). Tens of thousands of Spaniards protest labor reform. Reuters. March 11th. Retrieved from http://uk.reuters.com/article/2012/03/11/us-spain-labour-idUSBRE82A08S20120311.

Dougherty, K. (1994). *The contradictory college*. Albany: SUNY Press.

Douglas, J. (1970). *Youth in turmoil*. Chevy Chase, MD: National Institute of Mental Health.

Draper, H. (1965). *Berkeley: The new student revolt*. New York: Grove Press.

Drine, I. (2012). Youth unemployment and the Arab spring. *Making It Magazine*. November 17th. Retrieved from www.makingitmagazine.net/?p=6094

Drori, I. (2000). *The seam line: Arab workers and Jewish managers in the Israeli textile industry*. Stanford: Stanford University Press.

Dubas, J., Miller, K., & Petersen, A. (2003). The study of adolescence during the 20th century. *History of the Family, 8*, 375–397.

Dublin, T. (1975). Women, work, and the family: Female operatives in the Lowell mills, 1830–1860. *Feminist Studies, 3*(1/2), 30–39.

Dublin, T. (1981). *Women at work: The transformation of work and community in Lowell, Massachusetts, 1826–1860.* New York: Columbia University Press.

Duda, A. (2010). *When 'it's time' to say 'enough!':Youth activism before and during the Rose and Orange Revolutions in Georgia and Ukraine.* PhD Dissertation, University of Birmingham.

Dueck, J. (2007). A Muslim jamboree: Scouting and youth culture in Lebanon under the French mandate. *French Historical Studies, 30*(3), 485–516.

Durham, D. (2004). Disappearing youth: Youth as a social shifter in Botswana. *American Ethnologist, 31*(4), 589–605.

Economic Voice. (2013). Business engagement with schools is crucial to beat youth unemployment. December 13th. Retrieved from www.economicvoice.com/cipd-business-engagement-with-schools-is-crucial-to-beat-youth-unemployment/

Economist. (2013). Generation jobless. April 27th. Retrieved from www.economist.com/news/international/21576657-around-world-almost-300m-15-24-year-olds-are-not-working-what-has-caused

Egesberg, M. (2012). Is Spain's youth unemployment really as bad as they say? *Business Daily.eu.* August 3rd. Retrieved from http://businessdaily.eu/is-spains-youth-unemployment-really-as-bad-as-they-say/

Ehrenreich, B. (2009). *Bright-sided: How the relentless promotion of positive thinking has undermined America.* New York: Metropolitan Books.

Eisenbichler, K. (2002). *The premodern teenager: Youth in society 1150–1650.* Toronto: University of Toronto Press.

Eisenstadt, S.N. (1971). Contemporary student rebellions: Intellectual rebellion and generational conflict. *Acta Sociologica, 14*(3), 169–182.

Elkar, R. (1995). Young Germans and Young Germany. In M. Roseman (Ed.), *Generations in conflict: Youth revolt and generation formation in Germany, 1770–1968* (pp. 69–91). Cambridge: Cambridge University Press.

El Shakry, O. (2011). Youth as peril and promise: The emergence of adolescent psychology in postwar Egypt. *International Journal of Middle East Studies, 43*, 591–610.

Elson, D. (Ed.). (1995). *Male bias in the development process.* Manchester: Manchester University Press.

Enright, R., Levy, V., Harris, D., & Lapsley, D. (1987). Do economic conditions influence how theorists view adolescents? *Journal of Youth and Adolescence, 16*(6), 541–559.

Enríquez, C.G. (2013). Youth unemployment in Spain. Real Instituto Elcano Expert Comment 31. Retrieved from www.isn.ethz.ch/Digital-Library/Publications/Detail/?ots591=0c54e3b3-1e9c-be1e-2c24-a6a8c7060233&lng=en&id=163703

Erikson, E. (1968). *Identity, youth and crisis.* New York: W.W. Norton.

European Commission. (2010). *Employment in Europe 2010.* Brussels: European Commission.

Eurostat. (2013). Unemployment by sex, age and nationality. Retrieved from http://appsso.eurostat.ec.europa.eu/nui/show.do?dataset=lfsq_ugan&lang=en.

Ewen, S. (1976). *Captains of consciousness.* New York: Basic Books.

Falk, K., & Nissan, L. (2007). *A vision for and brief history of youth philanthropy.* Arlington: Association of Fundraising Professionals.

Fantasia, R. (1995). Fast food in France. *Theory and Society, 24*(2), 201–243.

Farrukh, S. (2012). Youth unemployment: A ticking time bomb. *Business Recorder.* September 26th. Retrieved from www.brecorder.com/supplements/88/1242228/

Fasick, F. (1994). On the 'invention' of adolescence. *Journal of Early Adolescence, 14*(1), 6–23.

Fass, P. (2008). Childhood and youth as an American/global experience in the context of the past. In J. Cole & D. Durham (Eds.), *Figuring the future* (pp. 25–47). Santa Fe: SAR Press.

FCYO – Funders' Collaborative on Youth Organizing. (2013). About FCYO. Retrieved from www.fcyo.org/aboutfcyo

Feiler, B. (2011). *Generation freedom: The Middle East uprisings and the remaking of the modern world.* New York: HarperCollins.

Feixa, C. (2012). Leisure. In N. Lesko & S. Talburt (Eds.), *Keywords in youth studies* (pp. 39–44). New York: Routledge.

Feixa, C. (2013). The #spanishrevolution and beyond. *Cultural Anthropology.* February 14th. Retrieved from http://culanth.org/fieldsights/68-the-spanishrevolution-and-beyond

Ferguson, K. (2007). Organizing the ghetto: The Ford Foundation, CORE and white power in the black power era, 1967–1969. *Journal of Urban History, 34*(1), 67–100.

Ferguson, N. (2011). The global temper tantrum. *Newsweek.* July 11th. Retrieved from www.newsweek.com/ferguson-global-temper-tantrum-68403

Feuer, L. (1969). *The conflict of generations: The character and significance of student movements.* New York: Basic Books.

Feuer, L. (1972). Student unrest in the United States. *Annals of the American Academy of Political and Social Science, 404*, 170–182.

Fillieule, O. (2013). Age and social movements. In D. Snow, D. Della Porta, B. Klandermans, & D. McAdam (Eds.), *Wiley-Blackwell encyclopedia of social and political movements* (pp. 1–3). London: John Wiley & Sons.

Finn, J. (2001). Text and turbulence: Representing adolescence as pathology in the human services. *Childhood, 8*(2), 167–191.

Fishman, J., & Solomon, F. (1964). Youth and social action: An introduction. *Journal of Social Issues, 20*(1), 1–27.

Fix, M. et al. (2009). *Migration and the global recession.* Washington, DC: Migration Policy Institute.

Flacks, R. (1967). The liberated generation: An exploration of the roots of student protest. *Journal of Social Issues, 23*(3), 52–75.

Flacks, R. (1971). *Youth and social change.* Chicago: Markham.

Fleetwood, S. (2008). Workers and their alter egos as consumers. *Capital & Class, 94*, 31–47.

Flores, H. (2013). Tuition, other fees up in 1,257 schools. *Philippine Star.* May 28th. Retrieved from www.philstar.com/headlines/2013/05/28/947197/tuition-other-fees-1257-schools

Foner, P. (1977). *The factory girls.* Urbana: University of Illinois Press.

Forland, T., Korsvik, T., & Christophersen, K. (2010). Protest and parents: A retrospective survey of sixties student radicals in Norway. *Acta Sociologica, 53*(3), 229–245.

Fornero, E. (2013). Italy's reforms are bearing fruit. *Wall Street Journal.* June 5th. Retrieved from http://online.wsj.com/article/SB10001424127887324063304578525231668975390.html

Forstater, M. (2010). *Implications of the global financial and economic crisis on the textile and clothing sector.* Geneva: ILO.

Foster, J. (1969). *Protest! Student activism in America.* New York: Morrow.

Frayer, L. (2012). In Spain, millions join strike to protest labor reforms. *Los Angeles Times.* March 29th. Retrieved from http://articles.latimes.com/2012/mar/29/world/la-fg-spain-austerity-strike-20120330

Freeman, R. (1976). *The over-educated American*. New York: Academic.

Fridell, G. (2007). Fair-trade coffee and commodity fetishism: The limits of market-driven social justice. *Historical Materialism, 15*, 79–104.

Friedman, T. (2004). Doing our homework. *New York Times*. June 24th. Retrieved from www.nytimes.com/2004/06/24/opinion/doing-our-homework.html

Friedman, T. (2011). The clash of generations. *New York Times*. July 16th. Retrieved from www.nytimes.com/2011/07/17/opinion/sunday/17friedman.html?_r=0

Fritsch, K. (2010). Occupy everything: A roundtable on US student occupations. *Upping the Anti*. Retrieved from http://uppingtheanti.org/journal/article/10-occupy-everything-a-roundtable-on-us-student-occupations/

Fuchs, C. (2012). Social media, riots and revolutions. *Capital & Class, 36*(3), 383–391.

Fuerst, J. (2010). Youth. In S. Pons & R. Service (Eds.), *A dictionary of 20th-century communism*. Princeton: Princeton University Press.

Fuller, G. (2003). *The youth factor: The new demographics of the Middle East and the implications for US policy*. Washington, DC: Brookings.

Fuller, G., & Pitts, F. (1990). Youth cohorts and political unrest in South Korea. *Political Geography Quarterly, 9*(1), 9–22.

Furlong, A. (2006). Not a very NEET solution: Representing problematic labour market transitions among early school-leavers. *Work, Employment & Society, 20*(3), 553–569.

Furlong, A. (Ed.). (2009). *Handbook of youth and young adulthood*. New York: Routledge.

Furlong, A. (2012). *Youth studies: An introduction*. London: Routledge.

Furlong, A., & Cartmel, F. (2007). *Young people and social change*. 2nd edn. Buckingham: Open University Press.

Furlong, A., Woodman, D., & Wyn, J. (2011). Changing times, changing perspectives: Reconciling 'transition' and 'cultural' perspectives on youth and young adulthood. *Journal of Sociology, 47*(4), 355–370.

Gaudet, S. (2007). *Emerging adulthood: A new stage in the life course*. Ottawa: Government of Canada.

Gavin, M. (2007). Africa's restless youth. *Current History*, May issue, 220–226.

Generations United. (2011). Unemployment struggles affect all ages. *Together*. November 9th. Retrieved from http://generationsunited.blogspot.co.uk/2011/11/unemployment-struggles-affect-all-ages.html

Georgiopoulos, G., & Behrakis, Y. (2013). Greek March unemployment rises, youth hardest hit. *Reuters*. June 6th. Retrieved from http://uk.reuters.com/article/2013/06/06/uk-greece-unemployment-idUKBRE9550I420130606.

Gibson, D. et al. (2012). Generations united for a better society. *Guardian*. September 30th. Retrieved from www.theguardian.com/society/2012/sep/30/generations-united-for-better-society

Gillis, J. (1974). *Youth and history: Tradition and change in European age relations, 1770-Present*. New York: Academic Press.

Ginwright, S., & Cammarota, J. (2002). New terrain in youth development. *Social Justice, 29*(4), 82–95.

Ginwright, S., Noguera, P., & Cammarota, J. (Eds.). (2006). *Beyond resistance! Youth activism and community change*. New York: Routledge.

Gitlin, T. (1993). *The sixties: Years of hope, days of rage*. New York: Bantam.

Goldberg, P.J., & Riddy, F. (Eds.). (2004). *Youth in the Middle Ages*. York: York Medieval Press.

Golden, I. (2012). DA youth wage subsidy march turns violent. *Wits Vuvuzela*. May 15th. Retrieved from http://witsvuvuzela.com/2012/05/15/da-youth-wage-subsidy-march-turns-violent/

Goldsen, R., Rosenberg, M., Williams, R., & Suchman, E. (1960). *What college students think.* Princeton: Van Nostrand.

Goldstone, J. (2002). Population and security: How demographic change can lead to violent conflict. *Journal of International Affairs, 56*(1), 3–22.

Goldthorpe, J., & Jackson, M. (2008). Education-based meritocracy. In A. Lareau & D. Conley (Eds.), *Social Class* (pp. 93–117). New York: Russell Sage.

Goretti, L., & Worley, M. (2012). Introduction: Communist youth, communist generations: A reappraisal. *20th Century Communism, 4*: 5–13.

Gorsuch, A. (2000). *Youth in revolutionary Russia: Enthusiasts, bohemians, delinquents.* Bloomington: Indiana University Press.

Goyette, K. (2008). College for some to college for all: Social background, occupational expectations and educational expectations over time. *Social Science Research, 37,* 461–484.

GPYD – Global Partnership for Youth Development. (2004). *Global Partnership for Youth Development.* Retrieved from www.bpdweb.com/gpyd/.

Gramsci, A. (1998). *Selections from the prison notebooks.* London: Lawrence & Wishart.

Grant, J. (1969). *Confrontation on campus.* New York: New American Library.

Gray, J. (2012). New youth wage 'condemns them to poverty.' *New Zealand Herald.* October 9th. Retrieved from www.nzherald.co.nz/business/news/article.cfm?c_id=3& objectid=10839349

Green, A. (1990). *Education and state formation.* New York: St Martin's Press.

Green, D., King, R., & Miller-Dawkins, M. (2010). *The global economic crisis and developing countries.* Oxford: Oxfam.

Green, L. (2003). Notes on Mayan youth and rural industrialization in Guatemala. *Critique of Anthropology, 23*(1), 51–73.

Greenberger, E., & Steinberg, L. (1986). *When teenagers work: The psychological and social costs of adolescent employment.* New York: Basic Books.

Griffin, C. (1993). *Representations of youth.* Cambridge: Polity Press.

Griffin, C. (1997). Youth research in the 1990s: Time for (another) rethink. *Sociological Research Online.* Retrieved from www.socresonline.or.uk/2/4/griffin.html

Gross, D. (2007). The golden ass. *Slate.* June 19th. Retrieved from www.slate.com/articles/business/moneybox/2007/06/the_golden_ass.html

Grossberg, L. (2001). Why does neo-liberalism hate kids? The war on youth and the culture of politics. *Review of Education/Pedagogy/Cultural Studies, 23*(2), 111–136.

Grubb, N., & Lazerson, M. (2005). *The education gospel.* Cambridge: Harvard University Press.

Gruber, J., Milligan, K., & Wise, D. (2009). *Social security programs and retirement around the world: The relationship to youth employment.* Working Paper 14647. Cambridge, MA: National Bureau of Economic Research.

Guardian. (2012). The graduate without a future. Comment is Free Series. Retrieved from www.guardian.co.uk/commentisfree/series/the-graduate-without-a-future

Gyimah-Brempong, K., & Kimenyi, M. (2013). *Youth policy and the future of African development.* Washington, DC: Brookings.

Hadjimatheou, C. (2012). Wasted talent: Greece's young unemployed majority. *BBC News.* March 23rd. Retrieved from www.bbc.co.uk/news/world-europe-17464528

Halaseh, R. (2012). Civil society, youth and the Arab spring. In S. Calleya & M. Wohlfield (Eds.), *Change and opportunities in the emerging Mediterranean* (pp. 253–272). Msida: University of Malta Press.

Hall, G.S. (1904). *Adolescence*. New York: Appleton.

Hall, S. et al. (1976). Youth: A stage in life? *Youth in Society, 17*, 17–19.

Halliday, F. (1969). Students of the world unite. In A. Cockburn & R. Blackburn (Eds.), *Student power: Problems, diagnosis, solution* (pp. 287–326). Harmondsworth: Penguin.

Hallward, P. (2012). Quebec's student protesters give UK activists a lesson. *Guardian*. June 1st. Retrieved from www.theguardian.com/commentisfree/2012/jun/01/quebec-protests-student-activists

Hanieh, A. (2009). Hierarchies of a global market: The South and the economic crisis. *Studies in Political Economy, 83*, 61–84.

Hanna, E. (2008). The English student movement: An evaluation of the literature. *Sociology Compass, 2*(5), 1539–1552.

Hardt, M., & Negri, A. (2011). Arabs are democracy's new pioneers. *Guardian*. February 24th. Retrieved from www.theguardian.com/commentisfree/2011/feb/24/arabs-democracy-latin-america

Harris, A., Wyn, J., & Younes, S. (2010). Beyond apathetic or activist youth: 'Ordinary' young people and contemporary forms of participation. *Young, 18*(1), 9–32.

Harvey, D. (2005). *A brief history of neoliberalism*. Oxford: Oxford University Press.

Harvey, D. (2009). Is this really the end of neoliberalism? *Counterpunch*. March 13th. Retrieved from www.counterpunch.org/2009/03/13/is-this-really-the-end-of-neoliberalism/

Harvey, E. (2005). The cult of youth. In G. Martel (Ed.), *A companion to Europe 1900–1945* (pp. 66–81). Oxford: Blackwell.

Heath, T. (2012). The secret of joy: Six lessons from Quebec's maple spring. *Truthout*. June 8th. Retrieved from http://truth-out.org/opinion/item/9671-the-secret-of-joy-six-lessons-from-quebecs-maple-spring

Hebdige, D. (1979). *Subculture: The meaning of style*. New York: Routledge.

Hebdige, D. (1988). *Hiding in the light*. New York: Routledge.

Heer, F. (1974). *Challenge of youth*. Tuscaloosa: University of Alabama Press.

Heidkamp, M., Corre, N., & Van Horn, C. (2010). *The 'new unemployables': Older job seekers struggle to find work during the great recession*. Chestnut Hill, MA: Sloan Center on Aging & Work.

Heirich, M. (1971). *The spiral of conflict: Berkeley 1964*. New York: Columbia University Press.

Heller, D., & Callender, C. (Eds.). (2013). *Student financing of higher education: A comparative perspective*. New York: Routledge.

Hendrixson, A. (2003). The 'youth bulge': Defining the next generation of young men as a threat to the future. *Different Takes, 19*, 1–4.

Hendrixson, A. (2012). The 'new population bomb' is a dud. *Differen Takes, 75*, 1–4.

Heyes, J., & Lewis, P. (2012). Employment protection under fire: Why labour market deregulation will not deliver quality jobs. Paper presented at the SPERI Conference, University of Sheffield, July 16th.

Heywood, C. (2010). Centuries of childhood: An anniversary – and an epitaph? *Journal of the History of Childhood and Youth, 3*(3), 341–365.

Hill, J. (2011). Endangered childhoods: How consumerism is impacting child and youth identity. *Media, Culture & Society, 33*(3), 347–362.

Hill, S. (2012). Youth unemployment is overstated. *Social Europe Journal*. July 25th. Retrieved from www.social-europe.eu/2012/07/youth-unemployment-is-overstated/

Hinton-Smith, T. (Ed.). (2013). *Widening participation in higher education: Casting the net wide?* Houndmills: Palgrave Macmillan.

Hoffman, D. (2010). Risky investments: Parenting and the production of the 'resilient' child. *Health, Risk and Society, 12*(4), 385–394.

Hollingshead, A.B. (1949). *Elmtown's youth.* New York: Science Editions.

Holmwood, J. (Ed.). (2011). *A manifesto for the public university.* London: Bloomsbury.

Honwana, A. (2012). 'Desenrascar a vide': Youth employment and transitions to adulthood. Conference Paper No. 29, Instituto de Estudos Sociais e Económicos, Maputo.

Honwana, A. (2013). Youth, waithood and protest movements in Africa. *African Arguments.* Retrieved from http://africanarguments.org/2013/08/12/youth-waithood-and-protest-movements-in-africa-by-alcinda-honwana/

Horn, G. (2007). *The spirit of '68: Rebellion in Western Europe and North America, 1956–1976.* Oxford: Oxford University Press.

Horne, J. (1986). Continuity and change in the state regulation and schooling of unemployed youth. In S. Walker & L. Barton (Eds.), *Youth, unemployment & schooling* (pp. 9–28). Milton Keynes: Oxford University Press.

Hosang, D. (2003). *Youth and community organizing today.* New York: Funders' Collaborative on Youth Organizing.

Howard, P., & Hussain, M. (2011). The upheavals in Egypt and Tunisia: The role of digital media. *Journal of Democracy, 22*(3), 35–48.

Howker, E., & Malik, S. (2010). *Jilted generation: How Britain has bankrupted its youth.* London: Icon Books.

Huang, Y. (2013). China's educated underemployment. EAI Background Brief No. 787. Retrieved from www.eai.nus.edu.sg/BB787.pdf

Hughes, N. (2011). 'Young people took to the streets and all of a sudden all of the political parties got old': The 15M movement in Spain. *Social Movement Studies, 10*(4), 407–413.

Humphreys, G. (2011). Racial discrimination and the global economic downturn. *World of Work, 72,* 9–12.

Huntingdon, S. (1996). *The clash of civilizations and the remaking of world order.* New York: Simon & Schuster.

Hvistendahl, M. (2011). Young and restless can be a volatile mix. *Science, 333,* 552–554.

Ibrahim, G. (2012). Testimonies of statements by professors on the American University of Cairo strike. *Al-Masryalyom.* September 24th. (In Arabic)

IDB & IFC – Islamic Development Bank & International Finance Corporation. (2012). *Education for employment: Realizing Arab youth potential.* Washington, DC: IFC.

ILO – International Labour Organization. (2009). *Global employment trends.* Geneva: ILO.

ILO. (2010). *Global employment trends for youth: Special issue on the impact of the global economic crisis on youth.* Geneva: ILO.

ILO. (2011). *Tackling youth unemployment challenges.* Turin: ILO.

ILO. (2012a). *Global employment trends for youth 2012.* Geneva: ILO.

ILO. (2012b). *The youth employment crisis: Time for action.* Geneva: ILO

ILO. (2013). *Global employment trends 2013.* Geneva: ILO.

International Student Movement. (2011). Education protests worldwide (September 2011). Retrieved from http://ism-global.net/protests_worldwide_sept2011

International Student Movement. (2012). Education protests worldwide (June 2012). Retrieved from http://ism-global.net/protests_worldwide_june2012

Irby, M. (Ed.). (2001). *Lessons learned, lessons shared: Reflections from the International Learning Group on youth and community development*. New York: Ford Foundation.

Issa, K. (2010). Student protests at the American University of Beirut: Identity, class and romanticism. *Al-Akhbar*. June 2nd. (In Arabic.)

IYF – International Youth Foundation. (2013a). IYF history. Retrieved from www.iyfnet.org/iyf-history

IYF. (2013b). Our global network. Retrieved from www.iyfnet.org/partners

IYF. (2013c). *Youth Livelihoods Alliance*. Retrieved from http://library.iyfnet.org/sites/default/files/library/2013_YLA_factSheet.pdf

Jacobs, A. (2010). China's army of graduates struggles for jobs. *New York Times*. December 11th. Retrieved from www.nytimes.com/2010/12/12/world/asia/12beijing.html?pagewanted=all&_r=0

Jaji, Z. (2012). Waithood and the coming revolution. *Leadership Magazine*. November 18th. Retrieved from http://leadership.ng/nga/zainab_jaji/40351/2012/11/18/waithood_and_coming_revolution.html?quicktabs_3=1

James, A. (1986). Learning to belong. In A. Cohen (Ed.), *Symbolising boundaries* (pp. 155–170). Manchester: Manchester University Press.

Jankowski, J. (1975). *Egypt's young rebels: 'Young Egypt,' 1933–1952*. Stanford: Hoover Institution Press.

Jarausch, K. (1975). Restoring youth to its own history. *History of Education Quarterly, 15*(4), 445–456.

JCWI – Joint Council for the Welfare of Immigrants. (2012). Exploding myths – The link between youth unemployment and immigration. February 8th. Retrieved from www.jcwi.org.uk/2012/02/08/exploding-myths-the-link-between-youth-unemployment-and-immigration

Jeffrey, C. (2009). Fixing futures: Educated unemployment through a North Indian lens. *Comparative Studies in Society and History, 51*(1), 182–211.

Jeffrey, C. (2010a). Geographies of children and youth I: Eroding maps of life. *Progress in Human Geography, 34*(4), 496–505.

Jeffery, C. (2010b). Timepass: Youth, class and time among unemployed young men in India. *American Ethnologist, 37*(3), 465–481.

Jeffrey, C. (2012a). Geographies of children and youth II: Global youth agency. *Progress in Human Geography, 36*(2), 245–253.

Jeffrey, C. (2012b). Geographies of children and youth III: Alchemists of the revolution? *Progress in Human Geography*, DOI: 10.1177/0309132511434902.

Jeffrey, C., & Dyson, J. (Eds.). (2008). *Telling young lives: Portraits of global youth*. Philadelphia: Temple University Press.

Jeffrey, C., & Young, S. (2012). Waiting for change: Youth, caste and politics in India. *Economy and Society, 41*(4), 638–661.

Jeffrey, C., Jeffery, P., & Jeffery, R. (2008). *Degrees without freedom? Education, masculinities and unemployment in Northern India*. Stanford: Stanford University Press.

Jenkins, P. (2013). Salz attacks warped top pay at Barclays. *Financial Times*. April 3rd. Retrieved from www.ft.com/cms/s/0/68c2c83c-9c40-11e2-ba3c-00144feabdc0.html#axzz2TWmbWlKF

Jeszeck, C. (2012). Unemployed older workers. Testimony before the Special Committee on Aging, US Senate, May 15th. Washington, DC: US Government Accountability Office.

Jobs, R. (2009). Youth movements: Travel, protest, and Europe in 1968. *American Historical Review*, 376–404.

Johansson, T., & Lalander, P. (2012). Doing resistance – Youth and changing theories of resistance. *Journal of Youth Studies, 15*(8), 1078–1088.

Johnson, R. (1979). 'Really useful knowledge': Radical education and working-class culture, 1790–1848. In J. Clarke, C. Critcher, & R. Johnson (Eds.), *Working-class culture* (pp. 75–102). London: Hutchinson.

Johnson-Hanks, J. (2002). On the limits of life stages in ethnography: The theory of vital conjunctures. *American Anthropologist, 104*(3), 865–880.

Johnstone, B., & Marcucci, P. (2010). *Financing higher education worldwide: Who pays? Who should pay?* Baltimore: Johns Hopkins University Press.

Joksic, M., & Spoerri, M. (2011). From resistance to revolution and back again: What Egyptian youth can learn from Otpor! when its activists leave Tahrir Square. Retrieved from www.carnegiecouncil.org/publications/articles_papers_reports/0087.html

Jones, G. (2009). *Youth.* Cambridge: Polity Press.

Jones, G., & Wallace, C. (1992). *Youth, family and citizenship.* Buckingham: Open University Press.

Jorgensen, T. (2009). The purest flame of the revolution: Working class youth and left wing radicalism in Germany and Italy during the Great War. *Labor History, 50*(1), 19–38.

Joya, A., Bond, P., El-Amine, R., Hanieh, A., & Henaway, M. (2012). *The Arab revolts against neoliberalism.* Toronto: Socialist Project.

JSF – Juventud Sin Futuro. (2013). We are not leaving, they are kicking us out. April 7th. Retrieved from www.jsfviena.net/en/que-reclamos

Junior Achievement. (2008). *JA Worldwide 2006–2007 annual report.* Colorado Springs: Junior Achievement.

Junior Achievement of Africa. (2013). Our supporters. Retrieved from http://jainafrica.org/our_supporters

Juris, J. (2012). Reflections on #occupy everywhere: Social media, public space and emerging logics of aggregation. *American Ethnologist, 39*(2), 259–279.

Kahane, R. (1997). *The origins of postmodern youth: Informal youth movements in comparative perspective.* New York: de Gruyter.

Kalman, S. (2003). Faisceau visions of physical and moral transformation and the cult of youth in inter-war France. *European History Quarterly, 33*(3), 343–366.

Kantor, J. (2013a). Class is seen dividing Harvard Business School. *New York Times.* September 9th. Retrieved from www.nytimes.com/2013/09/10/education/harvard-business-students-see-class-as-divisive-an-issue-as-gender.html?_r=0

Kantor, J. (2013b). Harvard Business School case study: Gender equity. *New York Times.* September 7th. Retrieved from www.nytimes.com/2013/09/08/education/harvard-case-study-gender-equity.html

Kapcia, A. (2005). Educational revolution and revolutionary morality in Cuba: The 'new man', youth and the new 'battle of ideas.' *Journal of Moral Education, 34*(4), 399–412.

Kaplan, R. (1996). *The ends of the earth.* New York: Random House.

Katz, M. (1976). The origins of public education: A reassessment. *History of Education Quarterly, 16*(4), 381–407.

Katz, M. (1995). *Improving poor people.* Princeton: Princeton University Press.

Katz, M., & Davey, I. (1978). School attendance and early industrialization in a Canadian city. *History of Education Quarterly, 18*(3), 271–293.

Kauffman Foundation. (2013a). Kauffman campuses initiative. Retrieved from www.kauffman.org/what-we-do/programs/entrepreneurship/kauffman-campuses-initiative

Kauffman Foundation. (2013b). Who we are. Retrieved from www.kauffman.org/about-foundation/foundation-overview.aspx

Kaveevivitchai, N. (2012). Young people: No jobs. *Bangkok Post*. October 15th. Retrieved from www.bangkokpost.com/learning/learning-from-news/317147/young-people-no-jobs

Kellner, D. (1997). Critical theory and British cultural studies: The missed articulation. In J. McGuigan (Ed.), *Cultural methodologies* (pp. 12–41). London: Sage.

Kelly, P. (2006). The entrepreneurial self and 'youth-at-risk', *Journal of Youth Studies*, 9(1), 17–32.

Keniston, K. (1971). *Youth and dissent: The rise of a new opposition*. New York: Harcourt Brace Jovanovich.

Kennelly, J. (2011). *Citizen youth: Culture, activism and agency in a neoliberal era*. New York: Palgrave Macmillan.

Kett, J. (1993). Discovery and invention in the history of adolescence. *Journal of Adolescent Health*, 14, 605–612.

Kett, J. (2003). Reflections on the history of adolescence in America. *History of the Family*, 8, 355–373.

Khalil, K. (2013). Political youth groups in Egypt post-revolution. *Bidayat*, summer issue.

Kim, J., & Sherman, R. (2006). Youth as important civic actors: From the margins to the center. *National Civic Review*, 124, 3–6.

Kim, S. (1997). *Class struggle or family struggle? The lives of women factory workers in South Korea*. Cambridge: Cambridge University Press.

Kington, T., Roberts, M., Connolly, K., Willsher, K., & Smith, H. (2012). European strikes: who is protesting and why? *Guardian*. November 14th. Retrieved from www.guardian.co.uk/business/2012/nov/14/european-strikes-who-protesting-why

Kirkpatrick, D., & Sanger, D. (2011). A Tunisian-Egyptian link that shook Arab history. *New York Times*. February 13th. Retrieved from www.nytimes.com/2011/02/14/world/middleeast/14egypt-tunisia-protests.html?pagewanted=all&_r=0

Kjeldgaard, D., & Askegaard, S. (2006). The glocalization of youth culture: The global youth segment as structures of common difference. *Journal of Consumer Research*, 33, 231–247.

Klatch, R. (1999). *A generation divided: The new left, the new right, and the 1960s*. Berkeley: University of California Press.

Klein, N. (1999). *No logo*. New York: Picador.

Klimke, M. (2009). *The other alliance: Student protest in West Germany and the United States in the global sixties*. Princeton: Princeton University Press.

Knupfer, A. (2001). *Reform and resistance: Gender, delinquency and America's first juvenile court*. New York: Routledge.

Koon, T. (1985). *Believe, obey, fight: Political socialization of youth in fascist Italy*. Chapel Hill: University of North Carolina Press.

Korany, B., & El Mahdi, R. (Eds.). (2012). *The Arab spring in Egypt: Revolution and beyond*. Cairo: University of Cairo Press.

Kotlikoff, L., & Burns, S. (2012). *The clash of generations*. Cambridge, MA: MIT Press.

Kraftl, P., Horton, J., & Tucker, F. (Eds.). (2012). *Critical geographies of childhood and youth: Contemporary policy and practice*. Bristol: Policy Press.

Krylova, A. (2007). Identity, agency, and the 'first Soviet generation.' In S. Lovell (Ed.), *Generations in twentieth-century Europe* (pp. 101–121). Basingstoke: Palgrave Macmillan.

Kuhar, M., & Reiter, H. (2012). Frozen transitions to adulthood of young people in Slovenia? *Sociologija*, 54(2), 211–226.

Kumar, A. (2011). Achievements and limitations of the UK student movement. In M. Bailey & D. Freedman (Eds.), *The assault on universities* (pp. 132–141). London: Pluto.

Kwon, S.A. (2013). *Uncivil youth: Race, activism and affirmative governmentality*. Durham: Duke University Press.

Lafer, G. (2002). *The job training charade*. Ithaca: Cornell University Press.

Lafrance, X., & Sears, A. (2012). Red square, everywhere: With Quebec student strikers, against repression. *The Bullet*. May 24th. Retrieved from www.socialistproject.ca/bullet/640.php

Lagorio, C. (2007). Marketing to kids. *CBS News*. May 14th. Retrieved from www.cbsnews.com/news/resources-marketing-to-kids/

LaGraffe, D. (2012). The youth bulge in Egypt: An intersection of demographics, security and the Arab spring. *Journal of Strategic Security, 5*(2), 65–80.

Lansley, S. (2012). The solution to youth unemployment lies in the coffers of big business. *Guardian*. 2nd April. Retrieved from www.guardian.co.uk/commentisfree/2012/apr/02/youth-unemployment-contract-scheme

Lanza, F. (2012). Springtime and morning suns: 'Youth' as a political category in twentieth-century China. *Journal of the History of Childhood and Youth, 5*(1), 31–51.

Laqueur, W. (1984). *Young Germany: A history of the German youth movement*. New Brunswick: Transaction.

LEAP Africa. (2013). About LEAP. Retrieved from www.leapafrica.org/index.php/about-leap/our-history

Leccardi, C., & Ruspini, E. (Eds.). (2006). *A new youth? Young people, generations and family life*. Aldershot: Ashgate.

Ledeen, M. (1969). Italian fascism and youth. *Journal of Contemporary History, 4*(3), 137–154.

Leidner, R. (1993). *Fast food, fast talk*. Berkeley: University of California Press.

Lerner, R. (2004). *Liberty: Thriving and civic engagement among America's youth*. Thousand Oaks, CA: Sage.

Lerner, R., & Steinberg, L. (2004). The scientific study of adolescent development. In R. Lerner & L. Steinberg (Eds.), *Handbook of adolescent psychology* (pp. 1–12). 2nd edn. Hoboken, NJ: John Wiley and Sons.

Lesko, N. (1996). Denaturalizing adolescence: The politics of contemporary representations. *Youth & Society, 28*(2), 139–161.

Lesko, N. (2001). *Act your age! A cultural construction of adolescence*. London: Routledge-Falmer.

Lesko, N., & Talburt, S. (Eds.). (2012). *Keywords in youth studies*. New York: Routledge.

Levenson, Z. (2011). Occupying education: The student fight against austerity in California. *NACLA Report on the Americas*, November issue, 25–28.

Levi, G., & Schmitt, J. (Eds.). (1997). *A history of young people in the West*. Cambridge: Harvard University Press.

Levin, H. (1983). Youth unemployment and its educational consequences. *Educational Evaluation and Policy Analysis, 5*(2), 231–247.

Lin, L. (2012). China's graduates face glut. *Wall Street Journal*. August 22nd. Retrieved from http://online.wsj.com/news/articles/SB1000087239639044354550457756675284720 8984

Linn, S. (2004). *Consuming kids: The hostile takeover of childhood*. New York: New Press.

Lipset, S.M. (1971). *Rebellion in the university*. New Brunswick, NJ: Transaction.

Lipset, S.M., & Altbach, P. (Eds.). (1969). *Students in revolt*. Boston: Houghton Mifflin.

Litow, S., & Wyman, N. (2013). Closing the ITC skills gap. *Sydney Morning Herald*. December 6th. Retrieved from www.smh.com.au/national/education/closing-the-itc-skills-gap-20131206-2ywar.html

Livingstone, D. (1999). *The education-jobs gap.* Toronto: Garamond Press.

Livingstone, D. (2009). *Education and jobs: Exploring the gaps.* Toronto: University of Toronto Press.

Lloyd, C. (Ed.). (2005). *Growing up global: The changing transitions to adulthood in developing countries.* Washington, DC: National Academies Press.

Lloyd, C., & Payne, J. (2002). *In search of the high skills society.* SKOPE Research Paper No. 32, University of Warwick.

Locke, C., & Te Lintelo, D. (2012). Young Zambians 'waiting' for opportunities and 'working towards' living well. *Journal of International Development, 24,* 777–794.

Loncle, P., Cuconato, M., Muniglia, V., & Walther, A. (Eds.). (2012). *Youth participation in Europe.* Bristol: Policy Press.

Lounsbury, J. (1998). How the junior high school came to be. In R.J. David (Ed.), *Moving forward from the past* (pp. 110–114). Columbus: National Middle School Association.

Low Pay Commission. (2011). *National minimum wage.* Norwich: The Stationery Office.

Lowrey, A. (2009). Europe's new lost generation. *Foreign Policy.* July 13th. Retrieved from www.foreignpolicy.com/articles/2009/07/13/europes_new_lost_generation

Luke, A. (2012). Creating the quiet majority? Youth and young people in the political culture of the Cuban revolution. *Bulletin of Latin American Research, 9,* 127–143.

Lukose, R. (2005). Consuming globalization: Youth and gender in Kerala, India. *Journal of Social History, 38,* 915–935.

Lüküslü, D. (2005). Constructors and constructed: Youth as a political actor in modernising Turkey. In J. Forbrig (Ed.), *Revisiting youth political participation* (pp. 29–36). Strasbourg: Council of Europe.

Luxenberg, S. (1985). *Roadside empires: How the chains franchised America.* New York: Viking.

Lynch, C. (1999). The 'good girls' of Sri Lankan modernity: Moral orders of nationalism and capitalism. *Identities, 6,* 55–89.

Lynch, M., Engle, J., & Cruz, J. (2010). *Subprime opportunity: The unfulfilled promise of for-profit colleges and universities.* Washington, DC: The Education Trust.

MacDonald, C., & Sirianni, C. (Eds.). (1996). *Working in the service society.* Philadelphia: Temple University Press.

MacDonald, R. (2011). Youth transitions, unemployment and underemployment. *Journal of Sociology, 47*(4), 427–444.

MacDonald, R. (2013). Underemployment and precarité: The new condition of youth? *LLinE,* Issue 1. Retrieved from www.lline.fi/en/article/research/20132/underemployment-and-precarit-the-new-condition-of-youth

MacLeod, D. (1982). Act your age: Boyhood, adolescence, and the rise of the Boy Scouts of America. *Journal of Social History, 16*(2), 3–20.

Mains, D. (2007). Neoliberal times: Progress, boredom and shame among young men in urban Ethiopia. *American Ethnologist, 34*(4), 659–673.

Majavu, A. (2010). No youth wage subsidy – Motlanthe. *Sowetan Live.* August 20th. Retrieved from www.sowetanlive.co.za/news/2010/08/20/no-youth-wage-subsidy—motlanthe

Makhubu, N., & Magome, M. (2012). SA's ticking time bomb. *IOL News.* Retrieved from www.iol.co.za/news/politics/sa-s-ticking-time-bomb-1.1244433#.UZceiI5OsfQ

Males, M. (1996). *The scapegoat generation.* Monroe, ME: Common Courage.

Males, M. (1999). *Framing youth.* Monroe, ME: Common Courage.

Mannheim, K. (1998). The sociological problem of generations. In *Essays on the sociology of knowledge* (pp. 163–195). London: Taylor & Francis.

ManpowerGroup. (2012). *Wanted: Energized, career-driven youth*. Milwaukee: Manpower-Group.

Marchand, M., & Runyan, A.S. (Eds.). (2000). *Gender and global restructuring: Sighting, sites and resistances*. New York: Routledge.

Marchart, O. (2004). New protest formations and radical democracy. *Peace Review, 16*(4), 415–420.

Marche, S. (2012). The war against youth. *Esquire*. March 26th. Retrieved from www.esquire.com/features/young-people-in-the-recession-0412

Marcucci, P., & Usher, A. (2012). *Global changes in tuition fee policies and student assistance*. Toronto: Higher Education Strategy Associates.

Marcuse, H. (1969). *An essay on liberation*. Boston: Beacon Press.

Marginson, S. (2006). Putting 'public' back into the public university. *Thesis Eleven, 84*, 44–59.

Marginson, S. (2011). Higher education and public good. *Higher Education Quarterly, 65*(4), 411–433.

Marquardt, R. (1998). *Enter at your own risk: Canadian youth and the labour market*. Toronto: Between the Lines.

Martin, A., & Lehren, A. (2012). A generation hobbled by the soaring cost of college. *New York Times*. May 12th. Retrieved from www.nytimes.com/2012/05/13/business/student-loans-weighing-down-a-generation-with-heavy-debt.html?adxnnl=1&adxnnlx=1385554696-fgL5TajIQcfhb9MTBno5Cw

Marx, K. (1852) *The eighteenth brumaire of Louis Bonaparte*. Retrieved from www.gutenberg.org/files/1346/1346-h/1346-h.htm

Marx, K., & Engels, F. (1848/1998) *The communist manifesto*. London: Verso.

Mason, P. (2011). Book review: Fight back! A reader on the winter of protest. *New Statesman*. May 12th. Retrieved from www.newstatesman.com/non-fiction/2011/05/fight-movement-protest-rights

Mason, P. (2012). *Why it's kicking off everywhere: The new global revolutions*. London: Verso.

Masquelier, A. (2013). Teatime: Boredom and the temporalities of young men in Niger. *Africa, 83*, 470–491.

Matthews, H. (2001). Citizens, youth councils and young people's participation. *Journal of Youth Studies, 4*(3), 299–318.

Matza, D. (1961). Subterranean traditions of youth. *Annals of the American Academy of Political and Social Science, 338*(1), 102–118.

Mawdsley, J., & Lerner, R. (2000). *Investing in the world's youth: A global initiative*. Battle Creek, MI: Kellogg Foundation.

Maynes, M.J. (2004). Gender, labor and globalization in historical perspective: European spinsters in the international textile industry, 1750–1900. *Journal of Women's History, 15*(4), 47–66.

Maynes, M.J. (2009). Girlhood in modern European history: (Proto-)industrialisation, consumption, marriage and selfhood, circa 1750–1900. Retrieved from http://hsozkult.geschichte.hu-berlin.de/index.asp?type=diskussionen&id=1216&view=pdf&pn=forum

Mayo, E., & Nairn, A. (2009). *Consumer kids: How big business is grooming our children for profit*. London: Constable Robinson.

McAfee, A. (2011). When entitlement meets unemployment. *HBR Blog Network*. August 29th. Retrieved from http://blogs.hbr.org/hbr/mcafee/2011/08/when-entitlement-meets-unemplo.html

McConnell, B. (2011). A leaderless revolution: Occupy economic democracy. *OpEdNews.com*. December 22nd. Retrieved from www.opednews.com/articles/A-Leaderless-Revolution-O-by-Brian-McConnell-111219-520.html

McDermott, K. (1985). 'All dressed up and nowhere to go': Youth unemployment and state policy in Britain. *Urban Anthropology*, 14(1), 91–108.

McIntyre, D. (2010). The layoff kings. *DailyFinance.com*. August 18th. Retrieved from www.dailyfinance.com/2010/08/18/the-layoff-kings-the-25-companies-responsible-for-700-000-lost/

McIntyre, J. (2012). Youth rising. *New Internationalist*. October Issue. Retrieved from http://newint.org/features/2012/10/01/young-people-mcintyre/

McLanahan, A. (2011). The living indebted: Student militancy and the financialization of debt. *Qui Parle, 20*(1), 57–77.

McLaughlin, M., Scott, R., Deschenes, S., Hopkins, K., & Newman, A. (2009). *Between movement and establishment: Organizations advocating for youth*. Stanford: Stanford University Press.

McLeod, J., & Wright, K. (2008). Social values and schooling: Curriculum, counselling and the education of the adolescent, 1930–1970s. Paper presented at the Australian Association for Research in Education Conference, Brisbane.

McNally, D. (2002). *Another world is possible: Globalization and anti-capitalism*. New York: Blackwell.

McNally, D. (2010). *Global slump: The economics and politics of crisis and resistance*. Oakland: PM Press.

Melin, A. (2013). Educated with a dead-beat job – The unseen legacy of Europe's crisis. *Reuters*. June 25th. Retrieved from http://uk.reuters.com/article/2013/06/25/us-eu-youth-underemployment-insight-idUSBRE95O0SN20130625

Mertens, S., Anfara, V., & Roney, K. (Eds.). (2009). *An international look at educating young adolescents*. Charlotte: Information Age Publishing.

Miles, S. (2000). *Youth lifestyles in a changing world*. Buckingham: Open University Press.

Milkman, R., Luce, S., & Lewis, P. (2013). *Changing the subject: A bottom-up account of Occupy Wall Street in New York City*. New York: Murphy Institute.

Miller, S. (2011). *Revisiting the conventional wisdom on youth unemployment*. Presentation at the United Nations Expert Group Meeting on the Challenge of Building Employment for a Sustainable Recovery, Geneva, June 24th.

Mills, M.B. (1997). Contesting the margins of modernity: Women, migration, and consumption in Thailand. *American Ethnologist, 24*(1), 37–61.

Mills, M.B. (2003). Gender and inequality in the global labor force. *Annual Review of Anthropology, 32*, 41–62.

Mizen, P. (2002). Putting the politics back into youth studies: Keynesianism, monetarism and the changing state of youth. *Journal of Youth Studies, 5*(1), 5–20.

Mizen, P., Bolton, A., & Pole, C. (1999). School age workers: The paid employment of children in Britain. *Work, Employment & Society, 13*(3), 423–438.2

Mo. (2013). Week of 'black protest' after student suicide triggered by inability to pay for tuition fees. *Interoccupy.net*. March 21st. Retrieved from http://interoccupy.net/reclaimeducation/manila-march-18-22-week-of-black-protest-after-student-suicide-triggered-by-inability-to-pay-for-tuition-fees/

Mohammed, I., & Wheeler, W. (2001). *Broadening the bounds of youth development: Youth as engaged citizens*. New York: Ford Foundation.

Moller, H. (1968). Youth as a force in the modern world. *Comparative Studies in Society and History, 10*(3), 237–260.

Morison, O. (2012). Youth unemployment in Europe: Less dire by another measure. *Globe and Mail*. August 21st. Retrieved from www.theglobeandmail.com/report-on-business/economy/economy-lab/youth-unemployment-in-europe-less-dire-by-another-measure/article4491822/

Morsy, H. (2012). Scarred generation. *Finance & Development, 49*(1). Retrieved from www.imf.org/external/pubs/ft/fandd/2012/03/morsy.htm

Mosca, I., & Wright, R. (2011). *Is graduate under-employment persistent? Evidence from the United Kingdom*. Discussion Paper No. 6177. Bonn: Institute for the Study of Labour.

Moses, E. (2000). *The $100 billion allowance: Accessing the global teen market*. New York: John Wiley & Sons.

Mukwaya, J. (2001). Preface. In *The national youth policy: A vision for youth in the 21st century*. Kampala: Ministry of Gender, Labour and Social Development.

Mulholland, H. (2012). Minimum wage frozen for under-21s. *Guardian*. March 19th. Retrieved from www.guardian.co.uk/society/2012/mar/19/minimum-wage-frozen-for-under-21s

Mullaney, L. (2012). Mars, Cranswick and ABF join £1bn youth plan. *Foodmanufacture.co.uk*. Retrieved from www.foodmanufacture.co.uk/Business-News/Mars-Cranswick-and-ABF-join-1bn-youth-plan

Mullen, A. (2010). *Degrees of inequality: Culture, class and gender in American higher education*. Baltimore: Johns Hopkins University Press.

Mungham, G. (1982). Workless youth as a 'moral panic.' In T. Rees & P. Atkinson (Eds.), *Youth unemployment and state intervention* (pp. 29–40). London: Routledge & Kegan Paul.

Munnell, A., & Wu, A. (2012). *Are aging baby boomers squeezing young workers out of jobs?* Boston: Center for Retirement Research, Boston College.

Munusamy, R. (2012). Goodbye youth wage subsidy, hello youth employment accord. *Daily Maverick*. August 17th. Retrieved from www.dailymaverick.co.za/article/2012-08-17-goodbye-youth-wage-subsidy-hello-youth-employment-accord/#.Ufi6GeBOSfQ

Murphy, C. (2011). The Twitter generation. *The Majalla*. September 23rd. Retrieved from www.majalla.com/eng/2011/09/article55226471

Musgrove, F. (1964). Youth and the social order. London: Routledge & Kegan Paul.

Nader, L. (1989). Orientalism, Occidentalism and the control of women. *Cultural Dynamics, 2*, 323–355.

Nasaw, D. (1981). *Schooled to order: A social history of public schooling in the United States*. Oxford: Oxford University Press.

Naseej. (2012). *Weaving our fabric in the Arab world*. Amman: Naseej.

Nasiripour, S., & Kirkham, C. (2013). Student loan defaults surge to highest level in nearly 2 decades. *Huffington Post*. September 30th. Retrieved from www.huffingtonpost.com/2013/09/30/student-loans-default_n_4019806.html

National Center on Education and the Economy. (1990). *America's choice: High skills or low wages*. Washington, DC: National Academies Press.

National Research Council. (2002). *Community programs to promote youth development*. Washington, DC: National Academies Press.

National Treasury. (2011). *Confronting youth unemployment: Policy options for South Africa*. Pretoria: National Treasury.

Nelson, L. (2012). The new politics of student debt. *Inside Higher Ed.* May 3rd. Retrieved from www.insidehighered.com/news/2012/05/03/how-student-debt-became-focus-presidential-campaign

Nenga, S., & Taft, J. (Eds.). (2013). *Youth engagement: The civil-political lives of children and youth.* Bingley: Emerald.

Neumann, M. (2011). *The Communist Youth League and the transformation of the Soviet Union, 1917–1932.* New York: Routledge.

Neumann, M. (2012). 'Youth, it's your turn!': Generations and the fate of the Russian revolution (1917–1932). *Journal of Social History, 46*(2), 273–304.

Newfield, C., & Lye, C. (2011). Introduction: Against the day. *South Atlantic Quarterly, 110*(2), 529–538.

News Taco. (2011). Undocumented youth occupy Wells Fargo in Oakland. *Causa Justa.* Retrieved from www.cjjc.org/news/63-occupy/238-undocumented-youth-occupy-wells-fargo-in-oakland

Newstalk ZB. (2013). Maccas, KFC say no to youth wage. April 8th. Retrieved from www.newstalkzb.co.nz/auckland/news/2091754323-maccas--kfc-say-no-to-youth-wage

Neyzi, L. (2001). Object or subject? The paradox of 'youth' in Turkey. *International Journal of Middle East Studies, 33,* 411–432.

Nielsen, N. (2012). More than half young Greeks are unemployed. *EU Observer.* August 9th. Retrieved from http://euobserver.com/social/117199

Nilan, P., & Feixa, C. (Eds.). (2006). *Global youth? Hybrid identities, plural worlds.* New York: Routledge.

Nixon, R. (2011). US groups helped nurture Arab uprisings. *New York Times.* April 14th. Retrieved from www.nytimes.com/2011/04/15/world/15aid.html?pagewanted=all&_r=0

Noelke, C. (2011). *The consequences of employment protection legislation for the youth labour market.* Working Paper No. 144. Mannheimer Zentrum für Europäische Sozialforschung, Mannheim.

Nsamenang, B. (1999). Eurocentric image of childhood in the context of world's cultures. *Human Development, 42,* 159–168.

Oakley, M. (2012). A lost generation? What about those aged over 50? *Touchstone.* July 6th. Retrieved from http://touchstoneblog.org.uk/2012/07/a-lost-generation-what-about-those-aged-over-50

O'Beacha'in, D., & Polese, A. (2010). 'Rocking the vote': New forms of youth organization in Eastern Europe and the former Soviet Union. *Journal of Youth Studies, 13*(5), 615–630.

O'Brien, A. (1982). Italian youth in conflict: Catholic Action and fascist Italy, 1929–1931. *Catholic Historical Review, 68*(4), 625–635.

Odem, M. (1995). *Delinquent daughters: Protecting and policing adolescent sexuality in the United States, 1885–1920.* Durham: University of North Carolina Press.

O'Donnell, M. (2010). Generation and utopia: Using Mannheim's concepts to understand 1960s radicalism. *Young, 18*(4), 367–383.

OECD. (2012). *Education at a glance 2012.* Paris: OECD.

Offer, D., & Schonert-Reichl, K. (1992). Debunking the myths of adolescence: Findings from recent research. *Journal of the American Academy of Child and Adolescent Psychiatry, 31,* 1003–1014.

O'Higgins, N. (2001). *Youth unemployment and employment policy: A global perspective.* Geneva: ILO.

O'Higgins, N. (2012). *This time it's different? Youth labour markets during 'the great recession.'* Bonn: IZA.

Oikonomakis, L., & Roos, J. (2013). 'Que no nos representan': The crisis of representation and the resonance of the real democracy from the indignados to Occupy. Paper presented at the Street Politics in the Age of Austerity Conference, University of Montreal, February 20th.

Ong, A. (1989). *Spirits of resistance and capitalist discipline: Factory women in Malaysia.* Albany: State University of New York Press.

Ong, A. (1991). The gender and labor politics of postmodernity. *Annual Review of Anthropology, 20,* 279–309.

ONS – Office of National Statistics. (2012). *Graduates in the labour market.* London: ONS.

Osgerby, B. (2002). 'A caste, a culture, a market': Youth, marketing, and lifestyle in postwar America. In R. Strickland (Ed.), *Growing up postmodern* (pp. 15–33). Lanham: Rowman & Littlefield.

Osgerby, B. (2008). Understanding the 'jackpot market': Media, marketing, and the rise of the American teenager. In P. Jamieson & D. Romer (Eds.), *The changing portrait of adolescents in the media since 1950* (pp. 27–58). Oxford: Oxford University Press.

Osterman, P. (1980). *Getting started: Youth labor market.* Cambridge: MIT Press.

Oxfam. (2011). *Power to the people? Reactions to the EU's response to the Arab spring.* Oxford: Oxfam.

Page, E. (2006). *Climate change, justice and future generations.* Cheltenham: Edward Elgar.

Palladino, G. (1996). *Teenagers: An American history.* New York: Basic Books.

Pangburn, D.J. (2011). Masses of young and old march across Spain in austerity protests. *Death and Taxes.* June 21st. Retrieved from www.deathandtaxesmag.com/107372/masses-of-young-and-old-march-across-spain-in-austerity-protests-video/

Papachristou, H. (2012). Over half of Greek youth unemployed. *Reuters.* March 8th. Retrieved from http://uk.reuters.com/article/2012/03/08/us-greece-unemployment-idUSBRE8270GX20120308

Passerini, L. (1997). Youth as a metaphor for social change: Fascist Italy and America in the 1950s. In G. Levi & J. Schmitt (Eds.), *A history of young people in the west: Stormy evolution to modern times* (pp. 281–342). Cambridge: Harvard University Press.

PBS. (2011). *Inside the April 6 movement.* Retrieved from www.pbs.org/wgbh/pages/frontline/revolution-in-cairo/inside-april6-movement/

Peacock, L. (2012). Greek youth unemployment hits 51.5pc. *Telegraph.* March 8th. Retrieved from www.telegraph.co.uk/finance/jobs/9132142/Greek-youth-unemployment-hits-51.5pc.html

Pechtelidis, Y. (2011). December uprising 2008: Universality and particularity in young people's discourse. *Journal of Youth Studies, 14*(4), 449–462.

Peiss, K. (1986). *Cheap amusements: Working women and leisure in turn-of-the-century New York.* Philadelphia: Temple University Press.

Penny, L. (2010). The day the teenagers turned on top shop. *New Statesman.* December 3rd. Retrieved from www.newstatesman.com/blogs/laurie-penny/2010/12/hope-young-education-angry

Perold, H. (Ed.). (2000). *Worldwide workshop on youth involvement as a strategy for social, economic and democratic development.* Washington, DC: Ford Foundation.

Petersen, A., & Mortimer, J. (Eds.). (1994). *Youth unemployment and society.* Cambridge: Cambridge University Press.

Pittman, K., Irby, M., & Ferber, T. (2000). Unfinished business: Further reflections on a decade of promoting youth development. In N. Jaffe (Ed.), *Youth development* (pp. 17–64). Philadelphia: Public/Private Ventures.

Platt, A. (1969). *The child savers: The invention of delinquency.* Chicago: University of Chicago Press.

PM News. (2013). Youth unemployment, A time bomb. *PM News.* Retrieved from http:// pmnewsnigeria.com/2013/04/23/youth-unemployment-a-time-bomb/

Pollock, J. (2011). Streetbook: How Egyptian and Tunisian youth hacked the Arab spring. *MIT Technology Review.* August 23rd. Retrieved from www.technologyreview.com/ featuredstory/425137/streetbook/

Pousadela, I. (2012). The Chilean student movement: An expanding space for civil society. Unpublished manuscript.

Power, N. (2012). Dangerous subjects: UK students and the criminalization of protest. *South Atlantic Quarterly, 111*(2), 412–420.

Price, R., McDonald, P., Bailey, J., & Pini, B. (Eds.). (2011). *Young people and work.* Farnham: Ashgate.

Punay, E. (2013). UP student kills self over tuition. *Philippine Star.* March 16th. Retrieved from www.philstar.com/headlines/2013/03/16/920420/student-kills-self-over-tuition

Pursley, S. (2013). The stage of adolescence: Anticolonial time, youth insurgency and the marriage crisis in Hashimite Iraq. *History of the Present, 3*(2), 160–197.

Pusey, A., & Sealey-Huggins, L. (2013). Transforming the university: Beyond students and cuts. *ACME, 12*(3). 443–458.

Quart, A. (2003). *Branded: The buying and selling of teenagers.* Cambridge: Perseus.

Raco, M. (2009). From expectations to aspirations: State modernisation, urban policy and the existential politics of welfare in the UK. *Political Geography, 28*, 436–444.

Radsch, C. (2012). *Unveiling the revolutionaries: Cyberactivism and the role of women in the Arab uprisings.* James Baker III Institute for Public Policy. Houston: Rice University.

Rampell, C. (2013). In hard economy for all ages, older isn't better … it's brutal. *New York Times.* February 2nd. Retrieved from www.nytimes.com/2013/02/03/ business/americans-closest-to-retirement-were-hardest-hit-by-recession.html

Record, A. (2002). Born to shop: Teenage women and the marketplace in the postwar United States. In E. Meehan & E. Riordan (Eds.), *Sex & money* (pp. 181–195). Minneapolis: University of Minnesota Press.

Reece, D. (2012). Prudential chief Tidjane Thiam says minimum wage is a 'machine to destroy jobs.' *Telegraph.* January 26th. Retrieved from www.telegraph.co.uk/finance/ financetopics/davos/9041442/Davos-2012-Prudential-chief-Tidjane-Thiam-says-minimum-wage-is-a-machine-to-destroy-jobs.html

Reed, A. (2000). Posing as politics and other thoughts on the American scene. *New York Times.* Retrieved from www.nytimes.com/books/first/r/reed-class.html

Rees, G., & Rees, T. (1982). Juvenile unemployment and the state between the wars. In T. Rees & P. Atkinson (Eds.), *Youth unemployment and state intervention* (pp. 13–28). London: Routledge & Kegan Paul.

Reese, W., Thorup, C., & Gerson, T. (2002). *What works in public/private partnering: Building alliances for youth development.* Baltimore, MD: International Youth Foundation.

Reich, R. (1991). *The work of nations.* New York: Vintage.

Reiter, E. (1991). *Making fast food: From the frying pan into the fryer.* Montreal: McGill-Queen's University Press.

Research and Destroy. (2009). *Communiqué from an absent future: On the terminus of student life*. Berkeley: Research and Destroy.

Reuters. (2013). Greek youth unemployment hits 64 per cent. *Telegraph*. May 9th. Retrieved from www.telegraph.co.uk/news/worldnews/europe/greece/10047453/Greek-youth-unemployment-hits-64-per-cent.html

Riley, N. (2009). Giving capitalism its due. *Wall Street Journal*. April 4th, A9.

Ritzer, G. (1996). *The McDonaldization of society*. Rev. edn. Thousand Oaks: Pine Forge.

Rivera, S. (2012). List of 2012 student protests regarding education in the US. Retrieved from http://teacherunderconstruction.com/2012/11/22/list-of-2012-student-protests-regarding-education-in-the-u-s/

Roberts, K. (2009). *Youth in transition: Eastern Europe and the West*. London: Palgrave.

Roche, J., Tucker, S., Flynn, R., & Thomson, R. (Eds.). (2004). *Youth in society: Contemporary theory, policy and practice*. 2nd edn. London: Sage.

Roelofs, J. (2003). *Foundations and public policy: The mask of pluralism*. Albany: SUNY Press.

Rooke, M. (1971). *Anarchy and apathy: Student unrest 1968–1970*. London: Hamilton.

Roos, J. (2011). La lucha sigue: The struggle of the indignados continues. *RoarMag.org*. July 27th. Retrieved from http://roarmag.org/2011/07/indignados-struggle-goes-on/

Rootes, C. (2013). Student movements. In D. Snow et al. (Eds.), *The Wiley-Blackwell encyclopedia of social & political movements* (pp. 4864–4869). London: John Wiley & Sons.

Roseen, D. (2013). Cultivating entrepreneurial spirits in youth to end extreme poverty. October 29th. Press release from States News Service.

Roseman, M. (1995). Introduction: Generation conflict and German history 1770–1968. In M. Roseman (Ed.), *Generations in conflict: Youth revolt and generation formation in Germany, 1770–1968* (pp. 1–46). Cambridge: Cambridge University Press.

Rosenbaum, J. (2011). The complexities of college for all: Beyond fairy-tale dreams. *Sociology of Education, 84*(2), 113–117.

Rosenberg, T. (2011). Revolution U. *Foreign Policy*. February 16th. Retrieved from www.foreignpolicy.com/articles/2011/02/16/revolution_u

Rosenfeld, S. (2012). *Subversives: The FBI's war on student radicals, and Reagan's rise to power*. New York: Farrar, Strauss & Giroux.

Rosenthal, M. (1986). *The character factory: Baden-Powell and the origins of the Boy Scout movement*. London: Collins.

Ross, A. (2013). Mortgaging the future: Student debt in the age of austerity. *New Labor Forum, 22*(1), 23–28.

Ross, C. (2012). *The Leaderless revolution*. New York: Simon & Schuster.

Ross-Thomas, E. (2010) Spain has first general strike in decade as Europe marches. *Bloomberg*. September 29th. Retrieved from www.bloomberg.com/news/2010-09-28/spain-girds-for-first-general-strike-in-8-years-to-protest-zapatero-cuts.html

Roth, J., & Brooks-Gunn, J. (2003). What exactly is a youth development program? *Applied Developmental Science, 7*(2), 94–111.

Rothstein, J., & Rouse, C. (2011). Constrained after college: Student loans and early-career occupation choices. *Journal of Public Economics, 95*, 149–163.

Rowell, S. (2012). School for revolutionaries: CANVAS modernizes nonviolent resistance. *Kennedy School Review*. April 1st. Retrieved from http://harvardkennedyschoolreview.com/school-for-revolutionaries/

Rowntree, J., & Rowntree, M. (1968). Youth as a class. *International Socialist Journal, 25*.

Royle, T. (2010). 'Low-road Americanization' and the global 'McJob': A longitudinal analysis of work, pay and unionization in the international fast-food industry. *Labor History, 51*(2), 249–270.

Royle, T., & Towers, B. (Eds.). (2002). *Labour relations in the global fast-food industry*. London: Routledge.

Ruddick, S. (2003). The politics of aging: Globalization and the restructuring of youth and childhood. *Antipode, 35*(2), 334–351.

Ruetschlin, C., & Draut, T. (2013). *Stuck: Young America's persistent jobs crisis*. New York: Demos.

Rustin, M. (2010). From the beginning to the end of neo-liberalism in Britain. *OpenDemocracy.net*. May 19th. Retrieved from www.opendemocracy.net/ourkingdom/mike-rustin/after-neo-liberalism-in-britain

Sachs, J. (2012). Rise of generation occupy. *Salon*. May 1st. Retrieved from www.salon.com/2012/05/01/rise_of_generation_occupy/

Sage, J., Smith, D., & Hubbard, P. (2012). The rapidity of studentification and population change: There goes the (student)hood. *Population, Space and Place, 18*, 597–613.

Said, E. (1983). Travelling theory. In *The world, the text and the critic* (pp. 226–247). Cambridge: Harvard University Press.

Salazar-Xirinachs, J.M. (2012). Generation ni/ni: Latin America's lost youth. *Americas Quarterly*. Retrieved from www.americasquarterly.org/salazar

Salinas, D., & Fraser, P. (2012). Educational opportunity and contentious politics: The 2011 Chilean student movement. *Berkeley Review of Education, 3*(1), 17–47.

Same Work Same Pay. (2012). Same Work Same Pay campaign launch. November 27th. Retrieved from www.scoop.co.nz/stories/PO1211/S00379/same-work-same-pay-campaign-launch.htm

Sánchez, F.R. (2012). *Youth unemployment in Spain*. Berlin: Friedrich-Ebert-Stiftung.

SAnews.gov.za. (2013). Wage subsidy targets youth unemployment. *SouthAfrica.info*. November 4th. Retrieved from www.southafrica.info/business/economy/development/employment-041113.htm#.UojBkqWSHwI%23ixzz2kuO3ayCk

Scales, P., & Leffert, N. (1999). *Developmental assets*. Minneapolis: Search Institute.

Schlosser, E. (2001). *Fast food nation*. Boston: Houghton Mifflin.

Schmidt, J. (2010). *Industrial violence and the legal origins of child labor*. Cambridge: Cambridge University Press.

Schor, J. (2004). *Born to buy: The commercialized child and the new consumer culture*. New York: Scribner.

Schumpeter. (2011). Young, jobless and looking for trouble. *Economist*. February 3rd. Retrieved from www.economist.com/blogs/schumpeter/2011/02/youth_unemployment

Schwab, K. (2013). The re-emergence of Europe: Tackling Europe's youth unemployment. *Huffington Post*. January 20th. Retrieved from www.huffingtonpost.com/klaus-schwab/the-reemergence-of-europe_3_b_2489823.html

Scones, P. (2013). With no money for college, 16-year-old freshman takes her own life. *Philippine Canadian Inquirer*. March 19th. Retrieved from www.canadianinquirer.net/portal.php?mod=view&aid=1382

Sears, A. (2014). Generation war or generational justice? *Briarpatch Magazine*. February 11th. Retrieved from http://briarpatchmagazine.com/blog/view/generation-war-or-generational-justice

Seccombe, K. (2002). 'Beating the odds' versus 'changing the odds': Poverty, resilience and family policy. *Journal of Marriage and the Family, 64*(2), 384–394.

Sender, H., & Langley, M. (2007). How Blackstone's chief became $7 billion man. *Wall Street Journal.* June 13th. Retrieved from http://online.wsj.com/article/SB118169817142333414.html

Serageldin, I. (2011). *The making of social justice: Pluralism, cohesion and social participation.* Nelson Mandela Annual Lecture, July 23rd, Johannesburg. Retrieved from www.nelsonmandela.org/news/entry/transcript-of-professor-ismail-serageldins-nelson-mandela-annual-lecture

Serracant, P. (2012). Changing youth? Continuities and ruptures in transitions into adulthood among Catalan young people. *Journal of Youth Studies, 15*(2), 161–176.

Seymour, R. (2012). Quebec's students provide a lesson in protest politics. *Guardian.* September 7th. Retrieved from www.theguardian.com/commentisfree/2012/sep/07/quebec-students-lesson-protest-politics

Shah, A., & Sardar, S. (2011). *Sandstorm: A leaderless revolution in the digital age.* New York: Global Executive Board.

Shierholz, H., Sabadish, N., & Finio, N. (2013). *The class of 2013: Young graduates still face dim job prospects.* Washington, DC: Economic Policy Institute.

Shoman, D. (2012). How best to tackle the youth unemployment crisis? World Economic Form on the Middle East. Retrieved from http://forumblog.org/2012/06/youth-unemployment-still-in-crisis/

Siegfried, D. (2006). Understanding 1968: Youth rebellion, generational change and postindustrial society. In A. Schildt & D. Siegfried (Eds.), *Between Marx and Coca-Cola: Youth cultures in changing European societies, 1960–1980* (pp. 59–81). New York: Berghahn.

Sika, N. (2012). Youth political engagement in Egypt: From abstention to uprising. *British Journal of Middle Eastern Studies, 39*(2), 181–199.

Singerman, D. (2007). *The economic imperatives of marriage.* Washington, DC: Wolfensohn Center for Development.

Skelton, T., & Valentine, G. (1997). *Cool places: Geographies of youth cultures.* New York: Routledge.

Slaughter, J. (1997). Can selling books ever be a 'good job'? *Labor Notes,* November issue, 3.

Smelser, N., & Halpern, S. (1978). The historical triangulation of family, economy, and education. *American Journal of Sociology, 84,* S288–S315.

Smith, C. (2006). *International experience with worker-side and employer-side wage and employment subsidies, and job search assistance programmes.* Pretoria: HSRC.

Smith, S. (2011). Youth in Africa: Rebels without a cause but not without effect. *SAIS Review, 31*(2), 97–110.

Soliman, S. (2011). *The autumn of dictatorship: Fiscal crisis and political change in Egypt under Mubarak.* Stanford: Stanford University Press.

Solomon, C., & Palmieri, T. (Eds.). (2011). *Spring time: The new student rebellions.* London: Verso.

Solomos, J. (1985). Problems, but whose problems?: The social construction of black youth unemployment and state policies. *Journal of Social Policy, 14*(4), 527–554.

Somma, N. (2012). The Chilean student movement of 2011–2012: Challenging the marketization of education. *Interface, 4*(2), 296–309.

Sommers, M. (2011). Governance, security and culture: Assessing Africa's youth bulge. *International Journal of Conflict and Violence, 5*(2), 292–303.

SPRA – Social Policy Research Associates. (2003). *Lessons in leadership: How young people change their communities and themselves.* Takoma Park, MD: The Innovation Center.

Springhall, J. (1977). *Youth, empire and society: A social history of British youth movements.* Hamden: Archon.

Stachura, P. (1981). *The German youth movement 1900–1945.* London: Macmillan.

Staeheli, L., & Nagel, C. (2012). Whose awakening is it? Youth and the geopolitics of civic engagement in the 'Arab awakening.' *European Urban and Regional Studies, 20*(1), 115–119.

Standing, G. (2011). *The precariat.* London: Bloomsbury.

Stanistreet, P. (2012). Anyone can teach, everyone can learn. *Adults Learning,* spring issue, 20–26.

Stanley, L. (2012). Dead, non-dead or walking dead? The global financial crisis and neo-liberalism. *British Politics and Policy at LSE.* December 27th. Retrieved from http://blogs.lse.ac.uk/politicsandpolicy/archives/29407

Stavropoulou, M., & Jones, N. (2013). *Off the balance sheet: The impact of the economic crisis on girls and young women.* Woking: Plan International.

Stewart, H. (2013). Britain's dole queues shrink but young people remain the hardest hit. *Guardian.* August 14th. Retrieved from www.theguardian.com/business/2013/aug/14/uk-unemployment-claimant-count.

Sukarieh, M. (2012). From terrorists to revolutionaries: The emergence of 'youth' in the Arab world and the discourse of globalization. *Interface, 4*(2), 424–437.

Sukarieh, M. (2013). On class, culture and the creation of the neoliberal subject: The case of Jordan. Unpublished Manuscript.

Sukarieh, M., & Tannock, S. (2008). In the best interests of youth or neoliberalism? The World Bank and the new global youth empowerment project. *Journal of Youth Studies, 11*(3), 301–312.

Sukarieh, M., & Tannock, S. (2009). Putting school commercialism in context: A global history of Junior Achievement Worldwide. *Journal of Education Policy, 24*(6), 769–786.

Sukarieh, M., & Tannock, S. (2011). The positivity imperative: A critical look at the 'new' youth development movement. *Journal of Youth Studies, 14*(6), 675–691.

Swain, H. (2013). Could the free university movement be the great new hope for education? *Guardian.* January 28th. Retrieved from www.theguardian.com/education/2013/jan/28/free-university-movement-excluded-learners

Swarthout, L. (2006). *Paying back, not giving back.* Boston: State PIRGs' Higher Education Project.

Sweetman, M. (2013). Ontario needs jobs, not more cuts. Rabble.ca. April 2nd. Retrieved from http://rabble.ca/news/2013/04/ontario-needs-jobs-not-more-cuts.

Taft, J. (2011). *Rebel girls: Youth activism and social change across the Americas.* New York: New York University Press.

Taft, J., & Gordon, H. (2013). Youth activists, youth councils and constrained democracy. *Education, Citizenship and Social Justice, 8*(1), 87–100.

Taibo, C. (2013). The Spanish indignados: A movement with two souls. *European Urban and Regional Studies, 20*(1), 155–158.

Talburt, S., & Lesko, N. (2012). An introduction to seven technologies of youth studies. In N. Lesko & S. Talburt (Eds.), *Keywords in youth studies* (pp. 1–10). New York: Routledge.

Talley, I. (2011). IMF warned of Egyptian youth jobless rate ahead of protests. *Wall Street Journal.* February 1st. Retrieved from http://blogs.wsj.com/economics/2011/02/01/imf-warned-of-egyptian-youth-jobless-rate-ahead-of-protests/

Tannock, S. (2001). *Youth at work: The unionized fast-food and grocery workplace*. Philadelphia: Temple University Press.

Tannock, S. (2003). Why do working youth work where they do? In L. Roulleau-Berger (Ed.), *Youth at work in the post-industrial city of North America and Europe* (pp. 285–303). London: Brill.

Tannock, S. (2006). Higher education, inequality & the public good. *Dissent*, spring issue, 45–51.

Tannock, S. (2013). Bad attitude? Migrant workers, meat processing work and the local unemployed in a peripheral region of the UK. *European Urban and Regional Studies*, DOI: 10.1177/0969776413481986.

Tannock, S., & Flocks, S. (2003). 'I know what it's like to struggle': The working lives of young students in an urban community college. *Labor Studies Journal*, *28*(1), 1–30.

Tapscott, D. (2011). The world's unemployed youth: Revolution in the air? *Guardian*. April 4th. Retrieved from www.guardian.co.uk/commentisfree/2011/apr/04/unemployed-youth-revolution-generational-conflict

Taylor, L., McMahill, D., & Taylor, B. (1960). *The American secondary school*. New York: Appleton-Century-Crofts.

Taylor, P. (2011). Youth unemployment – The headlines mislead. November 16th. Retrieved from http://philtaylor.org.uk/2011/11/youth-unemployment-the-headlines-mislead/

Teeter, R. (1995). Pre-school responses to the 19th century youth crisis. *Adolescence*, *30*(118), 291–300.

Te Riele, K. (2006). Youth 'at risk': Further marginalizing the marginalized? *Journal of Education Policy*, *21*(2), 129–145.

Tilly, L., & Scott, J. (1978). *Women, work and family*. New York: Holt, Rinehart & Winston.

Tinsley, M. (2012). *Too much to lose: Understanding and supporting Britain's older workers*. London: Policy Exchange.

Tipaldou, S. (2012). Spain: People flood the streets in labour law protests. *Counterfire*. February 28th. Retrieved from www.counterfire.org/index.php/articles/international/15584-spain-people-flood-the-streets-in-labour-law-protests

Tiraboschi, M. (2012). Young workers in recessionary times: A *caveat* (to continental Europe) to reconstruct its labour law? *International and Comparative Labour Studies*, *1*(1), 3–24.

Tirado, I. (1994). Nietzschean motifs in the Komsomol's vanguardism. In B. Rosenthal (Ed.), *Nietzsche and Soviet culture: Ally and adversary* (pp. 235–255). Cambridge: Cambridge University Press.

Tomlinson, S. (2008). Gifted, talented and high ability: Selection for education in a one-dimensional world. *Oxford Review of Education*, *34*(1), 59–74.

Touraine, A. (1968). Naissance d'un mouvement étudiant. *Le Monde*. March 7th.

Traynor, I. (2004). US campaign behind the turmoil in Kiev. *Guardian*. November 26th. Retrieved from www.theguardian.com/world/2004/nov/26/ukraine.usa

Trow, M. (1974). Problems in the transition from elite to mass higher education. In *Policies for Higher Education* (pp. 51–1010). Paris: OECD.

Tsaliki, L. (2012). The Greek 'indignados': The aganaktismeni as a case study of the 'new repertoire' of collective action. Paper presented at the In/Compatible Publics Conference, Berlin, January 31st.

Tuck, E., & Yang, K.W. (Eds.). (2014). *Youth resistance research and theories of change*. New York: Routledge.

Tugwell, P., & Petrakis, M. (2012). Merkel to be met by Greek anti-austerity protesters. *Bloomberg.* October 8th. Retrieved from www.bloomberg.com/news/2012-10-07/merkel-arrival-in-athens-to-be-met-by-anti-austerity-protesters.html

Turner, R. (1969). The theme of contemporary social movements. *British Journal of Sociology,* 20(4), 390–405.

Tyack, D. (1974). *The one best system: A history of American urban education.* Cambridge: Harvard University Press.

Uitermark, J., & Nicholls, W. (2012). How local networks shape a global movement: Comparing Occupy in Amsterdam and Los Angeles. *Social Movement Studies,* DOI 10.1080/14742837.2012.704181.

UKCES – UK Commission for Employment & Skills. (2012). *Youth inquiry evidence base.* London: UKCES.

UN – United Nations. (2011). *The global social crisis: Report on the world social situation 2011.* New York: United Nations.

Unemployed People's Movement. (2012). UPM statement on the youth wage subsidy and the clash between the DA and COSATU. *Abahlali BaseMjondolo.* May 18th. Retrieved from www.abahlali.org/node/8806

UNESCO. (2009). *Global education digest.* Montreal: UNESCO.

UNI Global Union. (2012). *Banking job loss survey.* Nyon: UNI Global Union.

UNICEF. (2011). Arab youth, key drivers of Arab development and democratization. November 18th. Retrieved from www.unicef.org/media/media_60552.html

UNICEF. (2012). UNICEF and Barclays renew partnership. November 27th. Retrieved from www.unicef.org.uk/Latest/News/Barclays-and-UNICEF-renew-partnership/

UNISON. (2012). Youth contract or youth con trick? Retrieved from www.unison-newcastle.org.uk/assets/files/Young%20Members/120509%20U27.pdf

USAID. (2012a). *Policy on youth in development.* Washington, DC: USAID.

USAID. (2012b). USAID launches new policy on youth in development. November 1st. Retrieved from www.usaid.gov/news-information/press-releases/usaid-launches-new-policy-youth-development

US Department of State. (2013). Youth councils: Empowering young people as agents of change. May 3rd. Retrieved from www.state.gov/j/gyi/releases/press/2013/208953.htm

USIP – United States Institute of Peace. (2010). Youth, violence and extremism. January 19th. Retrieved from www.usip.org/events/youth-violence-and-extremism

Utley, P. (1979). Radical youth: Generational conflict in the Anfang movement, 1912–January 1914. *History of Education Quarterly,* 19(2), 207–228.

van Dijk, R., de Bruijn, M., Cardoso, C., & Butter, I. (2011) Introduction: Ideologies of youth. *Africa Development,* 36(3&4), 1–17.

Vasagar, J. (2013). 'New deal' to tackle Europe's mass youth unemployment. *Telegraph.* May 24th. Retrieved from www.telegraph.co.uk/news/worldnews/europe/10078892/New-Deal-to-tackle-Europes-mass-youth-unemployment.html

Vedder, R., Denhart, C., & Robe, J. (2013). *Why are recent college graduates underemployed?* Washington, DC: Center for College Affordability and Productivity.

Venkatesh, S., & Kassimir, R. (Eds.). (2007). *Youth, globalization, and the law.* Stanford: Stanford University Press.

Waldram, H. (2011). Occupy together: How the global movement is spreading via social media. *Guardian.* October 14th. Retrieved from www.theguardian.com/news/blog/2011/oct/14/occupy-england-protests-gather-momentum-via-facebook

Walker, C., & Stephenson, S. (2010). Youth and social change in Eastern Europe and the former Soviet Union. *Journal of Youth Studies, 13*(5), 521–532.

Walker, R. (2010). The golden state adrift. *New Left Review, 66*, 5–30.

Walker, S., & Barton, L. (1986). *Youth, unemployment & schooling*. Milton Keynes: Oxford University Press.

Wallace, C., & Kovatcheva, S. (1998). *Youth in society: The construction and deconstruction of youth in East and West Europe*. New York: Palgrave.

Wanrooij, B. (1987). The rise and fall of Italian fascism as a generational revolt. *Journal of Contemporary History, 22*(3), 401–418.

Wanrooij, B. (1999). Youth, generation conflict and political struggle in twentieth-century Italy. *European Legacy, 4*(1), 72–88.

Watts, R., & Flanagan, C. (2007). Pushing the envelope on youth civic engagement: A developmental and liberation psychology perspective. *Journal of Community Psychology, 35*(6), 779–792.

Weber, T. (2012). Davos 2012: Youth unemployment 'disaster'. *BBC News*. January 28th. Retrieved from www.bbc.co.uk/news/business-16774301

WEF – World Economic Forum. (2011). Global shapers. Retrieved from www.weforum.org/community/global-shapers

WEF. (2012). *Addressing the 100 million youth challenge: Perspectives on youth employment in the Arab world in 2012*. Geneva: WEF.

Weiss, M., & Aspinall, E. (Eds.). (2012). *Student activism in Asia*. Minneapolis: University of Minnesota Press.

Westby, D. (1976). *The clouded vision: The student movement in the United States in the 1960s*. Lewisburg: Bucknell University Press.

White, G. (2013). Prudential boss Tijane Thiam's pay soars to £7.8m, despite FSA censure. *Telegraph*, April 5th. Retrieved from www.telegraph.co.uk/finance/newsbysector/banksandfinance/insurance/9974069/Prudential-boss-Tijane-Thiams-pay-soars-to-7.8m-despite-FSA-censure.html

White, M., & Smith, D. (1994). The causes of persistently high unemployment. In A. Petersen & J. Mortimer (Eds.), *Youth unemployment and society* (pp. 95–144). Cambridge: Cambridge University Press.

Whitney, S. (2009). *Mobilizing youth: Communists and Catholics in interwar France*. Durham: Duke University Press.

Willetts, D. (2010). *The pinch: How the baby boomers took their children's future – And why they should give it back*. London: Atlantic Books.

William T. Grant Foundation. (1988a). *The forgotten half: Non-college youth in America*. Washington, DC: William T. Grant Foundation.

William T. Grant Foundation. (1988b). *The forgotten half: Pathways to success for America's youth and young families*. Washington, DC: William T. Grant Foundation.

Williams, J. (2001). Ecstasies of the young: Sexuality, the youth movement and moral panic in Germany on the eve of the First World War. *Central European History, 34*(2), 163–189.

Williams, J. (2007). *Turning to nature in Germany: Hiking, nudism, and conservation, 1900–1940*. Stanford: Stanford University Press.

Williams, J. (2013). The teachings of student debt. In D. Heller & C. Callender (Eds.), *Student financing of higher education: A comparative perspective* (pp. 61–74). New York: Routledge.

Williams, P. (2007). Youth-subcultural studies: Sociological traditions and core concepts. *Sociology Compass*, *1*(2), 572–593.

Williams, P. (2009). The multidimensionality of resistance in youth-subcultural studies. *Resistance Magazine*, *1*, 20–33.

Williams, Z. (2012). Forget the nanny state. This is mollycoddling business. *Guardian*. September 19th. Retrieved from www.guardian.co.uk/commentisfree/2012/sep/19/youth-contract-mollycoddling-business

Willis, P. (1981). *Learning to labor*. New York: Columbia University Press.

Wilson, B. (2013). Youth, not oil, is Nigeria's most valuable resource. August 23rd. Retrieved from www.youthdevelopment.gov.ng/index.php/media-centre/interviews/379-youth-not-oil-is-nigeria-s-most-valuable-resource-wilson

Wolf, A. (2002). *Does education matter?* London: Penguin.

Wolf, D. (1992), *Factory daughters: Gender, household dynamics and rural industrialization in Java*. Berkeley: University of California Press.

Wolf, M. (2011). Why the world's youth is in a revolting state of mind. *Financial Times*. February 18th. Retrieved from www.ft.com/cms/s/0/6577ca92-3b94-11e0-a96d-00144feabdc0.html#axzz2VX2ga2Wn

Wolman, D. (2011). The techie dissidents who showed Egyptians how to organize online. *Atlantic*. February 3rd. Retrieved from www.theatlantic.com/technology/archive/2011/02/the-techie-dissidents-who-showed-egyptians-how-to-organize-online/70734/

Wood, J. (2012). The young and the restless. *BBC News*. October 23rd. Retrieved from www.bbc.co.uk/news/business-19997182

Work and Pensions Select Committee. (2012). *Youth unemployment and the youth contract*. London: House of Commons.

World Bank. (2006). *World development report 2007: Development and the next generation*. Washington, DC: World Bank.

Worsnop, R.L. (1990). Teens work to balance school and jobs. Retrieved from www.urbanministry.org/wiki/teens-work-balance-school-and-jobs

Wyn, J., & White, R. (1997). *Rethinking youth*. London: Sage.

Wyn, J., & Woodman, D. (2006). Generation, youth and social change in Australia. *Journal of Youth Studies*, *9*(4), 495–514.

YAF – Young America's Foundation. (2012). Youth misery index. Retrieved from www.yaf.org/youthmisery/index.html

Yahya, H. (2012). The global concept of the middle school. Retrieved from http://askdryahya.wordpress.com/2012/01/26/the-global-concept-of-the-middle-school-junior-high-ا-في-المتوسطة-المدرسة-مفهوم/

Youmans, W., & York, J. (2012). Social media and the activist toolkit: User agreements, corporate interests and the information infrastructure of modern social movements. *Journal of Communication*, *62*, 315–329.

YouthPolicy.org. (2013a). International youth sector. Retrieved from www.youthpolicy.org/mappings/internationalyouthsector/

YouthPolicy.org. (2013b). Overview of national youth policies. Retrieved from www.youthpolicy.org/nationalyouthpolicies/

Zelizer, V. (1985). *Pricing the priceless child: The changing social value of children*. New York: Basic Books.

Zhang, X. (2013). China's 'ant tribe' present social survival situation and personal financial advice. *Asian Social Science*, *9*(2), 24–35.

Zill, Z. (2012). Dimensions of the global youth revolt. *International Socialist Review, 81.* Retrieved from www.isreview.org/issues/81/feat-youthrebellion.shtml

Zimring, F. (2005). *American juvenile justice.* Oxford: Oxford University Press.

zurpolitik.com. (2009). *Occupied universities.* Retrieved from https://maps.google.at/maps/ms?ie=UTF8&hl=de&msa=0&msid=116283369278129786033.0004778dfa81fb402d565&ll=49.21042,8.876953&spn=23.014452,46.582031&z=4&source=embed

INDEX

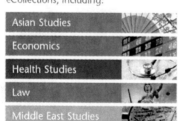